Mobile Intention Recognition

Peter Kiefer

Mobile Intention Recognition

Foreword by Christoph Schlieder

Springer

Peter Kiefer
University of Bamberg
Bamberg, Germany
peter.kiefer@uni-bamberg.de

This book has been accepted as a PhD thesis for a degree of Dr. rer.nat. by the Faculty of Information Systems and Applied Computer Sciences, University of Bamberg, Bamberg (Germany), under the original title: "The Mobile Intention Recognition Problem And An Approach Based On Spatially-Constrained Grammars".

ISBN 978-1-4899-8809-6   ISBN 978-1-4614-1854-2 (eBook)
DOI 10.1007/978-1-4614-1854-2
Springer New York Dordrecht Heidelberg London

Printed on acid-free paper

Springer is part of Springer Science+Business Media (www.springer.com)

For my parents.

For my parents.

Foreword

Understanding what the user of a mobile information system plans to do next – recognizing his or her intentions – is of crucial importance for the design of location-based services (LBS). Solutions to the mobile intention recognition problem are especially needed in application scenarios where the opportunities to interact with the mobile device via a keyboard or a touch-screen are limited. This is the case for the use of smart-phones in many outdoor activities such as riding a bike, skiing, or running. Even hikers prefer not to stop to interact with the device. Ideally, the LBS would analyze the spatial behavior of the user, identify the user's intentions to act, select the currently active intention, and finally provide the information services that assist the user in achieving the intended goal.

In his thesis, Peter Kiefer provides the first comprehensive treatment of the field. This includes not only a thorough review of the state of the art but also a formal characterization of the mobile intention recognition problem as opposed to the general intention recognition problem. Although the approach is formal, it is deeply rooted in the practical experience that the author of this book gained while designing LBS, especially tourist guides and location-based games.

The challenge of intention recognition consists in finding an adequate approach for representing the background knowledge about the structure of the spatial environment (e.g. the partonomic structure of a city) and the spatio-temporally constrained set of possible actions of the user. It is far from clear how to best combine this background knowledge with the behavioral data. Some obvious research issues are: Which spatial and temporal restrictions provide the relevant constraints for recognizing intentions in LBS? What is an adequate representational formalism for these constraints? Which computational mechanisms permit to solve the recognition problem? Peter Kiefer's thesis gives convincing answers to all these questions.

Here are some of the results which I think are particularly interesting: (1) a generic layered architecture for mobile services that perform intention recognition, (2) an analysis of behavioral pattern which shows that rule-based representation formalisms of different expressive power are needed to handle the problem, (3) two grammar formalisms, Spatially Constrained Context-Free Grammars (SCCFGs) and Spatially Constrained Tree-Adjoining Grammars (SCTAGs) which come with appropriate parsing algorithms that solve the intention recognition problem, (4) last, but not least, the implementation of the generic architecture as a framework for evaluating different approaches to intention recognition.

Peter Kiefer has written this thesis with the idea of presenting his research results in a larger context. In turns out that he succeeded writing a very readable book that is of value to those interested in LBS in general and intention recognition in particular. Because of the comprehensive and knowledgeable survey of the state of the art it may also serve as an introductory text to the field that is accessible not just to computer scientists but also to researchers from geographic information science.

Christoph Schlieder
Professor of Applied Computer Science, University of Bamberg

Acknowledgements

First, I would like to thank my supervisor Prof. Dr. Christoph Schlieder for his guidance throughout the years. He was not only a scientific teacher but also an encouraging and motivating mentor in all phases of my research on this thesis. Moreover, I very much enjoyed the diversity of non-thesis related projects I got involved in during my time as a research assistant at his chair.

I also thank Prof. Dr. Martin Raubal for the cordial welcome and the productive time at his lab at the University of California, Santa Barbara. A scholarship from the German Academic Exchange Service (DAAD) made it possible for me to collaborate with him for one month. I am looking forward to continuing this collaboration in the near future. Thank you to Prof. Dr. Ute Schmid and Prof. Dr. rer.nat. Guido Wirtz for joining my doctoral committee, and for their constructive remarks on my research in early phases of this work.

I sincerely thank all my colleagues at the Kulturinformatik lab who created an atmosphere I enjoyed very much working in. Cornelia Pickel for the daily coffee chat and for her administrative support in all matters of daily work. Klaus Stein for the scientific discussions on spatio-temporal behavior interpretation, for the LaTex help, and all those relaxing evenings at his place. Sebastian Matyas, my office-neighbour, for his unquestioning collegiality, and the conjoint research on the basic principles of location-based gaming. Some of the most memorable moments of these years are connected with the Geogames project.

Dominik Kremer for the discussions on spatial and philosophical concepts computer scientists sometimes tend to use rather unreflected, and for rewakening my interest in chess. Olga Yanenko and "the other Peter" (Wullinger) for the great team work in teaching. Claudia Heß for her friendly welcome and start-up help during my first months in the group. Last, but not least, Christian Matyas for having a similar conception of a perfect lunch break.

Thank you also to all students who worked in our lab during these years. I would especially like to name two of them, Manuel Beckmann and Jan Petendi, who were involved in the implementation of INTENSIVE.

Writing a PhD thesis is a passion that may easily lead to social isolation. A warm thank you to all friends who did not break ties although, recently, I have not been able to meet them very often. I am aware that there are better ways of returning the favor than mentioning you here. I cordially thank my family, especially my parents, for their ongoing love and support through all phases of my life. Nicole, thank you for your support and understanding.

Contents

1 Introduction 1
  1.1 From Location-Based to Intention-Aware Mobile Services 1
    1.1.1 Location-Based Services 1
    1.1.2 The Need for Intention-Awareness 3
    1.1.3 Non-Local Dependencies: The Visit/Revisit Problem .. 6
  1.2 Contributions 7
  1.3 Outline 8

2 Mobile Intention Recognition 11
  2.1 Intention-Aware Mobile Services 11
    2.1.1 The Context-Model of IAMSs 11
    2.1.2 Crossing the Semantic Gap 14
  2.2 Intentions and Intention Recognition 24
    2.2.1 Beliefs, Desires, Intentions, and Plans 24
    2.2.2 Intention Recognition and Plan Recognition 28
  2.3 The Mobile Intention Recognition Problem 31
    2.3.1 Spatio-Temporal Behavior Sequences 31
    2.3.2 Mobile Intention Recognition: A Definition 38
    2.3.3 Behavior Sequence Compositions 41
    2.3.4 The Problem of Interleaved Intentions 47
  2.4 Summary and Requirements for Mobile Intention Recognition 52

3 Related Approaches in Plan Recognition 55
  3.1 Finite State Machines 55
  3.2 Early Approaches to Plan Recognition 57
    3.2.1 Hypothesize and Revise 57
    3.2.2 Event Hierarchies 58
  3.3 Probabilistic Networks 59
    3.3.1 Static Probabilistic Networks 59
    3.3.2 Dynamic Probabilistic Networks................... 62
  3.4 Parsing Formal Grammars................................. 65

3.4.1   (Probabilistic) Context-Free Parsing 65
3.4.2   Spatially Grounded Intentional Systems 69
3.4.3   Towards More Context-Sensitivity 72
3.5   Combining Formal Grammars and Bayes 73
3.5.1   Probabilistic State-Dependent Grammars 73
3.5.2   Plan Tree Grammars and Pending Sets.............. 74
3.6   Summary... 77

4   Mobile Intention Recognition with Spatially Constrained
    Grammars 79
4.1   Parsing Spatial Behavior Sequences 79
4.1.1   A State Chart Parser for SGISs 79
4.1.2   Spatial Constraint Resolution 83
4.2   Non-Local Constraints: A Generalization of Spatial Grounding 88
4.2.1   Spatially-Constrained Context-Free Grammars 88
4.2.2   A State Chart Parser for SCCFGs 90
4.3   Intersecting Spatial Dependencies 93
4.3.1   Towards More Context-Sensitivity: A Parallel to NLP . 93
4.3.2   Spatially Constrained Tree-Adjoining Grammars 97
4.3.3   SCTAGs and the Mobile Intention Recognition Problem 101
4.3.4   A State Chart Parser for SCTAGs 104
4.4   Beyond Partonomies 124
4.5   Summary.. 125

5   Evaluation and Discussion 127
5.1   The Clothes Shop Example 127
5.2   Formalizing the Example with Spatial Grammars 129
5.2.1   IS and SGIS 129
5.2.2   SCCFG 130
5.2.3   SCTAG 130
5.3   Results and Discussion 131
5.3.1   Ambiguity Reduction with SGISs................... 131
5.3.2   Ambiguity Reduction with SCCFGs 134
5.3.3   Avoiding Inconsistency with SCTAGs 135
5.4   INTENSIVE: A Simulation and Testing Environment for
      the IAMS Framework 137

6   Conclusion and Outlook 145
6.1   Mobile Intention Recognition 145
6.2   Spatially Constrained Grammars 146
6.3   Future Research.. 149
6.3.1   Temporal Constraints 149
6.3.2   Look-Ahead Parsing 151
6.3.3   Probabilistic Spatially Constrained Grammars 151
6.3.4   Grammar Acquisition and Behavioral Corpora 152

6.3.5 Multi-Agent Intention Recognition...................153

References...155

Acronyms

LBS	Location-Based Service
LIG	Linear Indexed Grammar
MCSG	Mildly Context-Sensitive Grammar
NLP	Natural Language Processing
PCFG	Probabilistic Context-Free Grammar
POI	Point of Interest
PSDG	Probabilistic State Dependent Grammar
SCCFG	Spatially Constrained Context-Free Grammar
SCTAG	Spatially Constrained Tree-Adjoining Grammar
SGIS	Spatially Grounded Intentional System
TAG	Tree-Adjoining Grammar
VGI	Volunteered Geographic Information
VPP	Valid Prefix Property

Chapter 1
Introduction

1.1 From Location-Based to Intention-Aware Mobile Services

1.1.1 Location-Based Services

Location-based services (LBSs), i.e., services that adapt their behavior to the user's location, have become a part of many people's everyday lives. Applications, such as car, bicycle, and pedestrian navigation systems, GPS-based city tour guides, and friendfinder services, are getting more and more popular, and "impact individuals, organizations, and our society as a whole" (Raubal, 2011). Still most, if not all, current LBS products stay far beyond the general idea of context-aware services envisioned by the ubiquitous computing research community in the 1990's. Dey and Abowd (1999), for instance, introduce primary context as those types of context "that are, in practice, more important than others. These are location, identity, activity and time" (p. 4). Secondary are all other types of context, and "they can be indexed by primary context because they are attributes of the entity with primary context." (pp. 4-5). For finding out the weather forecast, for instance, the system needs the primary context information on location and time.

Simple LBSs typically adapt their behavior only to the primary context location, thus excluding the three other forms of primary context, identity, activity and time. A typical mobile tourist guide, for instance, has the same functionality at any time and for every tourist. This is often much too restrictive, and there is a widespread research interest in broadening this focus to other context information. Identity, for instance, is used by personalized maps (Meng et al, 2005, 2008) and geographic recommenders (Matyas and Schlieder, 2009). Approaches that integrate temporal context often use simple conditions specific for one scenario: a mobile phone might have the option to mute all sounds at night, and a mobile shopping guide might remind its user that she has only a limited amount of time left (Bohnenberger et al, 2005).

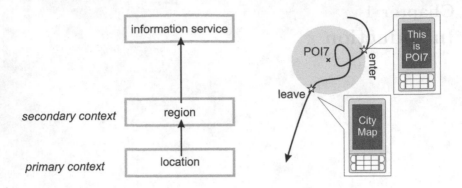

Fig. 1.1 Context-model of a location-based service (left). The enter/leave paradigm of proactive location-based services (right).

An integrated view of space and time is taken by approaches based on Time Geography which consider the complex space-time mechanics of moving in geographic space (Raubal et al, 2007).

However, a critical shortcoming of many systems is that they do not consider the primary context activity: "Activity [...] answers a fundamental question of what is occurring in the situation." (Dey and Abowd, 1999, p. 5). If the system knew exactly what the user is currently doing, or if it even knew what the user is intending to do in the future, it could adapt to the user's needs and offer a perfectly supportive service for the user's current state of mind. The sensors of a mobile device are certainly not able to read the user's mind. However, the behavioral data measured with those sensors available can be sufficient to at least build hypotheses on the user's intentions. These sensors do not necessarily need to be very sophisticated ones, such as wearable sensors or cameras. The combination of location and temporal context is often sufficient to guess what the user intends to do. Consider, for instance, a car suddenly decelerating while approaching an exit on the highway. A human observer would probably hypothesize that the driver has reached her goal, or stops to refuel or to have a break, and the same kind of inference could be performed by a mobile assistance system. In general, spatio-temporal properties of the user's trajectory, such as speed and acceleration, can be an important indicator on "what is occurring in the situation" (Dey and Abowd, 1999). This idea to exploit information gathered from trajectory and activity context to attribute intentions to the user is the idea framing this thesis.

1.1.2 The Need for Intention-Awareness

1.1.2.1 The on-enter/on-leave paradigm

The need for applications that recognize their user's intentions can be clarified with the context-model of LBSs displayed in Fig. 1.1 (left): the primary context location, i. e., a position in 2- or 3-dimensional euclidean space[1], is mapped to the secondary context region, and that region to an according information service. Regions are typically buffer zones around points of interest (POIs) somehow relevant for the application, but may also include larger regions, such as, "in Santa Barbara, CA, U.S.". This simple mapping is especially popular in *proactive* LBSs (Küpper, 2005, p. 3) that anticipate the user's information needs and trigger services automatically when the region context changes (on-enter/on-leave paradigm, see Fig. 1.1, right). On the contrary, *reactive* LBSs will start only when the user explicitly requests for it. In scenarios in which the interaction possibilities between user and device are restricted, proactive LBSs can often assist the user better than reactive ones. Such resource restrictions on the side of the user with respect to haptic and cognitive resources (Baus et al, 2002) occur, for instance, in navigation (Krüger et al, 2004), location-based gaming (Schlieder et al, 2006), and maintenance work (Kortuem et al, 1999). One strategy to improve the human/device interaction in these scenarios is to change the user interface, for instance, by providing audio (Holland et al, 2002) or wearable interfaces (Thomas et al, 1998). Still, this will often not help, or is at least only part of an optimal solution. For instance, audio commands via microphone may not be socially accepted in quiet places (such as a church or a public library)[2], and hard to process in very loud places (such as a factory or in a traffic context).

The focus of this thesis are applications that offer intelligent proactive services. The on-enter/on-leave paradigm of proactive LBSs works well under two assumptions: 1) the user enters the region only if she is interested in that region (i. e., she does not enter the region accidentally, or because she needs to cross the region to reach some other place). 2) There is only one information service associated with the region (i. e., only on "thing" afforded by the region

---

[1] $\mathbb{R}^2$ is assumed in the following as the methods developed in the later chapters of this thesis do not depend on whether the original input data was measured in 2D or 3D. For outdoor LBSs, the 2D position is derived by projecting the user's latitude/longitude to a plane. Services that use indoor positioning are also regarded as LBSs in the context of this thesis, aware that indoor positioning requires different sensors which implies different conditions with respect to accuracy and precision. Switching between indoor and outdoor also requires special attention to the changing reference system. These issues are not considered here. See Giudice et al (2010) for a current research agenda on merging indoor and outdoor spaces.

[2] The social implications of using location-based technologies in public spaces are a current research issue (e. g., De Souza E Silva and Frith, 2012).

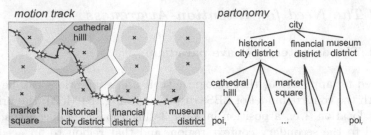

Fig. 1.2 The room-crossing problem of location-based services: a mobile user traverses a partonomy of regions, triggering several enter-/leave-events (similar to Schlieder and Werner, 2003, Fig.3).

[3]). The following discussions reveal why these two assumptions cannot be made for many mobile assistance scenarios, and why the context-model of Fig. 1.1 is too simplistic.

1.1.2.2 Spatial context ambiguity: the room-crossing problem

A simple example, discussed by Schlieder and Werner (2003) in the context of a mobile museum information system, illustrates that the first assumption is often not true: a museum visitor might traverse a number of trigger regions around exhibits although she is not interested in these exhibits. She might be searching for the exit or the restaurant. In that case the application should rather support her with an information service showing her a map of the whole museum or the museum wing instead of "spamming" her with information on the exhibits. This problem of determining the relevant spatial context in a partonomy (exhibit, museum wing, museum) was later called the *room-crossing problem* by one of the authors (Schlieder, 2005). Although it is called *room*-crossing problem it is also relevant for outdoor LBSs. Figure 1.2 demonstrates the problem for a mobile city-guide scenario: the tourist is looking for a museum and gets undesired information on several regions and POIs she approaches on the way. Navigation instructions would probably have been more helpful than, for instance, architectural information on a church on cathedral hill. You can see in Fig. 1.3 that room-crossing behavior not only occurs in theory, but that there is also empirical evidence: Veron and Levasseur (1991) describe a number of visitor types they have determined by observing visitors in the Centre Pompidou museum, Paris: the grasshopper type, for instance, hops from one exhibit to the next, omitting some exhibits in between though still coming close to them.

A mobile application implementing proactive LBSs that does not solve the room-crossing problem satisfactory is likely to annoy its users. Research on

---

[3] See Gibson, 1979, for the theory of affordances, and Jordan et al, 1998, for the role of affordances in GIScience (Geo Information Science).

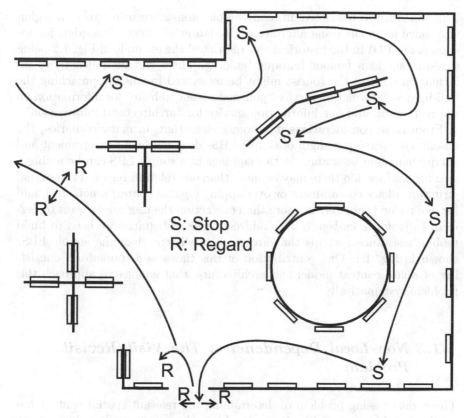

Fig. 1.3 A museum visitor's trajectory. Based on Veron and Levasseur (1991, p. 85), titled "Une Sauterelle" = "A Grasshopper".

human-computer interaction (HCI) has affirmed the intuition that, in general, intrusive systems that make errors are not accepted by the user. See, for instance, the empirical studies performed by Schaumburg with the Microsoft (R) Office (R) assistant (Schaumburg, 2001). This is especially problematic for ambient intelligent assistance systems[4], i.e., for systems that seamlessly integrate into a user's indoor environment and support her in performing some tasks.

1.1.2.3 Affordance ambiguity

The second assumption necessary for an on-enter/on-leave mechanism to be effective is that there exists only one information service for each region.

---

[4] See, for instance, the workshop titled "Lost in Ambient Intelligence" (Nijholt et al, 2004) at the Computer Human Interaction Conference (CHI'04).

This is much too restrictive in many mobile assistance scenarios as a region may have more than one affordance (Jordan et al, 1998). Consider, for instance, one POI in the historical city district of the example in Fig. 1.2 being a restaurant in a famous baroque building. There will be at least two information services the tourist might be interested in when approaching the building: an information service "gourmet review website" for information on the restaurant, and one information service for "architectural information".

From these considerations it becomes clear that, in many scenarios, the on-enter/on-leave paradigm of simple LBSs does not lead to convenient and adequate mobile assistance. Both mappings in a simple LBS can be ambiguous: for one location there may be more than one relevant region if the spatial structure allows containment or overlapping (*spatial context ambiguity*), and for one region there may be more than one action the user might want to perform (*affordance ambiguity*). To address these ambiguities we need to build mobile assistance systems that are more intelligent than the simple LBSs shown in Fig. 1.1. One contribution of this thesis is a framework, consisting of a new context model and architecture, that enables to approach this problem systematically.

1.1.3 Non-Local Dependencies: The Visit/Revisit Problem

The room-crossing problem of determining the relevant spatial context has until now only been considered as a local one: the user is attributed intentions depending on her behavior in the current spatial context, and on the behavior in a limited sequence of connected spatial contexts before. For instance, the intention of the user entering a POI in the museum district (Fig. 1.2) is, first of all, dependent on her behavior in the current POI. Second, it is dependent on her behavior in the previous spatial context (museum district without POI), the spatial context before (financial district), and so on.

This locality restriction on the spatial context that may be used to recognize intentions seriously limits the types of behavior sequences that can be represented and, consequently, leads to unsatisfactory results when algorithmically interpreting a behavior sequence as intentions. The types of behavior sequences concerned by this restriction occur frequently in mobile assistance and can prototypically be described by the Visit/Revisit pattern: the user first visits a region, i. e., shows certain behavior in that region, then behaves arbitrarily in some other spatial context, and later returns to the visited region. At the time of revisiting it is not sufficient to regard only a limited number of connected spatial contexts before. Modeling a dependency of the whole sequence of spatial contexts, however, leads to a combinatory problem because of the intermediate "behave arbitrarily". A mobile assistance systems engineer may frequently have the requirement to configure a system in a way that it recognizes the visit/revisit pattern, and sometimes also more than one visit/revisit per behavior sequence. However, the visit/revisit problem has not yet been considered as an interesting problem in the ubiquitous computing and mobile GIScience communities.

Patterns similar to the visit/revisit pattern are known in plan recognition, a sub-field of artificial intelligence (A.I.), as "interleaving" plans. Moreover, the natural language processing (NLP) community has identified similar structural dependencies in the syntax of natural languages, and developed representational formalisms and algorithms for them. The similarity of certain structural dependencies in plan recognition and NLP is a current topic in A.I. (Geib and Steedman, 2007). However, as the mobile intention recognition problem is a special (and spatial) case of general plan recognition, the requirements and possible algorithmic solutions differ. This thesis explores the problem of interleaving intentions for mobile intention recognition, and develops corresponding new representational formalisms which are specifically designed for spatio-temporal behavior, and more expressive than those used in mobile assistance up to now.

1.2 Contributions

This thesis contributes to the increasing interest of the GIScience community in building mobile systems that provide intelligent assistance. It regards intelligent mobile assistance from the perspective of the intention recognition problem, a well-known problem in A.I. The main contributions are as follows:

- The thesis presents a framework for a class of mobile services that recognize their user's intentions (Intention Aware Mobile Services). The framework consists of a context-model and an architecture for bridging the semantic gap between low-level trajectory data and high-level intentions.
- The mobile intention recognition problem is defined as a sub-class of the general intention recognition problem, and the fundamental differences between mobile and general intention recognition are analyzed. The problem of interleaved mobile intentions is identified and explored in the light of related work from plan and intention recognition.
- Two new representational formalisms based on formal grammars are defined which allow to express interleaved intentions with different degree of complexity. These formalisms integrate spatial constraints into formal grammars. The principles of interpreting mobile behavior by parsing spatially constrained grammars are discussed and exemplified with extensions to existing chart-parsers. With an exemplary use case it is shown that the new formalisms are able to represent a larger and more realistic class of mobile intention recognition problems than previous formalisms, and that parsing these higher-expressive grammars will return more plausible results.

This thesis differs from most research in intelligent mobile assistance systems by building on a formal and methodological background in intention/plan recognition, i. e., not on (low-level) activity recognition as most approaches do. A reader with an A.I. background, however, will probably be most interested in the implications of space and time on the intention recognition problem.

1.3 Outline

The rest of the thesis is structured as follows:

- *Chapter 2* introduces the mobile intention recognition problem intuitively and formally. It presents an architecture for Intention Aware Mobile Services that helps to cross the semantic gap between low-level trajectory data and high-level intentions. An excursion on the philosophical background on the term "intentions" helps to specify more precisely what is meant with "recognizing someone's intentions".
  The heart of chapter 2 is a discussion of the implications of space and time on mobile intention recognition, compared to (non-mobile) intention recognition. A problem occurring in many mobile intention recognition domains is identified: the problem of interleaved intentions, more specifically, crossing and nesting long-ranging space-intention dependencies. The chapter concludes with a summary and a listing of five requirements for mobile intention recognition.
- *Chapter 3* gives an overview on related work in plan and intention recognition. The literature review reveals that the problem of interleaved intentions has already been mentioned in early articles in general plan recognition, and is increasingly discussed in recent work. Likewise, the interpretation of human spatio-temporal behavior is a recent topic. However, mobile approaches typically interpret behavior on a lower semantic level than intentions. A systematic discussion of the specificities of space and time in mobile intention recognition is largely missing. The only exception, a spatial grammar formalism (Spatially Grounded Intentional Systems, SGIS), does not support interleaved intentions.
- *Chapter 4* contributes two new representational formalisms for interpreting mobile behavior in terms of intentions: Spatially Constrained Context-Free Grammars (SCCFG) and Spatially Constrained Tree-Adjoining Grammars (SCTAG). Depending on the complexity level of the underlying grammar, Context-Free or Tree-Adjoining, different kinds of interleaving intention patterns can be expressed. Certain variants of the "Visit-Revisit" pattern especially relevant for mobile intention recognition are shown to be expressable with SCTAGs, but not with SGISs or SCCFGs. Restrictions of the SCTAG formalism are discussed.

The principles of parsing spatially constrained grammars are discussed and exemplified by providing an incremental parsing algorithm for each of the formalisms. It is explained why the runtime of parsing with spatial constraints depends on the type of spatial model (partonomic vs. non partonomic).

- *Chapter 5* evaluates the expressiveness of the three formalisms SGIS, SCCFG, and SCTAG with an exemplary use case. The example of a customer in a clothes shop picking and dropping items proves that, given a realistic spatio-temporal behavior sequence, the SCTAG formalism performs best in terms of disambiguation and recognizable behavior patterns. The chapter also shortly introduces the software tool INTENSIVE, the INTENtion SImulation enVironmEnt, a desktop application that allows to easily build intention models and spatial models. INTENSIVE allows to analyze a real motion track recorded with a mobile assistance system, visualizing the intentions a given intention recognition algorithm would have recognized while the human agent was moving.
- *Chapter 6* concludes with the main results of the thesis and presents an outlook on future research perspectives in mobile intention recognition.

Chapter 2
Mobile Intention Recognition

Chapter 1 has discussed why the restricted context-model and architecture of simple LBSs do not allow for building intelligent proactive mobile services that recognize their user's intentions. Based on these considerations this chapter introduces *intention-aware mobile services* (IAMSs) as an extension of LBSs, and presents a context-model and architecture for this new class of services. A short excursion on the philosophical background of "intentions" sheds light on some aspects of intentions an IAMS system engineer needs to be aware of.

The second contribution of this chapter is a systematic investigation of the mobile intention recognition problem. The specificities of space and time for mobile intention recognition, compared to the non-spatial and non-temporal intention recognition problem, are discussed. At the end of this chapter, section 2.3.4 identifies the problem of interleaved intentions as an important problem in mobile intention recognition. This problem is going to frame the following chapters.

2.1 Intention-Aware Mobile Services

2.1.1 The Context-Model of IAMSs

Figure 2.1 shows the context model of IAMSs, again following Dey and Abowd's (1999) classification of primary and secondary context. It illustrates why these services are called "intention-aware": the information service is selected using the secondary context *intention*. As we see by comparing the models shown in Figs. 1.1, 2.1, and the general context model in Küpper (2005, Fig. 1.1), IAMSs are an extension of LBSs and a sub-class of context-aware services. This systematization of IAMSs as an own class between LBSs and context-aware services is new.

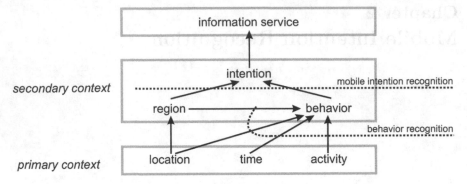

Fig. 2.1 Context-model of an intention-aware mobile service.

An ideal IAMS would always know its user's current intention, and map it to an information service. For instance, if the mobile tourist from the example in section 1.1.2 approached the restaurant in a historic building an ideal IAMS would somehow know whether the user's intention is *HaveFood* or *RegardBuilding* (this "somehow" will be specified later). This intention can then directly be mapped to "gourmet review website", or "architectural information" respectively. We could make this step even more intelligent by personalizing the information service, i.e., by adding primary context information on identity. The "gourmet review website" information service, for instance, might show personalized dinner recommendations depending on an online user profile. Accordingly, the "architectural information" service could select its information with respect to the user's previous knowledge and professional background. Aware that these parameterization and personalization steps are helpful they are not considered any further as they are out of scope.

As LBSs, IAMSs have location as primary context, but additionally time and activity (see Fig. 2.1). Dey and Abowd's (1999) idea of "activity" remains vague[1]. There is a lot of research titled *activity recognition* which, for instance, recognizes activities such as "lie", "nordic walk", "walk", "sit" from wearable sensors (e.g., Pärkkä et al, 2006). Other approaches titled "activity recognition" are dealing with the problem on a semantically higher level and regard activities such as "toilet usage", "preparing meals" (e.g., Storf et al, 2009). Some authors recognizing "activity" focus on the health aspect of being active, as the opposite live style to being inactive (e.g., Anderson et al, 2007). Bobick and Ivanov (1998) choose the similar term "action recognition" for combining basic gestures to a higher geometry ("drawing a square"). As these papers focus on methodology and somehow take the notion of "activity" for granted it seems hard to find a common terminology or precise definition of "activity". However, there is a difference between plan and activity recog-

---

[1] See chapter 1: "Activity [...] answers a fundamental question of what is occurring in the situation." (Dey and Abowd, 1999, p. 5).

nition which can be described well in the words of Geib and Goldman (2009, p. 1104): "Much of the work on activity recognition can be seen as discretizing a sequence of possibly noisy and intermittent low-level sensor readings into coherent actions that could be treated as inputs to a plan recognition system." As we will see in section 2.2 the plan recognition problem mentioned by Geib and Goldman is closely related to intention recognition.

In the context of this thesis, *activity* is defined based on Montello's classification of spatial scales (Montello, 1993): activity is primary context information about the user's interaction with the environment or device which takes place in figural space. According to Montello, a person can haptically manipulate objects in figural space without locomotion of the whole body. In contrast, vista and environmental space require a prior relocation before a haptic manipulation becomes possible. The activity used by an IAMS depends on the kinds of sensors available. For instance, an intelligent sofa in ambient assisted living (AAL) could have sensors that tell us not only that the person is located on it but also whether that person is "sitting" or "lying". Similarly, a wardrobe could be equipped with sensors that measure activities "open" and "close".

On the secondary context level IAMSs use regions, just as LBSs, and a new secondary context type: *behavior*. Behavior is regarded as qualitative context information about the user's interaction with the environment or device at any spatial scale, figural, visual, or environmental space (again based on Montello, 1993). There are two types of behavior:

- *Spatio-temporal behavior* is inferred from the user's locomotion (which is equivalent to interaction with the environment in visual and environmental space). The qualitativeness of behavior means that a stream of 2D coordinates is not behavior but its classification as "strolling", "walking", "sitting", or "running". The step of *behavior recognition* from a user's locomotion is explained in the following section 2.1.2.
- *Behavior in figural space* is inferred from the primary context activity. An activity can be interpreted as different behavior depending on location and time. For instance, some current mobile devices have sensors that will measure an activity "device is shaken". This may be mapped to the behavior "knee bending" if the user is located in a gymnasium, whereas the behavior "picking" would be more appropriate in a strawberry field. However, in many situations we will map activities to behaviors independent of location and time.

IAMSs are required to use at least spatio-temporal behavior. That means, an IAMS must always track the user's locomotion and use it for behavior and intention recognition. A system does not necessarily need to use behavior in figural space to be categorized as an IAMS.

From behaviors and spatial information, intentions are inferred. Intentions are also secondary context, but on a higher level than behaviors. Mapping behavior and space to intentions is called *mobile intention recognition* which is the central problem of this thesis. This problem is formally defined in section 2.3.

2.1.2 Crossing the Semantic Gap

An IAMS tries to infer user intentions from sensor measurements. This task of assigning meaning to raw data is a challenge that appears in several research fields of A.I., such as image recognition or NLP. Henry Kautz, who was one of the first computer scientists to formally approach the plan recognition problem, identified this semantic gap as one future research issue in the outlook of his PhD thesis: "The semantic gap between the output of the low-level processes and the high-level inference engines remains wide, and few have ventured to cross it." (Kautz, 1987, p. 127). For the interpretation of *mobile* behavior the semantic gap occurs especially between 2D position data and intentions: we cannot map a position directly to an intention. As discussed in section 1.1.2, the main reasons can be seen in the problems of spatial context and affordance ambiguity.

An established A.I. strategy for crossing semantic gaps is to cut the gap into pieces by introducing intermediate layers. This means turning a larger problem into several small ones, and allows us to remain flexible as we can easily experiment with algorithms for partial problems while keeping the rest static. A typical NLP system for speech recognition, for instance, will cut the semantic gap between an audio stream and its interpretation into layers for phonology, morphology, syntax, semantics, and pragmatics.

A way of crossing the semantic gap in an IAMS is shown in Fig. 2.2 (which is a modified version of the architecture proposed in Kiefer and Stein, 2008). The 2D position input is accumulated to a motion track with which the following tasks are performed: data refinement, segmentation, feature extraction, behavior classification, and intention recognition. The activity data (such as non-positional sensor readings in AAL) are also classified to behaviors. All processing needs to be done *incrementally*, i. e., the system has to recognize behavior and intentions on-the-fly using only past data.

The challenges and possible approaches for the steps from raw data to behaviors are described in the following. Note that these steps are preprocessing from the perspective of intention recognition and can easily be replaced with better methods when the related research fields advance. It is as well important to keep in mind that the best methods for these steps may (and probably will) depend on the use case.

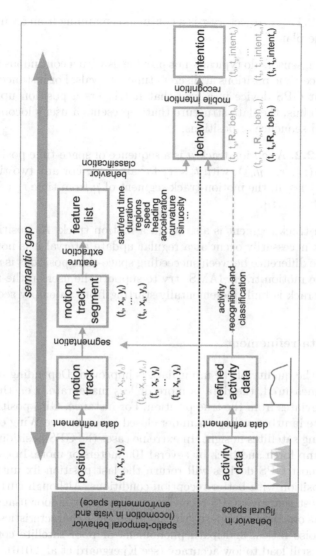

Fig. 2.2 Crossing the semantic gap between input data and intentions.

2.1.2.1 Trajectory and motion track

As the interest of this thesis are scenarios with limited interaction possibilities, such as biking at high speed, the user's ability to manually interact with the device and the environment in figural space is restricted. Thus, the system tries to get as much knowledge as possible out of the user's locomotion which is derived from primary contexts location and time. The user's locomotion history is called a *trajectory*, defined by Buchin et al (2010) as:

Definition 2.1. "A trajectory τ is a continuous mapping from a time interval $[t_0; t_n]$ to the plane."

Positioning sensors do typically not provide us with a continuous trajectory but with space-time positions at discrete time intervals. For instance, we could configure our GPS device in a way that it triggers a position update once per second. Thus, the data structure that represents a user's locomotion is a timestamped sequence of positions:

Definition 2.2. A motion track μ is a sequence of space-time positions $\langle (t_0, x_0, y_0), \ldots, (t_n, x_n, y_n) \rangle$, with $t_i < t_j$ for all $i < j$. For any two times t_k, t_l with $0 \leq k \leq l \leq n$, the motion track segment of μ from time t_k to time t_l is denoted with $\mu[t_k, t_l]$.

A motion track segment is also again a motion track. As positioning updates do not necessarily occur at a regular update interval it is not assumed that the time difference between succeeding space-time positions is a constant for the whole motion track. IAMSs try to support the user on-the-fly so that the motion track is built incrementally starting from an empty sequence.

2.1.2.2 Data refinement

In this step the quality of the input data is improved. Depending on the way position is measured, the data is more or less inaccurate, i.e., the position measured deviates from the true position. For instance, GPS positioning can be inaccurate in urban valleys or under closed canopies (see Wing et al, 2005) due to missing satellites in sight. In extreme cases the GPS position may even suddenly jump forth and back by several 100 meters or more. In case of total signal loss most GPS devices will return the last position fix until the user reaches a position with better reception conditions. Although current experiments suggest that new GPS receivers may, even for indoor usage, perform not as bad as one might suppose "the environment's characteristics" [such as] "signal-to-noise ratios, multipath phenomena or poor satellite constellation geometries" still lead to low accuracy (see Kjærgaard et al, 2010). A systematic overview on typical error sources in positioning is given in Küpper (2005, sections 6.4 and 6.5).

Methods that deal with positioning inaccuracy can generally be divided into four classes:

- *Heuristic methods*: we may, for instance, assume a maximum speed for the user and remove those position fixes not possible under this speed restriction. We could also remove those position fixes which have bad error indicators, such as number of satellites or horizontal dilution of precision (HDOP) in GPS.
- *Geometric methods*: these methods improve the quality of the motion track by taking into account its geometric properties. The idea is to make

the curve smoother. See, for instance, the overview on incremental line generalization algorithms in Stein (2003).

- *GIS-GPS unification methods*: these methods add knowledge about the environment in form of geographic (vector) data. A mobile biking tourist will, for instance, not cross a river (unless there is a bridge or ferry) and not move on the roof of buildings. See Taylor and Blewitt (2006) for GIS-GPS unification methods.
- *Probabilistic location estimation methods (Bayesian filtering)*: these methods represent the state of a dynamic system, like a moving agent, at time t as a probability distribution on a number of random variables (e. g., x, y, speed). Assuming that the Markov condition holds, i. e., that the state of the system at time t depends only on the state at time t - 1 (first order Markov assumption), and assuming a motion model, the filter computes the most probable values for the random variables at points in time for which no measurement exists. See Fox et al (2003) for an introduction, and Hightower and Borriello (2004) for a case study.

Methods from these classes may be combined. In many use cases the fine-grained structure of the motion track is important for the following segmentation and behavior classification steps. Thus, data refinement must be applied carefully to avoid over-generalization. Besides inaccuracy, an important challenge in positioning is fusing data from different sensors (especially for indoor positioning). The above-mentioned Bayesian filters are one method widely-used for sensor fusion (again, see Hightower and Borriello, 2004).

A completely different strategy for dealing with positioning problems has been proposed in HCI under the title "seamful design" (Chalmers and Galani, 2004). Positioning problems are called "seams" in this context. In contrast to the classical design principle of hiding these seams from the user (which is the strategy of the four methods discussed above), a seamfully designed mobile system would either reveal them to the user, or exploit them as a core feature of the system, e. g., by integrating them into the rules of a location-based game (LBG) (Barkhuus et al, 2005). As IAMSs try to draw as few user attention as possible the idea of overloading the user by revealing too much seam information is not viable. However, revealing serious positioning problems, such as loss of GPS signal for a long period of time, could be an additional feature of an IAMS.

Formally, the data refinement step maps a motion track μ to a new motion track μ'. The number of space-time positions in μ and μ' is not necessarily the same, as data refinement may insert (e. g., by smoothening the track along a road) or remove (e. g., bad signal quality) space-time positions. The data refinement step is triggered on a motion track $\mu[t_i, t_k]$ for each incoming position update (t_k, x_k, y_k), where $\mu[t_i, t_k]$ is created by appending (t_k, x_k, y_k) to the motion track one step before $\mu[t_i, t_{k-1}]$ (see Fig. 2.2).

2.1.2.3 Segmentation

The data refinement step appends space-time positions to a motion track buffer. The next step, segmentation, decides about the conditions when the algorithm regards the emerging motion track segment as finished. The segmentation step will typically check the following conditions for finishing a motion track segment:

- *Region segmentation*: finish the motion track segment if the user enters or leaves a region. By doing so the algorithm assumes Schlieder and Werner's *behavioral specificity assumption* to hold:

  "The interpretation process is simplified when the conceptualization of geographic space in thematic regions reflects the way in which spatial behavior is constrained by the regions. If this is the case, that is, if regions are defined by what you can do and cannot do there, we will say that the behavioral specificity assumption holds for the spatio-thematic regions in the application domain considered." (Schlieder and Werner, 2003, p. 7)

  This assumption is plausible for most application scenarios of IAMSs. A mobile tourist guide, for instance, defines its spatial structure around the POIs in the city (Fig. 1.2). The intentions the user can have, such as *VisitChurch*, are specific to these regions. As another example, the intentions of an AAL system user will usually be associated with the spatial structure of the home environment, such as rooms, and the areas around furniture, facilities, and devices these rooms contain.

  As the motion track is not continuous, the border of the region will, in general, segment the motion track between two space-time positions (t_k, x_k, y_k) and $(t_{k+1}, x_{k+1}, y_{k+1})$. In that case, the algorithm computes the space-time position (t_{k*}, x_{k*}, y_{k*}) between these two which is exactly on the border of the region (e. g., by using linear interpolation). The motion track segment $\mu[t_i, t_{k*}]$ is forwarded to the next processing step. The segment buffer is set to $\mu[t_{k*}, t_{k+1}]$ (which will be the start of the next segment).

- *Spatio-temporal criteria segmentation*: finish a motion track segment if the user's spatio-temporal behavior changes significantly. In the words of Yoon and Shahabi (2008, p. 1116), "[t]rajectory segmentation is the process of partitioning a given trajectory into a small number of homogeneous segments w.r.t. some criteria." The idea is to detect behavioral changes from the space-time properties of the user's trajectory. For instance, if the user has been moving straightly into one direction at a constant speed for some time, and then suddenly continues moving in a zig-zag-pattern, we can assume that this behavior change is a good indicator for a changing intention.

  A number of approaches for spatio-temporal criteria segmentation exists. One of the most recent, Buchin et al (2010), is a framework that allows to segment a motion track under a list of criteria, such as diame-

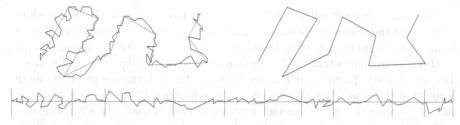

Fig. 2.3 Segmentation of a motion track with respect to criterion heading. Original motion track (top left), heading (top right), and unfolded visualization of segments without heading (bottom). Taken from Stein (2003, Fig.12.1)

ter, heading, speed, or curvature. A segmentation approach that converts the quantitative track data to a qualitative representation (called "qualitative motion vectors") before segmentation is proposed by Musto et al (2000). In the moving object data mining community trajectories are segmented for solving tasks such as the detection of similar moving objects. Elnekave et al (2008), for instance, use minimal bounding boxes to represent segments of spatio-temporal data. An example for segmentation with respect to the criterion heading is illustrated in Fig. 2.3.

Incremental spatio-temporal criteria segmentation can be described as follows: let motion track $\mu[t_i, t_{k+1}]$ not fulfill a given criterion C, whereas the motion track one space-time position before, $\mu[t_i, t_k]$, still fulfilled C. The motion track segment $\mu[t_i, t_k]$ is forwarded to the next processing step, and the motion track buffer is set to $\mu[t_k, t_{k+1}]$.

- *Activity disruption segmentation*: finish a motion track segment if the system recognizes an activity in figural space (indicated by the vertical arrow from activity to segmentation in Fig. 2.2). The algorithm ensures that the end time of the motion track segment is the start time of the activity, and the start time of the next motion segment is the end time of the activity (the activity seamlessly integrates into the motion track).
- *Fixed duration segmentation*: finish the motion track segment at least every r steps, or at the latest if the duration of the segment is longer than a certain constant d. This ensures that our IAMS remains responsive even if the user does not enter a new region or change her behavior.

2.1.2.4 Determining interesting behavior

In the next steps the motion track segment is described as behavior. If we asked a human observer to describe the behavior shown in a motion track segment verbally, she would probably come up with descriptions like "searching", "running", or "strolling". These descriptions depend on the scenario. For instance, the behavior "running" will not be applicable for a mobile biking scenario.

The domain expert will often be able to identify a finite set **B** of behaviors relevant for the respective domain of an IAMS. Alternatively, we might choose to assist the domain expert in identifying interesting behavior patterns with methods from spatio-temporal data mining (refer to Dodge et al, 2008; Roddick et al, 2001; Laube and Purves, 2006, as three examples from the huge amount of literature that exists in this research area). This, of course, requires that we have collected a sufficient amount of motion track data before.

The task is to map the motion track segment to one element from a given set of behaviors **B**. The algorithm divides this task into two steps: feature extraction and behavior classification.

2.1.2.5 Feature extraction

Feature extraction abstracts from the absolute space-time positions of the motion track segment $\mu[t_i, t_k]$ and describes it by features[2]. This includes very simple features, such as the average speed of the motion track, but also more sophisticated features that describe the detailed motion structure. Buchin et al (2010) define a number of criteria useful for segmenting a trajectory which can also be used as features (disk, diameter, heading, speed, curvature, sinuosity, curviness). The three most complex of these features are illustrated in Fig. 2.4: curvature, sinuosity, and curviness all describe certain aspects of the micro structure of a motion track segment. Each of them is defined for a point p on the segment with respect to an environment $[p_1, p_2]$. A value that describes, for instance, the curviness of the whole segment, can be defined as the medium curviness over all points in the segment, or as the maximum curviness difference.

Another approach for describing the micro structure of a motion track (which would relate to Buchin et al's sinuosity), is described in Stein (2003) and Stein and Schlieder (2004): they apply a line generalization algorithm until the minimal distance between any vertex of the original line l to the simplified line l' is less than a given maximal distance ϵ. The integral of a histogram mapping ϵ to the number of vertices in l' can be used to describe the sinuosity of a line (see Fig. 2.5).

The regions feature is always determined in the feature extraction step. That is, we find the set of regions from the spatial model of the domain in which all positions in the motion track segment are located[3].

---

[2] If features have been computed for a spatio-temporal criteria segmentation in the previous step we can, of course, re-use these values.

[3] As we always segment according to the entering and leaving of a region we can be sure that all points of a motion track segment are located in the same set of regions. Positions on the border of a region (especially those that were added as (t_{k*}, x_{k*}, y_{k*}) in the region segmentation step) are not used for computing the regions feature.

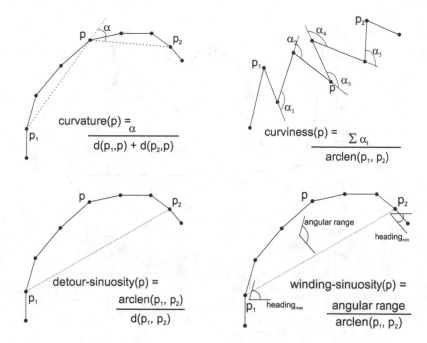

Fig. 2.4 Curvature (top left), curviness (top right), detour sinuosity (bottom left), and winding sinuosity (bottom right) of a motion track segment (based on Buchin et al, 2010).

2.1.2.6 Behavior classification

In the *behavior classification step* the feature list computed in the previous step is mapped to one behavior from **B** by using a function $behcl : F_1 \times \cdots \times F_n \to \mathbf{B}$. The function $behcl$ may, for instance, be specified using a decision tree or an artificial neuronal network (ANN). Depending on the use case it may be sensible to learn $behcl$ with machine learning methods (Mitchell, 1997). An example for a specification of $behcl$ can be found in Kiefer and Stein (2008, p. 7): the rules described in this paper yield in a decision tree which is illustrated in Fig. 2.6. The function $behcl_{kieferstein}$:

$$F_{\text{speed}} \times F_{\text{curvature}} \times F_{\text{diameter}} \to \{b_r, b_c, b_0, b_s, b_{cs}\}.$$

maps three features to a set of five behaviors, with domains $dom(F_{\text{speed}}) = \{low, medium, high\}$, $dom(F_{diameter}) = \mathbb{R}^+$, $dom(F_{curvature}) = \{low, high\}$, and behaviors riding ($b_r$), curving ($b_c$), standing ($b_0$), sauntering ($b_s$), and slow curving ($b_{cs}$). The result, a motion track annotated with behaviors, is shown in Fig. 2.7. We may also decide to use the feature $F_{regions}$ and classify behaviors differently depending on the region in which the motion track segment is located.

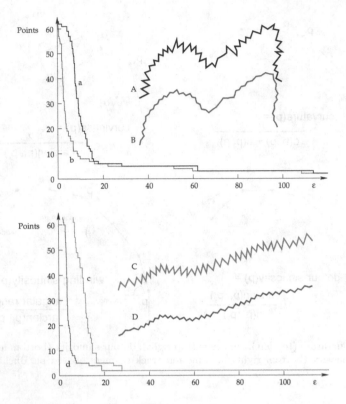

Fig. 2.5 The ϵ-points curve abstracts from the gross structure of the motion track and reveals the micro structure: tracks A, B, C, D, and related ϵ-points curves a, b, c, d (taken from Stein, 2003, Fig. 12.2).

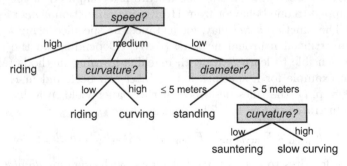

Fig. 2.6 Behavior classification with a decision tree.

As the stream of processing spatio-temporal behavior in Fig. 2.2 shows, the classified behavior beh_n is annotated with the regions feature, and timestamps for start and end time. This information is simply copied from the motion track segment.

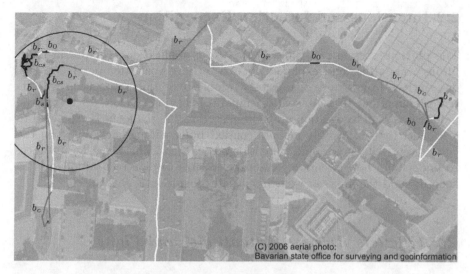

Fig. 2.7 Segmented motion track with classified behavior sequence (the user enters from the right). Taken from Kiefer and Stein (2008, Fig. 4)

2.1.2.7 Activity recognition and classification

The behavior in figural space (bottom in Fig. 2.2) is derived from the primary context activity. As mentioned above, there are many approaches in the literature which recognize user activity in figural space using different sensors, such as wearable sensors (e. g., Pärkkä et al, 2006) or sensors embedded in the environment, like "contact switches, break-beam sensors, and pressure mats." (Wilson and Atkeson, 2005, p. 63). Application areas are also rather diverse and not always focused on information services. Examples include the documentation of a hospital worker's services (Sánchez et al, 2008), and the measuring of the gas usage in a household (Cohn et al, 2010).

As the main focus of this thesis is the spatio-temporal behavior inferred from the user's locomotion the details of these methods which can be added between refined activity data and behavior in the processing model depicted in Fig. 2.2 are not discussed any further. The output of activity recognition and classification is annotated with start time, end time, and the location information on where the activity happened. This location is either determined by the positioning method used for the trajectory or, for fixed sensors, from the position of the sensor.

2.2 Intentions and Intention Recognition

The previous section motivated IAMSs from application scenarios in ubiquitous computing, and explored how to retrieve spatio-temporal behavior descriptions from a user's trajectory. Mobile intention recognition will attribute intentions to these spatio-temporal behaviors. Before discussing the mobile intention recognition problem in section 2.3, the focus is expanded to a broader (not exclusively mobile) context by providing background on the key concepts "intention" and "intention recognition". This helps, for instance, to understand how intention recognition relates to plan recognition, and to keep in mind the limits of what intention recognition is able to achieve.

2.2.1 Beliefs, Desires, Intentions, and Plans

2.2.1.1 Rational agents

Recognizing a user's intentions in an IAMS by using observations of her spatio-temporal behavior is only possible if we have a model of agency for our domain. This model includes information on what users typically *intend* to do when using our system, and a model of how these intentions manifest themselves as behavior, e. g.: if the user has the intention to visit a museum, she will move towards the museum, stop in the vicinity of the museum, optionally take a photo of the facade, wait in the entrance queue, and so on. In general: "if intention I, then behaviors a, b, and c". This simple model of agency hides away the complex processes that take place in the user's mind. Still, it is important for an IAMS engineer to remember that these processes exist and how they may influence the usability of an IAMS.

Modeling these complex processes is also essential for computer scientists who try to build rational software agents, i. e., agents that act like rational humans. The probably most influential model of rational agents is the Belief/Desire/Intention (BDI) architecture (see Bratman et al, 1988). It is specifically relevant for mobile intention recognition because intentions play a major role in this model. The two other main concepts, belief and desire, explain why an agent has certain intentions, and how these intentions are reflected in actions. Figure 2.8 illustrates how beliefs and desires contribute to the forming of an intention. In the tourist example these concepts can be identified as follows:

There could be several reasons why the user has the intention to visit the museum: maybe she desires to get the cultural experience which will allow her to perceive the world in a new perspective. Or, maybe she feels that the museum visit is somehow socially compulsory for a typical vacation in that city, and wants to be able to compare her impressions of, say, the famous Mona Lisa painting in Paris with those impressions her friends at

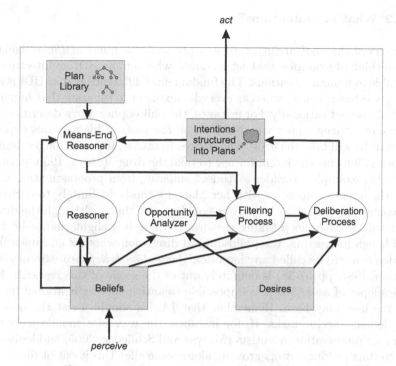

Fig. 2.8 Architecture of a BDI agent. Based on Bratman et al (1988, Fig. 1)

home had during their visits in Paris. Satisfying these *desires* contributes to her individual utility function of a fulfilling life, whatever that utility function may look like.

Besides the user's desires, there is another factor that impacts the formation of an intention: the user's beliefs about the world, i. e., the facts she assumes or knows to be true. For instance, the user will only intend to visit the museum today if she believes at least the following facts to be true: "the museum is open", "I can afford to pay the entrance fee", "I will, given some means of transportation, be able to reach the museum early enough to see the Mona Lisa before closing time, under the assumption that (as my aunt told me) you never wait longer than 30 minutes in the queue at the Louvre entrance". As the user of an IAMS moves in environmental space, beliefs about spatio-temporal constraints constitute a very important part of her beliefs. From the perspective of Time Geography these are beliefs about authority constraints (opening times), coupling constraints (seeing the Mona Lisa is only possible at the Louvre), and capability constraints (maximum speed, transportation mode) (see Hägerstrand, 1970; Miller, 2005)[4].

---

[4] See also the discussions in section 6.3.1 of the last chapter.

2.2.1.2 What are intentions?

The focus of the BDI architecture was primarily to build *artificial* agents. We can think of examples that let us doubt whether the BDI architecture is applicable to human intentions. The fundamental difference is that BDI is assuming a *rational* agent, whereas everyday experience suggests that humans do not always act rationally. For instance, the philosopher Moya describes the example of a "drug-addict who believes, on the basis of his previous experience, that he will take the drug, who desires to take it, has no stronger desire, etc., but still forms the intention *not* to take the drug" (Moya, 1990, p. 144). As another example, consider a student suffering from procrastination who forms the intention to start with her Master's thesis "definitely tomorrow". As a counter-argument to Moya, one could answer that – although the drug-addict will *probably* keep taking the drug – there is a slight chance he will not. Though interesting, the philosophical discussion whether an impossible intention can still be called an "intention" (*intention-belief inconsistency*, see Bratman, 1987, pp. 37-38) is definitely out of the scope of this research. For the developer of an IAMS it is impossible to anticipate any irrational intentions the user may have. Remember that IAMSs should assist the user in some domain-specific tasks. If, for instance, the user of a mobile mapping system for preservation scientists (Matyas and Schlieder, 2005) suddenly decides to start picking flowers growing along some alley this is out of the scope of the system and not supported by any information service. However, when designing an IAMS it is important to keep in mind that there sometimes may be unforeseen intentions for which a default strategy should be implemented. The mapping system, for instance, could just show an overview map and wait until the user returns to explicable behavior. An AAL system supporting people with cognitive diseases, such as Alzheimer, could notify the patient ("are you sure you want to ...?") or call a nurse.

It seems that, in the scope of IAMSs, sticking to the BDI architecture of rational agents and practical reasoning is a more target-oriented approach to discuss the question "what is intention?". But before, let us consider why the concept of intention is needed at all: Michael Bratman, one author of the above-mentioned article on BDI agents, is – in the first instance – a philosopher. In his more philosophical articles about human intentions he picks up the basic concepts of the BDI architecture (see Bratman, 1990, 1999) although, as said above, the focus of the BDI architecture was primarily to build artificial agents. One of his arguments, especially interesting here, deals with the question why the concept of intention is needed, for human and artificial agents: "Why bother with future-directed intentions anyway? Why not just cross our bridges when we come to them?" (Bratman, 1990, p. 18). In other words: why does an agent not decide about her actions by directly optimizing her utility function (desires), given certain facts (beliefs)? The reason, according to Bratman, is that agents are resource-limited. The thinking or computation necessary to optimize the utility function is too time consuming to be performed constantly. Thus, for instance, it is more efficient to commit early to the intention to visit the museum, maybe even before the vacation, than to walk around Paris, constantly thinking about all possible actions, their outcomes, and how they contribute to desires. Committing to an intention frees resources for other things, overall increasing productivity. For instance, I would have been a rather unproductive PhD thesis writer if I would constantly have thought about whether it makes sense to write a PhD thesis or not.

Wooldridge defines intentions using these considerations on resource constraints:

> "Agents cannot deliberate indefinitely. They must clearly stop deliberating at some point, having chosen some state of affairs, and commit to achieving this state of affairs. [...] We refer to the states of affairs that an agent has chosen and committed to as its *intentions.*" (Wooldridge, 2000, p. 22-23)

The relation between intentions and plans becomes clear in one of the roles Wooldridge assigns to intentions: "*Intentions drive means-ends reasoning*: If I have formed an intention, then I will attempt to achieve the intention, which involves, among other things, deciding *how* to achieve it." (Wooldridge, 2000, p. 25). The means-ends reasoning is called planning. Thus, a plan is a "recipe [...] for achieving the chosen state of affairs" (Wooldridge, 2000, p. 22). The BDI architecture structures intentions into plans. Bratman offers a deeper insight on the relation between intentions and plans by stating that "plans typically have a hierarchical structure" and that they play a role in reasoning "from a prior intention to further intentions" (Bratman, 1990, p. 19). This is plausible for IAMSs. For instance, an agent having the intention to visit a museum will reason about a possible plan to achieve this state of affairs. The plan will have a structure, such as "goto the museum", "wait in line", "pay entrance fee", "see Mona Lisa", where for each of these steps there may be another sequence of sub-plans, forming a hierarchy. The intermediate elements in this hierarchical plan structure are again intentions which finally lead to behavior at the bottom of the hierarchy. These behaviors are also part of the plan.

The example shows another principle: a "prior" intention (visit museum) may lead to "further" intentions which are rather unpleasant (waiting in line). The museum visitor might argue: "I do not have the intention to wait in line, I just have to" so that "wait in line" could be neither an intention, nor a behavior, but some category of its own. This problem has been discussed as "package deal" by Bratman (1990), and as the difference between "intended and intentional action" by Moya (1990). Both ask the question whether a soldier who bombs a village, killing enemy soldiers and children, has only the intention to kill the soldiers, or can automatically be attributed to have the intention to also kill the children. This discussion of accountability, again, is rather an ethical one and out of the scope of this thesis. However, we conclude that there may be *undesired intentions* in mobile intention recognition which come as a package with desired intentions.

One last aspect about the nature of intentions that a developer of an IAMS should be aware of is that there are also habitual behavior patterns, which means that "intentions are not necessarily conscious mental episodes, even if they sometimes are. If, as I arrive at the University as I do every day, someone asks me whether I had the intention to come to the University that day, I will answer yes [...] although I may not remember having gone through a process of forming that intention" (Moya, 1990, 132). There are many scenarios where an IAMS should support these kinds of unconscious intentions. For instance, Moya's car navigation system could recognize his intention to go to the university, and offer appropriate navigation instructions. Behaviors, at the bottom of the hierarchical plans, are also usually unconscious. Moya might, for instance, have a conscious intention to get into his car in the morning, but will definitely not consciously deliberate about how to change his spatial position towards the car, including speed, heading, and so on. An IAMS that recognizes and supports intentions the user is not aware of works perfectly well as it offers seamless support without the user having to tell the system her intentions.

This glimpse into the literature on rational agents and philosophy shows that there are many interesting discussions on the concept of intention. However, it is not the objective of this section to provide an exhaustive overview. To summarize the issues about intentions an IAMS engineer should be aware of:

- Artificial and human agents are resource-limited. Intentions serve as an intermediate level between beliefs and desires on the one, and actions on the other side.
- Intentions are pro-attitudes, directed towards some future state of affairs.
- Plans hierarchically structure intentions and behavior. These plan structures include that the user having an intention may automatically imply her having further intentions.
- Not all intentions are desired. Some intentions may appear in a "package deal" with a prior intention.
- Intentions, behaviors, and planning processes are not necessarily conscious.
- An IAMS may have to deal with intentions that seam irrational for the system.

2.2.2 Intention Recognition and Plan Recognition

The BDI architecture can help to build rational agents with mental states, processes that operate between these states, and processes that produce the agent's actions. Intention and plan recognition try to analyse these processes in reverse. By observing the outcome of the actions (the agent's behavior)

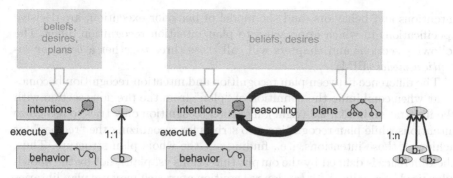

Fig. 2.9 Simplifications of the BDI architecture.

they try to find out mental states. Schlieder (2005, p. 43) states that "the fine-grained models of goal-directed behavior that have been proposed by cognitive psychologists such as the ACT-R architecture (Anderson and Lebiere, 1998) or the BDI architecture used in mulit-agent systems research [...] prove to be inadequate for describing user intentions in the context of location-based services." The reason is the complexity of these models: intention/plan recognition on the BDI architecture would need (reverse) models for all processes shown as squared boxes in Fig. 2.8. It is hard to build a model for each of these processes, especially if complex reasoning is concerned, but it is even harder due to the multiple dependencies between the blocks. The role of perception is particularly hard to handle as we cannot know what the agent perceives.

On the opposite, we could simplify the BDI architecture by putting beliefs, desires, and plans into a black box, and caring only about intentions and behavior (Fig. 2.9, left). Taking the room-crossing problem of section 1.1.2 as an example, we would turn the mapping "approach exhibit → information about the exhibit" into

approach exhibit at high speed → intention: pass the exhibit → overview map.

This 1:1-mapping between behavior and intention, however, is still not intelligent enough as it disregards the plan structure. The intention to pass the exhibit, for instance, might not be the best level of explanation as the intention to pass the exhibit may come in a package with a number of intentions, such as searching the restaurant or the exit.

Thus, we need to include more of the agent's mental state into our considerations. Figure 2.9 (right) shows an architecture that still hides most of the complexity of BDI while maintaining information on plan structures. The mapping between behaviors and intentions is now 1:n which allows, for instance, to infer that passing by the exhibit cannot be part of the plan to search the cafeteria if the agent has visited the cafeteria just a few moments ago. The way in which plans are represented, the reasoning process assumed between intentions and behaviors, and the model of behavior execution, are decisive specifications in which approaches to plan/intention recognition differ. The following sections and chapters will call these three together a *behavior intention model* (BIM).

The difference between plan recognition and intention recognition becomes clear when combining the definition of "plan" from the previous section with the illustration in Fig. 2.9 (right): intention recognition only tries to recognize intentions while plan recognition also strives for recognizing the "recipes" for achieving those intentions, i. e., finding out the whole plan structure. Thus, the difference is defined by the output (intentions vs. plan), not by the knowledge used internally. An intention recognition approach may use plan libraries to structure intentions. However, in the end, the intention recognition performs well if it recognizes the correct intention, not necessarily the correct plan. This means that plan recognition is the harder problem as there may be more than one plan structure that explains a certain intention. For the problem of supporting a mobile user, intention recognition in most cases is sufficient as it is more important to present the right information services in any given moment, than to provide a detailed explanation why this intention occurs.

Carberry (2001) characterizes plan recognition problems according to the attitude of the agent towards the system (the same characterization applies to intention recognition):

- *Intended plan recognition*: the agent knows that she is observed and acts cooperatively, i. e., chooses her behavior in a way that she thinks the system will interpret correctly. Examples are frequent in HCI if the user assumes that the system does not work well enough to recognize, for instance, her mumbling into the microphone, thus trying to speak extraordinarily clearly. This may appear in an IAMS but is definitely not the optimum as we want to minimize the attention the user needs to spend on the device.
- *Adversarial plan recognition*: the agent knows that she is observed, and attempts to hinder the system from recognizing the correct intentions (deception). This kind of situation occurs in security settings, such as monitoring passengers at the airport for terror prevention, and is rarely discussed in the literature (see Geib and Goldman, 2001; Mulder and Voorbraak, 2003). It is not relevant for IAMSs.
- *Keyhole plan recognition*: the observation of the agent has no impact on her behavior. This either means the agent does not know being observed, or she knows but does not care being observed, or – and this is the optimal case in an IAMS – she knows, cares, and thinks the system is working quite well.

As another characterization, plan/intention recognition can be divided into *online* and *offline* recognition (Bui, 2003): online recognition works incrementally and on-the-fly. Offline recognition is applied ex-post on previously recorded and finished behavior observations. Mobile intention recognition falls into the former category.

2.3 The Mobile Intention Recognition Problem

The previous sections have introduced IAMSs as mobile assistance systems which recognize their user's intentions (section 2.1) and provided background information on intentions, plans, and intention recognition (section 2.2). In the following the specificities of *mobile* intention recognition will be discussed. The mobile intention recognition problem will be defined as a special sub problem of the general intention recognition problem. This section also describes the problem of interleaved intentions which frequently occurs in mobile intention recognition, and for which new methods are developed in chapter 4.

2.3.1 Spatio-Temporal Behavior Sequences

The processing architecture introduced in Fig. 2.2 is specifically designed for intention recognition from motion track data. It describes the steps in which a user's trajectory is processed, crossing the semantic gap from position data to intentions. However, what makes the last processing step – intention recognition – a *mobile* one is not so much the fact that many of the input behaviors originate from a trajectory, but rather that all input behaviors are annotated with temporal and spatial information, independent from whether they were derived from the trajectory or from activity sensors. The spatial and temporal information in mobile intention recognition have several implications discussed in the following.

2.3.1.1 Temporal information in mobile intention recognition

One might argue that all human behavior happens at some point in time (or during a certain time interval), and conclude that the temporal aspects of mobile intention recognition do not make it special in any way. However, there are scenarios with incomplete information in which we want to infer intentions although we have no temporal information. Jarvis et al (2005), for instance, develop plan recognition methods for finding out whether a person or group has the intention to carry out a terrorist attack. A knowledge base might have the information that A) a person has taken flight lessons, and B) the same person has bought a gun, but – due to the unreliable sources from which the data was collected – no temporal information on when this happened, or even on the ordering of A) and B). Other examples for the absence of temporal information can be found in research on understanding discourse semantics which tries to infer human intentions from spoken or written text, such as "I want you to sing me a song. It's 'Yankee Doodle Dandy' in the key of C." (Sidner, 1985). In many texts like this, temporal information is missing and, quite often, temporal information is not relevant to interpret a sentence correctly.

IAMSs use sensors that annotate temporal information to all observations. Thus, the observations in mobile intention recognition are ordered. The definition of motion track (definition 2.2) also implies that this temporal order is strict and total. As the motion track is segmented incrementally with no overlap there is also a strict total temporal order on motion track segments, leading to a strict total temporal order on those behaviors derived from the trajectory. The activity disruption segmentation ensures that, finally, there is a strict total temporal order on all behaviors, including those inferred from activity, yielding in a behavior sequence:

Definition 2.3. Let B denote a finite set of behaviors. A *behavior sequence* is a sequence $\beta = \langle b_0, \ldots, b_n \rangle$ of behaviors from B. A behavior sequence has an implicit strict total temporal order. The sub sequence $\langle b_i, \ldots, b_j \rangle$ $(0 \leq i < j \leq n)$ is denoted with $\beta[i,j]$.

In case the intention recognition algorithm needs the absolute temporal information, the timestamps of start and end time can be annotated to each behavior, resulting in a temporal behavior sequence:

Definition 2.4. A *temporal behavior sequence* is a sequence $\beta_t = \langle (t_{s0}, t_{e0}, b_0), \ldots, (t_{sn}, t_{en}, b_n) \rangle$ of behaviors $b_0 \ldots b_n \in B$. We say a behavior b_i *took place* in the time interval $[t_{si}, t_{ei}[\subset T, t_{si} < t_{ei}$. A temporal behavior sequence has a strict total temporal order, i. e., $t_{ei} \leq t_{s(i+1)}$, for each two succeeding elements from β_t.

A duration of 0 is not allowed for any behavior. These definitions imply that, for any moment in time, the user shows at most one behavior. The way segmentation was described in section 2.1.2 ensures that the end time of any behavior is the start time of the next behavior. Thus, the behavior sequence in an IAMS is temporally complete, i. e., there is *exactly* one behavior for any moment in time:

Definition 2.5. A *temporally complete behavior sequence* β_{tc} is a temporal behavior sequence with $t_{ei} = t_{s(i+1)}$ for each two succeeding elements from β_{tc}.

Note that temporal completeness does not necessarily imply that the behavior sequence is terminated, i. e., more behaviors should be expected. The temporal completeness contrasts mobile intention recognition from many approaches in general plan recognition which lay special focus on dealing with

a.   {enter, exchange, exit, pay}

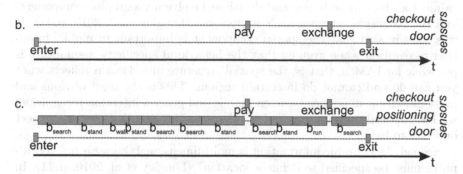

Fig. 2.10 a. Behavior observations without temporal information; b. Temporally ordered behavior sequence; c. Temporally complete behavior sequence

incomplete observations. Figure 2.10 illustrates the three levels of temporal information on behaviors in intention recognition for a clothes shopping example:

a) We know that the user has entered and exited the shop, payed one article, and exchanged one article.
b) From the ordering of the behavior we can see that the "pay" behavior was before the "exchange" behavior.
c) We know the spatio-temporal behavior between "pay" and "exchange": the user has searched (for some other articles) and probably exchanged the article she bought in the "pay" behavior with another article.

It is clear that serious positioning problems that cannot be handled in the data refinement step may impede temporal completeness: for instance, if the GPS signal is lost for a long period of time, such as five minutes, the resulting motion track segment may become meaningless if it does not even roughly approximate the user's real trajectory. Due to the fast technological advancements in positioning technology and data refinement algorithms, it is not too unsafe to assume that these situations are likely to become more and more rare in the near future.

To conclude, behaviors in mobile intention recognition come as ordered and temporally complete sequences. As we will see later this reduces the problem complexity.

2.3.1.2 Spatial information in mobile intention recognition

"Spatial is special" is one of the main statements of the introductory chapter in Longley et al's textbook on GIScience (Longley et al, 2010). The book lists a number of reasons, two of which can directly be transfered to explain why spatial information makes also mobile intention recognition special: first, "almost all human activities and decisions involve a geographic component, and the geographic component is important" (Longley et al, 2010, p. 11). It was already said that the spatial component is important in mobile intention recognition when arguing that the behavioral specificity assumption is plausible for IAMSs, that is, the spatial structure in a domain reflects what you can do and cannot do in certain regions. This is the most obvious and most important difference between mobile and general intention recognition: we have spatial information, and it relates to the intentions we can expect our user to have.

Second, "geographic information is multidimensional, because *two* coordinates must be specified to define a location" (Longley et al, 2010, p. 11). In the previous sections "region" was used for describing the place where a motion track segment or a behavior happened. These regions were picked from a "spatial model". To be more precise:

Definition 2.6. A *spatial model* SM = ($\boldsymbol{R}$, $\boldsymbol{SRT}$, $\boldsymbol{SR}$) consists of a finite set of *regions* $\boldsymbol{R}$, a finite set of (binary) *spatial relation types* $\boldsymbol{SRT}$, and a finite set of *spatial relations* $\boldsymbol{SR} \subseteq \boldsymbol{SRT} \times \boldsymbol{R} \times \boldsymbol{R}$ that specifies whether a spatial relation type holds for two regions.

Regions are written as capital R with subscript. The geometry $geom(R_i)$ of a region R_i is a polygon in $\mathbb{R}^2$. Valid polygons are

- simple polygons
- polygons with holes (if P_1 and P_2 are valid polygons with $P_2 \subset P_1$, then $P_1 \setminus P_2$ is a valid polygon)
- multi-ring polygons (if P_1 and P_2 are valid polygons with $P_1 \cap P_2 = \varnothing$, then $P_1 \cup P_2$ is a valid polygon)[5]

Sets of regions $\subset \boldsymbol{R}$ are written as bold $\boldsymbol{R}$ with subscript. It is required that $\boldsymbol{SRT}$ contains at least the relation types of the RCC-8 calculus (Randell et al, 1992), see Fig. 2.11: {*disjoint, touch, overlap, equals, covers, coveredBy, contains, containedBy*}. A functional notation will be used to specify whether a relation holds between two regions, i.e.: $srt: \boldsymbol{R} \times \boldsymbol{R} \to \{true, false\}$ takes the value *true* if $(srt, R_1, R_2) \in \boldsymbol{SR}$

Every spatial model has an all-encompassing region $R_\Omega \in \boldsymbol{R}$, with $\forall R_i \in \boldsymbol{R}$: $contains(R_\Omega, R_i) \lor covers(R_\Omega, R_i) \lor equals(R_i, R_\Omega)$[6]. Additional spatial relation types may include distance and direction relations, such as *north-of* or *far-away* (see Frank, 1992), or other spatial relations from qualitative

---

[5] A multi-ring polygon can also be defined as a polygon with a hole, where the hole cuts the polygon into two unconnected pieces.

[6] R_Ω is not an infinite region, and thus the *covers* relation may hold with its child regions. R_Ω is the top-level region containing all regions relevant for the domain, such as the city in Fig. 1.2. As we are not interested in intentions outside of our domain we assume that no behavior happens outside of R_Ω. (Without this assumption we could also say that a user located outside R_Ω has the intention $GotoR_\Omega$, and present a navigation information service accordingly.)

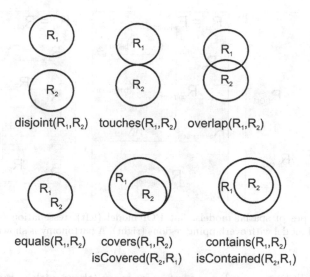

disjoint(R₁,R₂)   touches(R₁,R₂)   overlap(R₁,R₂)

equals(R₁,R₂)   covers(R₁,R₂)   contains(R₁,R₂)
             isCovered(R₂,R₁)   isContained(R₂,R₁)

Fig. 2.11 Spatial relation types in the RCC-8 calculus (Randell et al, 1992).

spatial reasoning (e. g., Skiadopoulos et al, 2007; Deng et al, 2007). Domains may impose constraints on the spatial model. Three types of spatial models are especially interesting for IAMSs (see Fig. 2.12):

- *Flat POI model*: regions (except R_Ω) may not overlap, cover, or contain other regions:
  $\forall R_1, R_2 \in \mathbf{R}: \neg\ overlap(R_1, R_2) \land ((contains(R_1, R_2) \lor covers(R_1, R_2))$
  $\rightarrow (R_1 = R_\Omega))$
  This is the spatial model type used by simple LBSs which have only on-enter/on-leave regions around POI (see Figs. 1.1 and 2.12, left).
- *Tessellation*: as the flat POI model, but with the additional condition that R_Ω is fully covered:
  $$\bigcup_{R_i \in \mathbf{R} \setminus \{R_\Omega\}} geom(R_i) = geom(R_\Omega)$$

  Small-sized indoor environments are sometimes structured as a tessellation. For instance, rooms and corridors will fully cover an apartment whereas, quite often, neither sub-regions (like areas around furniture) nor super-regions are modeled (see Fig. 2.12, center).
- *Partonomy*: no two regions are equals or overlap:
  $\forall R_1, R_2 \in \mathbf{R}: (R_1 \neq R_2) \rightarrow (\neg\ overlap(R_1, R_2) \land \neg\ equals(R_1, R_2))$

A partonomy was already used in the city guide example in Fig. 1.2 (left). A graph with regions as nodes, and relations *contains* and *covers* as edges yields in the *partonomy tree* (see Fig. 1.2, right). Partonomy is the most relevant spatial model type for intention recognition as many structured indoor and outdoor domains use this type. Flat POI model

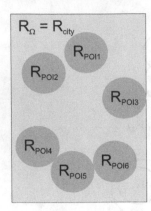 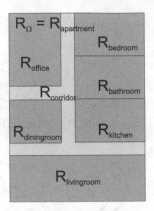 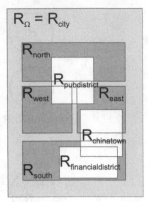

Fig. 2.12 Types of spatial models: flat POI model (left), tessellation (center), and general spatial model with overlapping regions (right). A partonomy is shown in Fig. 1.2.

and tessellation are sub types of partonomy (those with partonomy tree depth 1).

Deciding whether a spatial position (x, y) is in a given polygon (point-in-polygon problem) can efficiently be solved with algorithms from computational geometry (e. g., Huang and Shih, 1997). With an appropriate data processing a modified version of the swath algorithm efficiently computes the set of polygons which contains (x, y). As explained in section 2.1.2 each behavior in an IAMS is annotated with the set of regions in which it happened, which leads to an extension of temporal behavior sequences (definition 2.4):

Definition 2.7. Let B denote a finite set of behaviors, SM = (R, SRT, SR) denote a spatial model. A *spatio-temporal behavior sequence* is a sequence β_{st} = $\langle (t_{s0}, t_{e0}, R_0, b_0), \ldots, (t_{sn}, t_{en}, R_n, b_n) \rangle$ of behaviors $b_0 \ldots b_n \in B$. We say a behavior b_i *took place* in the set of regions $R_i \subseteq R$ during the time interval $[t_{si}, t_{ei}[\subset T, t_{si} < t_{ei}$. A spatio-temporal behavior sequence has a strict total temporal order, i. e., $t_{ei} \leq t_{s(i+1)}$, for each two succeeding elements from β_{st}.

The property of temporal completeness is defined according to definition 2.5. If SM is a partonomy $\langle (t_{s0}, t_{e0}, R_0, b_0), \ldots, (t_{sn}, t_{en}, R_n, b_n) \rangle$ can be chosen as a simplified notation for spatio-temporal behavior sequences, i. e., the region set R_i is replaced by the region $R_i \in R_i$ which is furthest away from R_Ω in the partonomy tree (the "smallest" region). R_i can be reconstructed by ascending the partonomy tree from R_i to R_Ω.

The 2-dimensionality of space makes the mobile intention recognition problem special. The reason is the *spatial continuity property* that holds if the sequence is temporally complete: as the user cannot fly she must traverse the regions in a sequence consistent with the spatial model, i. e., the values that are allowed for two succeeding region sets R_i and R_{i+1} can be restricted. For determining the consistency of a transition from R_i to R_{i+1} the tessellation

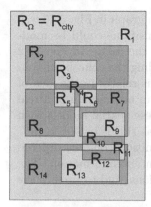 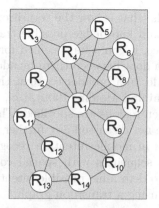 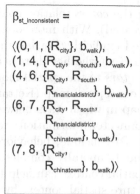

Fig. 2.13 Left: turning the general spatial model in Fig. 2.12, right, into a tessellation. Center: creating a transition graph for the tessellation (loop edges are omitted for reasons of clarity). Right: a spatio-temporal behavior sequence inconsistent with the spatial model.

tes(SM) of a spatial model is used: all geometries from $\mathbf{R}$ are intersected until a set of simple polygons remains from which a set of regions $\mathbf{R}_{tes}$ is created[7]. The function *reg*: $\mathbf{R}_{tes} \setminus \{R_\Omega\} \to 2^{\mathbf{R}}$ assigns each (non-Ω) region from the tessellation model *tes(SM)* the set of regions from the original model *SM* which contain it. The *transition graph tg(tes(SM))* is a graph with nodes $\mathbf{R}_{tes} \setminus \{R_\Omega\}$ and edges between those regions between which the user can travel. Each node in the transition graph has a loop edge to itself because the user may decide not to cross a region border. Figure 2.13 (left, center) illustrates how we derive a transition graph from a general spatial model. With the transition graph we can, finally, define spatial consistency:

Definition 2.8. A spatio-temporal behavior sequence $\beta_{st} = \langle (t_{s0}, t_{e0}, \mathbf{R}_0, b_0), \ldots, (t_{sn}, t_{en}, \mathbf{R}_n, b_n) \rangle$ is *spatially consistent* with the spatial model SM if, for each two succeeding region sets $\mathbf{R}_i$ and $\mathbf{R}_{i+1}$, there exists an edge between two regions R_{b1} and R_{b2} (both $\in \mathbf{R}_{tes}$) in the transition graph tg(tes(SM)), with reg(R_{b1}) = $\mathbf{R}_i$ and reg(R_{b2}) = $\mathbf{R}_{i+1}$.

Figure 2.13 (right) demonstrates a spatio-temporal behavior sequence inconsistent with the spatial model from Fig. 2.12 (right): $\beta_{st\_inconsistent}$ traverses the transition graph in an inconsistent manner $\langle R_1, R_{14}, R_{13}, R_{12}, R_{10} \rangle$ which would require the user to fly from R_{12} to R_{10}. It depends on the domain how the edges in the transition graph are determined. If no domain knowledge about obstacles, such as walls or rivers, is available it may be assumed that the user may transit between two regions in *tes(SM)* if the *touches*

---

[7] As, by definition, any spatial model must have an all encompassing region, we add R_Ω to $\mathbf{R}_{tes}$. We also must add the remainder of R_Ω after all intersections: $R_\Omega \setminus \bigcup_{R \in \mathbf{R}, R \neq R_\Omega} R$.

or the *covers* relation holds (that is how the transition graph in Fig. 2.13 was created). With more domain knowledge possible transitions could be modeled explicitly. For instance, it could be specified for the rooms in Fig. 2.12 (center) whether there is a door between them by adding the concept of *connectors* to the spatial mode. In a broader context, this relates to the idea of a conceptual map (Kettani and Moulin, 1999), i. e., an abstraction of a real map in which ways between regions are specified. These spatial models with connector information are not discussed any further as this is out of scope.

To conclude, behaviors in mobile intention recognition come as ordered and temporally complete sequences with spatial context information. The spatial context can help to determine possible intentions, and to predict the future spatial context by using a transition graph.

2.3.2 Mobile Intention Recognition: A Definition

In the next step intentions are recognized incrementally from the spatio-temporal behavior sequence. Intention recognition is triggered for each behavior that comes in from the preprocessing, i. e., the *current intention* I_i (from a finite set of possible intentions **I**) is recognized for each input (t_{si}, t_{ei}, R_i, b_i). An intention recognition algorithm that considers only current information from the time interval $[t_{si}, t_{ei}[$ will, in general, not work very well. For instance, the user of an AAL system who is entering the kitchen may have one of several intentions, such as *PrepareDinner*, *CleanKitchenFloor*, and many others. If it is sure that she had the intention *CleanCorridorFloor* before, the plan library may tell that this is part of an intention to clean the whole apartment and decide for *CleanKitchenFloor* (see the discussions about plan and intention recognition in section 2.2.2). Intention recognition needs more than local information about the spatio-temporal behavior sequence, possibly the whole $\beta_{st}[0,i]$ known up to now[8]. With these considerations the mobile intention recognition problem can be defined formally:

Definition 2.9. Let B denote a finite set of behaviors, I denote a finite set of intentions, SM = (R, SRT, SR) denote a spatial model. The *mobile intention recognition problem* consists in selecting the *current intention* $I_i \in I$ which explains the current behavior b_i in a temporally complete spatio-temporal behavior sequence $\beta_{st} = \langle (t_{s0}, t_{e0}, R_0, b_0), ..., (t_{si}, t_{ei}, R_i, b_i) \rangle$, where β_{st} is consistent with SM.

---

[8] The notation of partial spatio-temporal behavior sequences between indices i and j, $\beta_{st}[i,j]$, is chosen in analogy to motion track segments (definition 2.2).

2.3.2.1 Closed world assumption, inexplicability, and ambiguity

Both sets, $\mathbf{B}$ and $\mathbf{I}$, are specified by the domain expert. A good strategy for defining these intentions is to consider the information services the IAMS will have and specify the intentions supported by these services. As in classical software development, structured and unstructured interviews with the users of the system (as part of the use case analysis) can give useful hints to determine which intentions the users would like to have supported. $\mathbf{B}$ and $\mathbf{I}$ being finite implies a *closed world assumption*: the goal is not to recognize *any* intention a human might have but only those relevant for the application. The closed world assumption also comprises that the user of the system exclusively shows behavior consistent with her intentions. As a consequence, when faced with reality, there may be situations where the user shows *inexplicable* behavior, i. e., intention recognition is not able to select a current intention from $\mathbf{I}$. Inexplicable behavior does not necessarily need to be irrational (see section 2.2.1.2) but may also just be out of the domain. A spatio-temporal behavior sequence can also be inexplicable if the preprocessing did, for some reason, not work correctly.

Besides inexplicability, there is the problem of *ambiguity* which occurs if a given spatio-temporal behavior sequence has more than one possible interpretation, i. e., a whole set of intentions $\mathbf{I}_i \subseteq \mathbf{I}$ can be considered as hypotheses for the current intention. The kitchen example above, without the background knowledge about the corridor cleaning, is one example. In previous sections it was mentioned that the behavior sequence is generally not terminated: the user is still on her way and expected to show more behavior in the near future. As a consequence an IAMS tries to recognize intentions even if β_{st} consists of only one element. It is intuitively clear that a one-elementary input sequence, such as $(t_{so}, t_{eo}, R_{kitchen}, b_{entering})$, will very often be ambiguous as there are plenty of possible continuations. Thus, ambiguity is a central problem of mobile intention recognition and requires special attention.

2.3.2.2 Mobile intention recognition algorithms

A perfect mobile intention recognition algorithm, applied to a perfect behavior sequence, given a perfect model of the world, would solve the intention recognition problem perfectly in any incremental step for the whole runtime of the application, thus mapping each $\beta_{st}[0,i]$ ($0 \leq i \leq n$, where n is the total number of behaviors that occur during runtime) to one intention I_i. This would yield in an *intention sequence* $\iota[0,n] = \langle (t_{s0}, t_{e0}, \mathbf{R}_0, I_0), \ldots, (t_{sn}, t_{en}, \mathbf{R}_n, I_n) \rangle$. However, any real intention recognition algorithm will have to deal with inexplicability and ambiguity. Thus, in any time slice i the algorithm will return a set of hypotheses $\mathbf{I}_i$, where each element in $\mathbf{I}_i$ could explain $\langle (t_{si}, t_{ei}, \mathbf{R}_i, b_i) \rangle$. The result of the algorithm over the whole runtime is then an

algorithm   mobileIntentionRecognition(
                            spatio-temporal behavior sequence $\beta_{st}[0,n]$,
                            domain model $DM = ($**B**, **I**, SM, $BIM)$) **returns**
                            an intention hypotheses sequence $\rho[0,n]$
begin
        initialize(DM)
        $\rho \leftarrow$ an empty intention hypotheses sequence

        for (int i = 0; i $\leq$ n; i++) **do**
        $(t_s, t_e, \mathbf{R}_{in}, b) \leftarrow \beta_{st}[i,i]$
        $\mathbf{I}_{hypotheses} \leftarrow$ recognize($(t_s, t_e, \mathbf{R}_{in}, b)$)
        ρ.append($(t_s, t_e, \mathbf{R}_{in}, \mathbf{I}_{hypotheses})$)
        selectAndShowInfoService($\mathbf{I}_{hypotheses}$, $\mathbf{R}_{in}$)
        end for

        return ρ
end algorithm

abstract procedure   initialize(domain model DM)

abstract function   recognize(space-time behavior $(t_s, t_e, \mathbf{R}_{in}, b)$) **returns**
$\mathbf{I}_{hypotheses}$

abstract procedure   selectAndShowInfoService(intentions $\mathbf{I}_{curr}$, regions $\mathbf{R}_{curr}$)

Fig. 2.14 The general structure of mobile intention recognition algorithms.

intention hypotheses sequence $\rho[0,n] = \langle(t_{s0}, t_{e0}, \mathbf{R}_0, \mathbf{I}_0), ..., (t_{sn}, t_{en}, \mathbf{R}_n, \mathbf{I}_n)\rangle$[9].

Figure 2.14 illustrates the general structure of a mobile intention recognition algorithm. **B**, **I**, SM, and behavior intention model BIM are combined to a domain model DM. One important task when specifying a mobile intention recognition algorithm is to define the representational formalism for the BIM. In the initialize() procedure the algorithm prepares all internal data structures it needs to be ready for the first behavior input. For instance, the computation of a transition graph could be performed in initialize(). The recognize() function is the heart of the algorithm and incrementally determines intention hypotheses. Although it takes only the current space-time behavior as input, it may keep track of all previous space-time behaviors in its internal data structures. Procedure selectAndShowInfoService() triggers the information service.

---

[9] Two succeeding intentions $\mathbf{I}_i$ and $\mathbf{I}_{i+1}$ in an intention sequence ι may be the same. As the intention has not changed, the IAMS will in most cases also not change the information service. If the intention has not changed, but the region sets $\mathbf{R}_i$ and $\mathbf{R}_{i+1}$, it will sometimes make sense to choose a new information service. Same applies accordingly to succeeding hypotheses sets in an intention hypotheses sequence ρ.

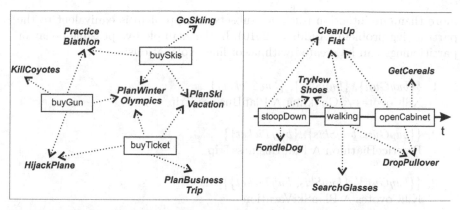

Fig. 2.15 Partitioning of observations to intentions in general intention recognition (left). Composition of a behavior sequence in mobile intention recognition (right).

The algorithm shows that each set of hypotheses $\mathbf{I}_i$ in $\rho[0,n]$ is computed with the restricted knowledge available at time slice i (i. e., $\beta_{st}[0,i]$). Even though the knowledge gained later (i. e., $\beta_{st}[i+1, n]$) may help to reduce the ambiguity of $\mathbf{I}_i$ in retrospect, and even though this ambiguity reduction may (and will) be used to improve later hypotheses ($\rho[i+1,n]$), from the perspective of evaluating an algorithm, the degree of ambiguity at time slice i is decisive as this is the moment when the IAMS needs to choose an information service. $|\mathbf{I}_i|$ is called the *degree of ambiguity* for the space-time behavior at time slice i, where $|\mathbf{I}_i| = 0$ is called inexplicability, $|\mathbf{I}_i| = 1$ means no ambiguity, and $|\mathbf{I}_i| > 1$ means ambiguity (with higher values for higher ambiguity). $|\mathbf{I}_i|$ will be used in chapter 5 for evaluating the performance of different algorithms.

2.3.3 Behavior Sequence Compositions

2.3.3.1 From partitioning to composition: the influence of ordering

Consider the non-mobile intention recognition problem displayed in Fig. 2.15 (left): the system has recorded a set of three behaviors (called "observations" for the non-mobile problem): {*buyGun, buySkis, buyTicket*}. One of the hardest challenges for intention recognition is to build subsets of these observations in a manner that: 1) all observations are used, and 2) the grouping is consistent with the BIM. For now it is assumed that the BIM does not imply any restrictions, i. e., all subsets of behaviors can be grouped together. Figure 2.15 (left) shows an example in which explanations for all subsets of behaviors exist. If it is further assumed that no behavior is used to explain more than one intention (disjunct subsets) the problem is equivalent to the partitioning problem (Audibert, 2010). In the example five possible behavior partitionings can be created with according explanations:

1. $\{\{buyGun\}, \{buySkis\}, \{buyTicket\}\}$
   KillCoyotes $\wedge$ GoSkiing $\wedge$ PlanBusinessTrip

2. $\{\{buyGun, buySkis\}, \{buyTicket\}\}$
   PracticeBiathlon $\wedge$ PlanBusinessTrip

3. $\{\{buyGun\}, \{buySkis, buyTicket\}\}$
   KillCoyotes $\wedge$ PlanSkiVacation

4. $\{\{buyTicket, buyGun\}, \{buySkis\}\}$
   HijackPlane $\wedge$ GoSkiing

5. $\{\{buyGun, buySkis, buyTicket\}\}$
   PlanWinterOlympics

In general, the number of possible partitionings for a set with cardinality n is equal to the nth *Bell number* B_n (see Audibert, 2010; Sloane, 2010). The Bell number B_n can be calculated recursively from all previous Bell numbers (where $B_0 = 0$):

$$B_{n+1} = \sum_{k=0}^{n} \binom{n}{k} B_k$$

or using the Dobinski formula:

$$B_n = \frac{1}{e} \sum_{k=0}^{\infty} \frac{k^n}{k!}.$$

Bell numbers grow extremely fast, e.g., $B_5 = 52$, $B_{10} = 115\,975$, $B_{20} \approx 5.172 \cdot 10^{13}$.

Spatio-temporal behavior sequences β_{st}, on the other hand, are ordered. Let us now assume that the user does not have any interleaved plans, which means behaviors can only be grouped into an explanatory sub sequence if they are neighbors in β_{st}. Separated behaviors, such as *stoopDown* and *openCabinet* in the example of Figure 2.15 (right), cannot be part of one intention if the intermediate behavior (*walking*) does not explain the same intention. This leads to four possible explanations for the example:

1. $\langle\langle stoopDown\rangle, \langle walking\rangle, \langle openCabinet\rangle\rangle$
   $\langle$FondleDog, SearchGlasses, GetCereals$\rangle$

2. $\langle\langle stoopDown, walking\rangle, \langle openCabinet\rangle\rangle$
   $\langle$TryNewShoes, GetCereals$\rangle$

3. $\langle\langle stoopDown\rangle, \langle walking, openCabinet\rangle\rangle$
   $\langle$FondleDog, DropPullover$\rangle$

4. $\langle\langle stoopDown, walking, openCabinet\rangle\rangle$
   $\langle$CleanUpFlat$\rangle$

The number of such explanations possible for a sequence of length n can be determined with simple combinatorics: there are (n - 1) positions at which the sequence can be cut, and the number of cuts is an integer between 0 and (n - 1). This yields in

$$C_n = \sum_{k=0}^{n-1} \binom{n-1}{k} = 2^{n-1}$$

which is still exponential but growing much slower than the Bell sequence, e. g., $C_5 = 16$, $C_{10} = 512$, $C_{20} = 524\,288$. C_n is called the number of possible *compositions* in number theory. It is the number of ways in which an integer n can be represented as a sum of positive integers (where the order of the summands matters). To be more precise about the different growth of B_n and C_n, consider $\frac{B_{n+1}}{B_n}$, and $\frac{C_{n+1}}{C_n}$ respectively, which express the percental growth of the two sequences: $\frac{C_{n+1}}{C_n} = 2$, i. e., the sequence C_n is logarithmically linear. In contrast, Asai et al (2000) have shown that B_n is logarithmically convex, i. e., $\frac{B_{n+1}}{B_n}$ is not a constant, but grows with the sequence: $\frac{B_{n+1}}{B_n} \geq \frac{B_n}{B_{n-1}}$ for all $n \geq 0$. Strict convexity, i. e., $\frac{B_{n+1}}{B_n} > \frac{B_n}{B_{n-1}}$, has not been proved yet but verified for $n \leq 1500$ computationally (Bouroubi, 2007). It is clear that, for realistic input sequence lengths in mobile intention recognition, B_n grows much faster than C_n.

Though a worst case scenario has been considered in which no additional grouping restrictions from the BIM are available, and in which the algorithm tries out all groupings in a (somehow stupid) bottom-up manner, this tremendous difference in number of possible explanations is intrinsic to the two problems of general and mobile intention recognition. It influences the degree of ambiguity one can expect. Section 3.2.2 will show that Kautz (1991) has already identified this as one problem about his general plan recognition approach. An additional source of ambiguity for general and mobile recognition arises from observation/behavior groupings for which more than one intention exists. For instance, the behavior *openCabinet* could be the only part of several intentions as the user may want to get a number of different things from the cabinet. This kind of ambiguity is relevant for intention

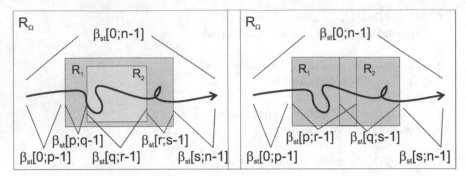

Fig. 2.16 Spatial composition of a spatio-temporal behavior sequence in a partonomy (left) and a spatial model with overlap (right).

recognition in practice but, as the set of all intentions $\mathbf{I}$ is finite, when estimating the complexity in terms of possible partitionings/compositions this kind of ambiguity would appear as a constant factor.

2.3.3.2 Spatial composition restrictions: the room-crossing problem revisited

Let us now integrate grouping restrictions from the BIM. At this point, we are not interested in those grouping restrictions that come from pre- and post-conditions in the plan library, such as, "the user must fill water into the bucket before he can clean the floor". We rather consider spatial grouping restrictions by disallowing all those compositions for a spatio-temporal behavior sequence $\beta_{st}[0;n\text{-}1]$ in which one or several sub sequences cross a region boundary, i. e., all spatio-temporal behaviors in each sub sequence must have the same set of regions: $\beta_{st}[p;q\text{-}1] = \langle (t_{sp}, t_{ep}, \mathbf{R}_{pq}, b_p), \ldots, (t_{s(q\text{-}1)}, t_{e(q\text{-}1)}, \mathbf{R}_{pq}, b_{q\text{-}1}) \rangle$.

Figure 2.16 (left) shows an example in a small partonomy: the regions R_1 and R_2 cut $\beta_{st}[0;n\text{-}1]$ into five pieces. The number of compositions for $\beta_{st}[0;n\text{-}1]$ without spatial restrictions is $C_n = 2^{n-1}$, and with spatial restrictions

$$C_p \cdot C_{q\text{-}p} \cdot C_{r\text{-}q} \cdot C_{s\text{-}r} \cdot C_{n\text{-}s} = 2^{p\text{-}1} \cdot 2^{q\text{-}p\text{-}1} \cdot 2^{r\text{-}q\text{-}1} \cdot 2^{s\text{-}r\text{-}1} \cdot 2^{n\text{-}s\text{-}1} = 2^{n\text{-}5}$$

It is easy to show that, in general, the number of possible compositions for a spatio-temporal behavior sequence of length n crossing k region boundaries is $C_{n-k} = 2^{n-k-1}$ if the intention changes at each boundary.

However, as illustrated in the room-crossing example in section 1.1.2 the user's intention does not change at every region boundary as the correct interpretation for a behavior sequence is not necessarily determined by the smallest current region. In Fig. 2.16 (left) the correct interpretation could also be found only in R_1 which means the sequence could be cut at positions p and s (instead of cutting at p, q, r, and s). In the worst case, the correct interpretation for the whole sequence could be in R_Ω which means that a

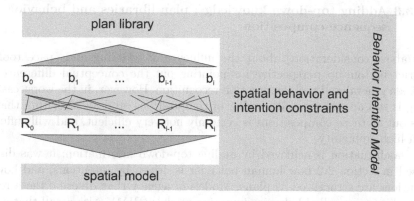

Fig. 2.17 Connecting plan library and spatial model.

composition at region boundaries cannot be assumed. For this worst case the maximum complexity of 2^{n-1} cannot be avoided. Because of the room-crossing problem no further statements from a bottom-up perspective are possible. However, we can say that, the more closely the BIM connects regions and behaviors the more ambiguity is reduced (in terms of possible groupings) by powers of two. A close connection between regions and behaviors means that the behaviors $\langle b_p \ldots b_{q-1} \rangle$ in a sequence $\beta_{st}[p;q\text{-}1]$ can only be interpreted in one region $R_z \in \mathbf{R}_{pq}$ (and not in overlapping, parent or child regions). If there is no close connection, a room-crossing problem will probably appear.

One remark about overlapping regions (see example in Fig. 2.16, right): if we again assume that no behavior is interpreted in parent regions we can either cut at p and r, or at q and s, i. e., the behavior sequence in the middle $\beta[r;q\text{-}1]$ can be interpreted as part of the intention in either region R_1 or R_2. When calculating the number of possible groupings we must subtract this middle part once (as it has been counted in both cuts), yielding

$$C_p \cdot (C_{r\text{-}p} \cdot C_{s\text{-}r} + C_{q\text{-}p} \cdot C_{s\text{-}q} - C_{q\text{-}p} \cdot C_{r\text{-}q} \cdot C_{s\text{-}r}) \cdot C_{n\text{-}s} = 2 \cdot 2^{n-4} - 2^{n-5}$$

The 2 is a constant factor so that the complexity in this case is 2^{n-4}. This relates to C_{n-k} when crossing three region borders with three times changing intentions (see above). (In a partonomy k = 3 appears if the relations *touches* or *covers* hold.) We conclude that overlapping regions have a higher complexity than partonomic structures. The amount of increase depends on the way the regions overlap and how the user crosses them.

2.3.3.3 Adding top-down knowledge: plan libraries and behavior sequence composition

The above considerations about the influence of ordering and space took a strict bottom-up perspective for pointing out the conceptual differences between general and mobile intention recognition. However, in the worst case there is still an exponential number of compositions, and an algorithm that tries out all these compositions is certainly not very efficient, and will suffer from high ambiguity.

Disambiguation is achieved by adding top-down information: it was discussed in section 2.2 how human behavior is driven by intentions, and how intentions are structured as plans. Models of agency that describe these relationships were called behavior intention models (BIM). Also recall that an intelligent BIM will not just map behavior to intentions, but induce a plan structure. This structural information restricts the number of possible behavior compositions. There were several examples in this chapter, like "the user must fill water into the bucket before he can clean the floor" or the steps necessary for seeing Mona Lisa.

We will see in chapter 3 that BIM are often called "plan libraries" in the related problem of plan recognition, and that types of plan libraries differ in the structural complexity they can represent. This influences the number of possible behavior compositions. For instance, Schlieder (2005) pointed out for mobile intention recognition that "[t]he representational formalism describing the behavior-intention mapping must be more expressive than a finite state mechanism", i. e., it must support behavior sequences such as $enter^n$ $leave^n$ (entering and leaving of nested regions in a partonomy).

For now, the complexity of the plans that can be represented is not the focus but the connection of these plans with space: plan libraries and space do not only individually restrict the number of possible compositions, but can also be related to each other. These *spatial behavior and intention constraints* define which behaviors/intentions are possible in which regions. This idea was referenced to as "behavioral specificity assumption" in section 2.1.2. For instance, we do not only know that the Mona Lisa visitor will show a *queuing* behavior before entering the exhibition but also that this will happen in the spatial region $R_{queuingarea}$. A *queuing* behavior outside of $R_{queuingarea}$ will not be interpreted as intention *BuyTickets* but maybe as *BuyFood* (for the spatial region $R_{snackbar}$). Thus, the BIM in mobile intention recognition consists of a plan library, a spatial model, and constraints that connect these two models (see Fig. 2.17). This fundamental idea is independent from the way in which plans are represented, and from the type of spatial model in a certain domain.

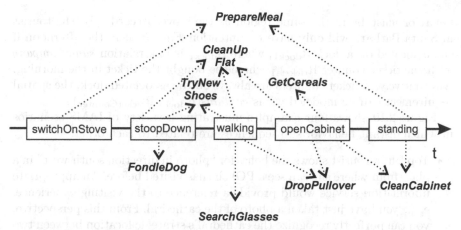

Fig. 2.18 A behavior sequence composition with interleaving intentions.

2.3.4 The Problem of Interleaved Intentions

The previous sections assumed that the user does not have any interleaved intentions. This allowed us to reduce the bottom-up worst case complexity for behavior grouping from B_n (partitioning) to 2^n (composition). This section explains why this assumption is often too restrictive, and illustrates with examples that long-ranging space-intention dependencies appear as problems in many IAMS scenarios. Handling these dependencies is the main focus of the formalisms developed in chapter 4.

2.3.4.1 Examples

Consider the AAL example in Fig. 2.18 (which is an extension of the example in Fig. 2.15, right): the user switches on the stove, does some other household stuff, and is finally *standing*. As a cook usually checks the cooked meal after some time, adding spices or other ingredients, we may assume that this *standing* is part of the *PrepareMeal* intention. This pattern $\langle doX_1, do\text{-}SomethingCompletelyDifferent, doX_2 \rangle$, where X_1 and X_2 are related to the same intention, can be found quite frequently in IAMSs. A tourist in Santa Barbara (California, U.S.), as another example, might reserve tickets for a whale watching tour in the morning, go for lunch and shopping at noon, and join the whale watching tour in the afternoon.

Both examples show that space is an important indicator for deciding whether an interleaving intention exists or not. For instance, the *standing* behavior can only be part of the *PrepareMeal* intention if the user is standing in front of the stove (more precisely: in front of the *same* stove), which means – due to spatial consistency – that the cabinet opened in the previous behavior must be in the same region as the stove. Accordingly, the tourist in Santa Barbara will only have the intention *EnterBoat* in the afternoon if she is located on a dock R_{dock1}, where R_{dock1} is in a relation *sameCompany* with the ticket counter $R_{tickets1}$ where she bought the ticket in the morning. Alternatively, if ticket counters are always on the associated dock, the spatial requirement can be modeled we as $contains(R_{dock}, R_{ticketCounter})$.

Figure 2.19 shows four examples illustrating a variety of IAMS scenarios in which distant behavior sub sequences are related to each other:

- Top left: a tourist shows the behavior "photo in direction south-west" in a place from where she can see a POI she has visited before. An appropriate information service would provide a reference to the visiting experience, e. g.,"you have just taken a photo of the cathedral. From this perspective, you can perfectly recognize the cathedral's strategic location between two rivers which I explained this morning."
- Top right: the whalewatching tour example. The tourist has bought a ticket in $R_{tickets1}$. Thus, her entering behavior in R_{dock2} is *not* interpreted as *EnterBoat* intention, but her entering of R_{dock1} some time later. It may be unusual to call the *sameCompany* relation a *spatial* relation. However, we could easily adjust the example by adding a multi-ringed parent region $R_{company1}$ which contains R_{dock1} and $R_{tickets1}$. The spatial relation *sameCompany* could then be translated into *hasSameDirectParent*. The spatial relation *contains* between dock and ticket counter is also possible.
- Bottom left: a tourist reaches a city by bus, does some sightseeing or shopping, and later tries to find the way back to the bus terminal. The *FindBus* intention is recognized if she shows a *searching* behavior in a region which *touches* the target region. This is an example for the pattern "find way back" found in many scenarios, and illustrates that a dependency between behavior sub sequences may range over the whole behavior sequence.
- Bottom right: an example from an ambient shopping environment in which regions are defined around shelves, with sensors at the clothes hangers for behavior *pick*. The shopper picks an article from R_{shelf3}, possibly more articles from other shelves, enters the fitting rooms, and later returns to R_{shelf3}. We can now assume that he is not satisfied with the article and tries to grab a different size.

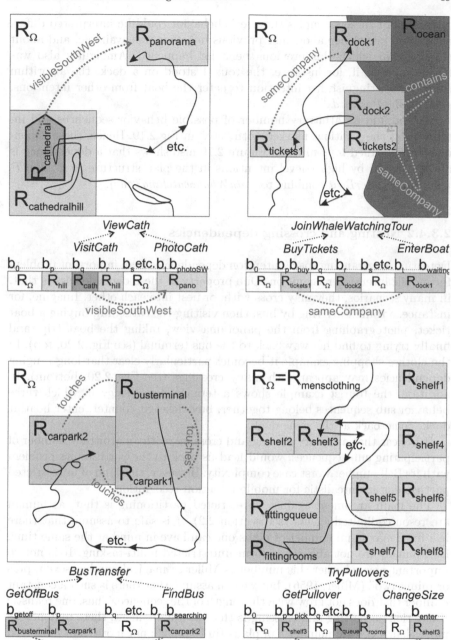

Fig. 2.19 Four mobile intention recognition scenarios with long-ranging space-intention dependencies.

In each of these examples the user's behavior could be interpreted differently if no knowledge about her previous behavior was available, and about the space in which this previous behavior happened. Ambiguity also was higher because if, for instance, the tourist stood on a dock, the algorithm could not distinguish her intention to enter the boat from other intentions, such as *BuyPostcard*.

We can add an arbitrary number of possible behavior sequences and intentions at the positions marked with "etc." in Fig 2.19. Hence, these dependencies are called *long-ranging*. Figure 2.19 also shows that a dependency is always caused by higher level intentions in the plan structure (e. g., *BuyTickets* and *EnterBoat* combine to *JoinWhalewatchingTour*).

2.3.4.2 Nesting and crossing dependencies

Detecting long-ranging space-intention dependencies is an important problem for mobile intention recognition. One property of these dependencies is that, in many scenarios, they may cross with, or nest into each other. Imagine, for instance, a tourist arriving by bus, then visiting the cathedral, buying a boat ticket, photographing from the panorama view, taking the boat trip, and finally trying to find her way back to the bus terminal (see Fig. 2.20, top). In the clothes shopping example it becomes particularly clear that long-ranging dependencies may appear with many crossings (see Fig. 2.20, bottom). In addition, the tourist example shows a ternary dependency in which three behavior sub sequences belong together: buy ticket at counter, enter boat at dock, come back at the same dock.

It is clear that arbitrary nesting and crossing, with an arbitrary number of participating sub sequences, would lead us back to the partitioning problem with its Bell number worst case complexity. However, this kind of unrestricted partitioning is unrealistic for mobile intention recognition.

The main argument against unrestricted partitioning is that, as human are resource-limited agents (see section 2.2), it is safe to assume that there is a fixed maximum number of plans one can have in mind at the same time, i. e., human are not able to perform unrestricted multi-tasking. It is not so important now whether this number is Miller's "magical number seven, plus or minus two" (Miller, 1956), but we can assume that there is such a constant number that does not grow with the length of the sequence. Thus, one realistic restriction on nesting and crossing is that, at any moment, there may not be more than a certain number c of plans (in Fig. 2.20: not more than c "dotted lines" in any moment).

Alternatively, it could be argued that crossing plan structures are cognitively more complex, and thus use a higher constant for nesting than for crossing plans. A third approach would be to restrict the number of dependencies involving more than two behavior sub sequences, or to even forbid these ternary or higher degree dependencies. This section does not settle on

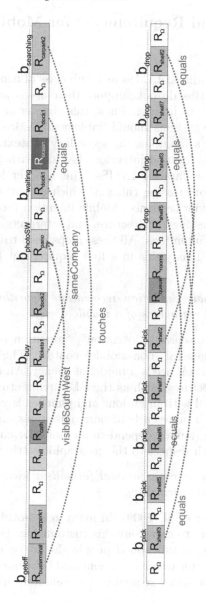

Fig. 2.20 Nesting and crossing of long-ranging space-intention dependencies.

one fixed assumption now. It rather concludes that in mobile intention recognition, spatio-temporal behavior sequences are not always strictly composed into groups with their temporal neighbours, but that long-ranging space-intention dependencies exist with a limited amount of nestings and crossings. Chapters 3 and 4 will discuss the kinds of nesting and crossing supported by different formalisms.

2.4 Summary and Requirements for Mobile Intention Recognition

This chapter has introduced IAMSs as a sub class of context-aware services. We have seen that LBSs do not support their users sufficiently well if interaction possibilities are limited. Thus, this chapter suggested that proactive mobile assistance systems should implement IAMSs instead of LBSs by integrating their user's intentions as secondary context. The semantic gap between sensor acquisition and intentions is wide, with position data as the most important sensor data for IAMSs. This chapter has proposed a processing architecture for crossing this gap which converts a trajectory into a spatio-temporal behavior sequence. Mobile intention recognition crosses the last step in this processing architecture, and interprets the spatio-temporal behavior sequence as intentions. All these steps need to be performed incrementally and online. This yields in a first requirement for mobile intention recognition[10]:

Requirement 1 *Mobile intention recognition algorithms should run efficiently on the limited ressources of a mobile device.*

This chapter also discussed "intention", "intention recognition", and related concepts in a general (non-mobile) context. The discussion revealed that intention recognition needs a model of agency. An argument was made that cognitive architectures, such as the BDI architecture, are too complex, and a simplified model with intentions and plans as key concepts was introduced. The connection between behaviors, intentions, and plans is specified in a BIM. The BIM is domain dependent and must be customized for a given system, especially with respect to the geographic setting.

Requirement 2 *The representational formalism used for the BIM should support easy geographic portability.*

As argued in Kiefer et al (2009), in many real world scenarios we would like the domain expert to carry out this customizing. For instance, an AAL system for supporting handicapped people should be customizable by the nurse as she knows better which intentions and behaviors may appear for her patient, and which behavior sequences are definitely irrational and require medical intervention.

Requirement 3 *The representational formalism used for the BIM should be cognitively understandable, i. e., modifiable by a domain expert.*

Requirement 4 *The representational formalism used for the BIM should support the formulation of exclusive, definite assertions, i. e., behavior sequences that should definitely be interpreted as one intention, or be classified as irrational.*

---

[10] Requirements are not ordered by importance.

A large part of this chapter was dedicated to the specificities of mobile intention recognition, compared to general intention recognition. The fundamental difference is that, in the mobile case, each observation is annotated with spatial and temporal information. These spatio-temporal behavior sequences are temporally complete and ordered, and consistent with region neighbourhood in a spatial model. A bottom-up worst case consideration revealed that the ordering information tremendously reduces the problem complexity compared to general intention recognition, because grouping behaviors to intentions in the mobile case is equivalent to composition, not partitioning.

This last statement was shown to be valid only if intentions do not interleave. A discussion of IAMS scenarios showed that this is not true in general as there may be long-ranging dependencies that nest into, and cross each other. Handling these dependencies with the goal of avoiding ambiguity and inexplicability is the main focus of the following chapters.

Requirement 5 *The representational formalism used for the BIM should allow us to express long-ranging space-intention dependencies which may – to a certain degree – nest into and overlap with each other.*

Chapter 3
Related Approaches in Plan Recognition

This chapter provides an overview on related work in plan and intention recognition. Related approaches are explored with respect to solving the mobile intention recognition for IAMS, i. e., in the light of the requirements introduced in section 2.4. Note that an understanding of the spatial grammar formalism in section 3.4.2 will help to get familiar with basic ideas used in chapter 4.

Related work in activity recognition is not the focus of this chapter but mentioned if it results from the discussion. Other fields of research more distantly related to this thesis, like ambient environments, mobile, pervasive, and ubiquitous computing, were touched on in the previous chapters and are not deepened here.

3.1 Finite State Machines

Finite state machines (FSMs) have, to the best of the author's knowledge, not been proposed with the claim to approach the problems of plan or intention recognition, but in related areas on a semantically lower level.

For instance, models with the expressiveness of FSMs have gained some popularity in the mobile computing community under the title "behavior interpretation". Ashbrook and Starner's (2002; 2003) research had probably the highest impact in this direction. They detect the places important in someone's daily life from a trajectory recorded over several days or weeks by clustering locations of GPS loss. From the transition history between these places they build a Markov model which expresses the probability that the user is going to visit a certain place, given the history of previously visited places (where the size of the history depends on the order of the Markov model). Although unsupervised learning makes this approach attractive the semantic level of interpretation is very low. The intentions that can be predicted are of the form *GotoX*, where X are places of daily life, such as *Gro-*

ceryStore or *Work*, but the system does not hypothesize about the reason for going to these place. We have seen in the previous chapter (section 2.2) that intentions are structured hierarchically by plans. The "*GotoX*-level" of recognizing intentions is on a very low level in the plan hierarchy. It may be sufficient for systems that offer only navigational assistance but not for more complex use cases in which the assistance system should support high-level intentions.

The representation of transitions between locations in a weighted graph can also be used for the interpretation of behavior aggregated over plenty of users which may open up new opportunities for researchers in the social sciences. See, for instance, Girardin et al (2008)'s study with photographers' footprints in the city of Rome.

Dee and Hogg (2004) try to detect inexplicable behavior in video surveillance settings (like, e. g., a car park). The motivation behind this approach is not assistance but the detection of interesting behavior through (unobstrusive) surveillance where inexplicability is assumed to be a good measure for interestingness. Similar as Ashbrook and Starner they restrict intentions to *GotoX* goals, whereas in their approach these goals are structured hierarchically: if X is not visible from the current position the *GotoX* goal is assumed to be split up into several *Goto* subgoals along the way. If the observed person does not follow the path with the least cost (typically the shortest path) through a weighted graph of goals her behavior is labeled as inexplicable. Although these goals are more structured than in Ashbrook and Starner's approach the splitting of *Goto* goals into other *Goto* goals is still semantically not sufficient for intelligent mobile assistance.

Higher-level intentions, such as *VisitMonaLisa*, *BuyTickets*, or *WaitIn-Queue*, could in principle also be recognized with FSMs. As one possible modeling, we could choose intention and region information as states (nodes), and behaviors as transitions (directed edges). By choosing a finite set of intentions for each FSM-state (with the meaning that the user has all these intentions at the same time, as parent and child intentions) instead of only one current intention we could account for hierarchical intentions (as long as the hierarchy is bounded). However, FSMs are not able to recognize nested sequences, such as $a^n b^n$ (e. g., Schlieder 2005's $enter^n leave^n$), and also not sequences in which several dependencies overlap, like those occurring in many mobile intention recognition scenarios (see examples in Figs. 2.19 and 2.20). If, for instance, the tourist in the example from Fig. 2.19 (top left) enters $R_{panorama}$, and the system should distinguish between whether the tourist has shown a certain behavior in the cathedral before or not, an FSM would need to "remember" an arbitrarily long sequence of spatio-temporal behaviors which would either lead to an infinite number of states (which contradicts FSM) or, with assumptions on maximum sequence length, hierarchy depth, and restrictions on the spatial model, at least to an immense number of states with complicated state variables. Thus, FSMs do not fulfill requirement 5 from section 2.4.

3.2 Early Approaches to Plan Recognition

This section summarizes two selected approaches to plan recognition from the 1970's and 1980's. The first one, Schmidt et al (1978), demonstrates why researchers in those days have started to discuss the plan recognition problem. The second one, Kautz (1987), with his claim and aim to treat the problem on a very general level, is particularly characteristic for many approaches, not only from the early days but also today.

3.2.1 Hypothesize and Revise

Schmidt et al (1978) are generally cited as the first authors who identified the plan recognition problem as a problem in its own right: "The problem of plan recognition is to take as input a sequence of actions performed by an actor and to infer the goal pursued by the actor and also to organize the action sequence in terms of a plan structure" (Schmidt et al, 1978, p. 52).

Their focus was on how to use A.I. for the construction and testing of a psychological theory. They incrementally presented textual descriptions of an agent's actions in an evolving small story, and asked a human observer what she thinks the agent is planning. They described how an observer would start with a single hypothesis for a plan which she would later incrementally revise and make more detailed. Even observations of actions that do not fit with the initial hypothesis would often be "explained away" with explanations like "the agent did not know that precondition X was not true" or "the agent changed her initial plan because of Y". This hypothesize and revise paradigm was then implemented in a system called BELIEVER.

The hypothesize and revise algorithm is described rather informally in the paper and complexity is not discussed. Many decisive details remain open: "We have yet to define a Rule Applying Algorithm (RAA) which will select and try suitable revisions among [the above-mentioned] suggestions" (Schmidt et al, 1978, p. 70). The reason for the informality can be seen in the different focus: while Schmidt et al. aim at describing the plan recognition process in the mind of a human observer psychologically plausible, the focus of most later plan and intention recognition approaches (including this thesis) is to develop methods that create the correct output, without the claim of reproducing the interna of the human plan recognition process realistically. Geib and Goldman (2009) about Schmidt et al (1978): "The earliest work in plan recognition [...] was rule-based; researchers attempted to come up with inference rules that would capture the nature of plan recognition. However without an underlying formal model these rule sets are difficult to maintain and do not scale well." (p. 1103)

3.2.2 Event Hierarchies

Whilst Schmidt et al (1978) are criticized for their lack of formality, a very formal approach to plan recognition has been developed by Kautz in the context of his PhD research (Kautz and Allen, 1986; Kautz, 1987, 1991). His theory is appreciated by Geib and Goldman (2009) to have "framed much of the work in plan recognition to date". The theory is especially remarkable for its generality.

Plans in Kautz's theory are represented as so-called *event hierarchies* which are first-order logic (FOL) representations that encode two types of relationships between plans: specialization and decomposition. The plan *VisitLouvre*, for instance, could be defined as a specialization of the plan *VisitMuseum*. The *VisitMuseum* plan could be decomposed into *GotoMuseum*, *BuyTicket*, *TourMuseum*. A circumscription process transforms these event hierarchies, and other general domain-dependent background knowledge, into a graph representation, and plan recognition is turned into a problem of graph covering: find the part of the graph that contains the minimum of independent explanations, given the observations. The graph of the winter Olympics example in section 2.3.3 (Fig. 2.15, left), for instance, is a graph similar to those of Kautz (with only decomposition relationships), and determining the minimum of independent explanations for this example would yield in the intention *PlanWinterOlympics*. Woods (1990) criticizes the minimum covering criterion as not applicable for all domains, and as "encoded into the basic representation of the problem in such a way that the entire formalization needs to be scrapped if one wants to consider any other criterion" (p. 137). In our example, the observed person in Fig. 2.15, left, could just as well have the intentions *HijackPlane* $\land$ *GoSkiing*.

Especially important in the context of this thesis: decomposition in event hierarchies does not necessarily imply ordering. For instance, formally, the *GotoMuseum*, *BuyTicket*, and *TourMuseum* plans could appear in any order if not explicitly specified. The previous chapter discussed the differences in complexity between general and mobile plan/intention recognition which arise from the number of possible observation groupings (Bell numbers vs. 2^n). Kautz has already identified this as one major problem of his approach:

> "Some of the most intimidating complexity results arise from the group-observations algorithm. The non-dichronic algorithm finds all consistent partitions of the set of observations. In the worst case, all *partitions* are possible — any subset of the observed events could be part of the same End event. Then Hypoths will contain B(n) hypotheses, where n is the number of observations." (Kautz, 1987, p. 122)[1]

The algorithmic part of Kautz's approach is also deemed critical by Woods (1990):

---

[1] It seems that Kautz uses the term "partitioning" in the same sense as section 2.3.3 introduced "composition".

"My major disappointment with Kautz's paper is that he doesn't give the same care and rigor to presenting and proving the capabilities of his algorithm that he gives to the formal model theory." (p. 137)

To conclude, Kautz's event hierarchies are too general for the special case of mobile intention recognition which leads to unnecessarily complex algorithms (too complex algorithms violate requirement 1). It is also questionable whether predicate calculus statements are cognitively understandable for domain experts (requirement 3): "the embedding of the ideas within the notations of the predicate calculus seems consistently to make them less clear and less intuitive than the corresponding English statements of the principles" (Woods, 1990, p. 136).

3.3 Probabilistic Networks

The previously discussed approaches to plan recognition were soon criticized for their inability to handle the likeliness of plans. For instance, Charniak and Goldman (1993) argued that "the problem of plan recognition is largely a problem of inference under conditions of uncertainty" (p. 54). In the winter Olympics example (Fig. 2.15, left), for instance, a Bayesian theorist might argue that the interpretation *GoSkiing ∧ HijackPlane* is much less likely than *KillCoyotes ∧ PlanSkiVacation* as there are (luckily) more people in this world who plan a ski vacation than a hijack. He might add that this likeliness will change if we had some other evidence in favor of the observed person being a terrorist, or general context information (such as, the destination location of the plane ticket is not a ski region in summer). It is clear that this kind of inference needs special approaches for reasoning under uncertainty.

The rest of this section summarizes the most relevant approaches to plan recognition with probabilistic networks. As the focus of this thesis are formal grammars those approaches that reason under uncertainty with formal grammars are treated separately (sections 3.4 and 3.5).

3.3.1 Static Probabilistic Networks

3.3.1.1 Bayes networks and Dempster-Shafer

The first authors to propose a Bayesian approach to plan recognition were Charniak and Goldman (1993). As Kautz (1987), they start with a predicate-calculus-like representation of plans. From these rules they create a *plan recognition Bayesian network* which is a certain class of Bayesian networks.

A Bayesian network is a directed acyclic graph (DAG) with nodes corresponding to random variables and arcs representing probabilistic influence.

An arc is directed in a way that mirrors the causality between the two random variables in the domain. A conditional probability distribution at each node gives the probability of the random variable taking certain values for all combinations of the values of its parent nodes. The specific strength of Bayesian networks is that nodes between which no (transitive) connection through arcs exists are assumed to be conditionally independent. Thus, a much fewer number of conditional probabilities must be determined than entries would be necessary in a complete probability table. Bayesian networks are textbook knowledge in A.I. (see, for instance, Pearl, 1988).

The plan recognition Bayesian networks used by Charniak and Goldman (1993) have nodes which represent random variables on "*thing* being of instance *type*". A set of seven rules defines the preconditions for adding these nodes to the network, with information on actions, slot-filler constraints, and observed objects. The network grows with every new observation and by creating new hypotheses. For instance, the observation of a *going*-action could lead to a hypothesis that this is part of a *GoTo-LiquorShop* action. As the observed agent could go to an almost arbitrary number of places, the hypothesizing may lead to explosive network growth: "As with most AI problems, then, we find that a formal description of the problem is only the first step. We also need to specify a way to restrict our attention" (Charniak and Goldman, 1993, p. 67). Their solution is a marker passing technique (a kind of spreading activation) for reasoning that restricts the creation of hypotheses (Carroll and Charniak, 1991). As we have seen in section 2.3.3, "restricting our attention" is also a problem in mobile intention recognition, and using knowledge about the relationships between space and intentions is one way of doing this.

An approach to plan recognition with reasoning under uncertainty that uses the Dempster-Shafer theory of evidential reasoning was suggested by Carberry (1990). Dempster-Shafer was also used for mobility prediction by Samaan and Karmouch (2005) who argue that "[t]he main advantage of the underlying theory of evidence over other approaches is its ability to model the narrowing down of a hypothesis with the accumulation of evidence and to explicitly represent uncertainty in the form of ignorance or reservation of judgement" (p. 539). The basic difference to traditional probability theory is that the probabilities are not assigned to single elements of the universe of discourse but to subsets. The Dempster-Shafer rule of combination defines how evidence from independent sources can be combined. The theoretical background of Dempster-Shafer can be found in Shafer (1990). The details are ommitted here as we are more interested in Bayes and Dempster-Shafer on an abstract level (see the following discussion), and on dynamic probabilistic networks (section 3.3.2).

3.3.1.2 Some general remarks on reasoning under uncertainty in mobile intention recognition

Dempster-Shafer and Bayes both have the benefit of reducing ambiguity by weighting hypotheses with probabilities, or evidence respectively. However, the notes that were imagined to be made by a Bayesian theorist on the terrorist/ski vacation example at the beginning of section 3.3 reveal the drawbacks of reasoning under uncertainty for plan/intention recognition:

1. Probabilities are conditional on a number of context variables (weather, season, time of day, ...). Even for an expert it is often difficult to consider them all.
2. Probabilities are often hard to determine, especially for very rare incidents, such as terror attacks. It is also well-known that humans are particularly weak in estimating conditional probabilities.
3. Besides estimating probabilities themselves, humans are also typically not very good in interpreting probabilities that were determined automatically through some kind of learning (which collides with requirement 3).
4. Probabilities are dependent on the person observed (terrorist/no terrorist), and very often it is not possible to train a personal model. A mobile tourist assistance system, for instance, is required to be ready for use immediately.
5. It does not make sense to model something with probabilities if we know it for sure. It may be even dangerous: not noticing a terror plan because of low probabilities is one obvious example.

   In addition, remember the motivation for requirement 4 in section 2.4: a nurse who customizes an AAL system for mentally handicapped people, for instance, knows for sure that not switching off the stove before going to bed is an inconsistent behavior sequence, and no "magic black box" probability mechanism should ever be able to override this definite expert knowledge.

   The spatial specificity assumption typically holding in mobile intention recognition (see section 2.1.2) also imposes fixed knowledge-based constraints which are not dependent on probabilities: you can play baseball in the baseball field but not on the plane. We know this for sure and can save the overhead of probabilistic modeling and reasoning.

The discussion in the 90s between authors in favor of Dempster-Shafer and Bayes respectively was mostly centered around some of these fundamental arguments. For instance, Carberry (1990) argues against Bayes' rule that "complex probability computations are extremely difficult to explain and justify to a lay person. Yet if an information system is to be viewed by users as intelligent and cooperative, it must appear rational and must be able to explain its reasoning" (p. 472). Charniak and Goldman (1993) answer that "we have yet to see an argument that Dempster's role of combination is more intuitively comprehensible than Bayes' rule" (p. 56).

In a later paper Carberry (2001) argues that "it appears that Charniak and Goldman's system is not sensitive to the order in which actions are observed, something that should affect plan recognition in longer stories" (pp. 37f). This missing of ordering is, of course, a major counter-argument against Bayes networks, not only for Carberry's use case of story understanding, but as well for mobile intention recognition. Indeed, both approaches described in this section are not designed for the number of observations we find in mobile intention recognition. The plan recognition Bayesian networks, for instance, maintain every observation in the system which makes the network grow quickly, and inference increasingly hard over time as new observations may be combined with old observations in an arbitrary way.

We will see in the following that many recent approaches in mobile behavior interpreation prefer *dynamic* probabilistic networks over static ones due to their computational attractiveness in dynamic scenarios.

3.3.2 Dynamic Probabilistic Networks

3.3.2.1 The basic idea

Dynamic Bayes Networks (DBNs)[2] are Bayes networks which consist of several time slices, where the internal structure of the network for each time slice over time is the same. The partial network at time slice t contains random variables (and dependencies between them) which describe the state of the world at time t. The world dynamics is modeled as inter-slice dependencies. For each new observation at t_i, a time slice is added and connected to the random variables in the previous time slice t_{i-1} via inter-slice dependencies. Note that this process of adding new time slices implies a 1st order Markov assumption: "the future is conditionally independent of the past given the present" (Kjaerulff, 1992).

Inside of each time slice the nodes are typically structured into layers. Especially in behavior interpretation there is always an observation layer at the bottom to which values are assigned from the sensor readings. The observation is conditionally dependent on the unobserved random variables on top of the observation layer. With this structure, DBNs are a special type of Hidden Markov Models (HMM): "[DBNs] generalize HMMs by allowing the state space to be represented in factored form, instead of as a single discrete random variable." (Murphy, 2002). Many approaches use the dependencies between observation layer and world state for coping with the problems of uncertainty, noisy sensors, and sensor fusion (e. g., Brandherm and Schwartz, 2005).

---

[2] Also called dynamic belief networks or dynamic probabilistic networks.

A whole family of approaches for the interpretation of mobile behavior using layered DBNs has been published by Patterson, Liao et al.: a first variant of their system uses a DBN with seven nodes in each time slice for recognizing a person's mode of transportation ($\in$ {bus, car, foot}) from GPS readings (Patterson et al, 2003). One year later they presented an extended version of this DBN which additionally recognizes trip segments and goals (Patterson et al, 2004; Liao et al, 2004). Finally, the journal version of this research adds nodes which recognize the novelty of the behavior on top of the DBN (Liao et al, 2007). The aim of their system, called OpportunityKnocks, is to help cognitively-impaired people use public transportation safely. The probabilities in the network have been trained with previously recorded mobile behavior of a specific person so that it is able to recognize behavior untypical for that person like, e. g., getting on the wrong bus. Detecting transportation routines is also the goal of Gogate et al (2005) who use Hybrid Dynamic Mixed Networks which are another kind of DBNs.

As explained in section 3.1, the recognition of *GotoX* goals is not sufficiently semantically rich. Likewise, the recognition of transportation mode is rather a recognition of activities than one of plans or intentions. Other related applications of DBNs include the recognition of a player's quest in a multiuser dungeon game (Albrecht et al, 1997), sensor validation and attribution of actions to several agents (Nicholson and Brady, 1994), autonomous vehicle driving (Forbes et al, 1995), and wheelchair maneuver assistance (Demeester et al, 2008). None of these uses plan structure information, and none recognizes intentions on a sufficiently high semantic level. Even Tahboub (2006), who calls his approach "intention recognition", is on a rather low semantic level and quite restricted with exactly four intentions: move to an object, move away from an object, move parallel to an object, do nothing regarding an object.

3.3.2.2 DBNs for mobile intention/plan recognition

The main reason why standard DBNs do not recognize complex and hierarchical intentions has been mentioned above: the 1st order Markov assumption (Kjaerulff, 1992). With all the background information about intentions, plan hierarchies, and nested/intersecting dependencies that was introduced in chapter 2, it should be clear that the future is *not* independent of the past, given the present. Even if we would assume an n-th order Markov assumption for DBNs, i. e., if we would allow for longer inter-slice dependencies, these would not cover an arbitrary past, but be bounded by n. Besides the Markov assumption, also "[t]ypically for these dynamic networks [...] a temporal window is imposed to constrain the state space to some extent" (Albrecht et al, 1997). Slices falling out of the window can be combined to a compact belief state representation via "backward smoothing" (Kjaerulff, 1992). This belief state of the past cannot capture an arbitrary long region/behavior sequence which would be necessary for long-ranging space-intention dependencies.

To cope with the problem of missing hierarchies, Bui et al (2002) propose the Abstract Hidden Markov Model (AHMM) for "policy" recognition which allows for hierarchies in the policies. One interesting aspect about this approach, at least in the context of this thesis, is that AHMMs were applied to behavior in spatial regions in a partonomy:

> "the analysis [...] shows that policy recognition can be carried out more efficiently if the domains of the intermediate abstract policies form a partition of the state-space [...], due to fact that the belief state of the DBN can be represented more compactly in this case." (Bui et al, 2000)

As we will see later, this is a similar intuition as followed by the spatial grammars in this thesis. However, the AHMM approach is not optimal. The authors themselves criticize AHMM in a successor paper:

> "The AHMM is equivalent to a special class of PSDG [(Probabilistic State Dependent Grammar)^3] where only production rules of the form X $\rightarrow$ YX and X $\rightarrow \oslash$ are allowed. The first rule models the adoption of a lower level policy Y by a higher level policy X, while the second rule models the termination of the policy X." (Bui, 2003, p. 1310)

Bui (2003), now titled "plan recognition", proposes a way out of this simple expressiveness: the Abstract Hidden Markov Memory Model (AHMEM). This model allows the policy to have an internal memory, i.e., additional nodes in the DBN, which is updated in a Markov fashion. Although the AHMEM can recognize production rules of the form X $\rightarrow$ Y$_1$ ... Y$_m$ X it was argued in Kiefer (2009) that it is not able to capture long-ranging dependencies between regions. The memory compensates the 1st order Markov assumption to some degree but not totally. The argument is similar to that discussed in section 3.1 in the context of FSMs: the global state variable in an AHMEM would need to "remember" an arbitrarily long sequence of spatio-temporal behaviors, just as in FSMs.

Finally, an approach strongly related to Bui's work should be mentioned: the Cascading Hidden Markov Model (CHMM) (Blaylock and Allen, 2006). CHMMs allow for faster inference than AHHMs, but lose expressiveness which makes them impractial for our requirements. However, the motivation behind CHMM is interesting as it concerns the efficiency of AHMM inference: Blaylock and Allen (2006) doubt that Bui's AHMM would still run efficiently if there was no partonomy:

> "only certain policies are valid in a given state (location), which helps reduce the ambiguity. The domain was modeled such that lower-level policies become impossible as the agent moves to another room, which makes it fairly clear when they then terminate. Although the algorithm was successful for this tracking task, it is unclear how effective estimation of policy termination would be in general" (Blaylock and Allen, 2006)

---

^{3} PSDGs will be explained in section 3.5.1.

Besides the limited expressiveness, the other drawbacks of using a probabilistic approach for mobile intention recognition listed in section 3.3.1 apply accordingly to DBNs and HMMs: it is difficult to capture all necessary random variables and their dependencies for a domain-specific DBN (structural aspect), and probabilities are hard to determine if no corpus of (individual) training data exists (probabilistic aspect). The last argument, "why use probabilities if we know something for sure?", applies even more for DBNs as only approximate inference on DBNs works efficiently (Murphy and Paskin, 2001; Murphy, 2002)[4].

3.4 Parsing Formal Grammars

Formal grammars are generally well-suited for the description and recognition of patterns (Gonzalez and Thomason, 1978). Starting with Chomsky (1959) one of their main fields of application was NLP (Jurafsky and Martin, 2000) where they are used to describe structural regularities, especially in syntax. However, the interest for using grammars in pattern recognition fields outside of NLP has grown as "they are intuitively simple to understand, and have very elegant representations." (Chanda and Dellaert, 2004). This distinguishes them from FOL representations (section 3.2.2) and probabilistic networks of realistic size (section 3.3); recall also requirement 3 that the representational formalism for an BIM should be cognitively understandable. In addition, efficient parsing algorithms for formal grammars exist which favors the fulfillment of requirement 1. This section introduces related work on human behavior interpretation with formal grammars.

3.4.1 (Probabilistic) Context-Free Parsing

3.4.1.1 Intentional systems: a context-free grammar for representing hierarchical plans

We have seen in sections 2.3.3 and 3.1 that the expressiveness of a formalism for mobile intention recognition should be higher than that of an FSM, i.e., higher than the expressiveness of a type-3 grammar (regular grammar) in the Chomsky hierarchy (Chomsky, 1959). A type-2 grammar that recognizes intentions from behaviors can be defined similar to Schlieder (2005, p. 11) as:

---

[4] Algorithms for DBNs inference are not discussed here as this is out of scope. See Murphy (2002) for an elaborate discussion on DBN inference. The same applies to algorithms for learning the parameters of a DBN/HMM. This is typically done with Expectation-Maximization, see Bilmes (1998) for a tutorial.

Definition 3.1. An *intentional system (IS)* is a production system (B, I, P, S) with terminals B denoting behaviors, non-terminals I denoting intentions and start symbol S $\in$ I called the highest-level intention. P is a set of productions from I to $(I \cup B)^+$. All three sets are finite.

An IS is a normal Context-Free Grammar (CFG) with intentions as non-terminals and behaviors as terminals. It is one possible representational formalism for the BIM in a mobile recognition algorithm (see section 2.3.2), but a very simple one as the connection between intentions and space is ignored (Fig. 2.17).

In line with textbooks on formal grammars, the letter $\mathbf{P}$ is chosen to denote the set of production rules (because "production" starts with a "P"). However, the letter $\mathbf{P}$ could also mean *p*lan library as the rules in $\mathbf{P}$ are plans that structure intentions and behaviors hierarchically. More precisely, $\mathbf{P}$ contains the structural information on "mini-plans" which are necessary for building larger plans (see the discussion on the relation between plans and intentions in section 2.2). These larger plans are the parse trees created by applying the production rules. The plan hierarchies that can be created with ISs are, in principle, not depth-bounded as recursive productions rules are possible. This allows for rather complex and high-level plan representations, in opposite to many of the formalisms presented in the previous sections. An assumption on a maximum plan depth is not required.

The plan recognition problem for an IS consists in finding the correct parse tree, given a behavior sequence β. If $\beta[0,i]$ is unfinished (which it is most of the time in mobile intention recognition) the plan recognition problem consists in finding the correct incomplete parse tree, where these parse trees must be separable in a fully-expanded left hand side with $\beta[0,i]$ as terminals in the leaf nodes, and a non-expanded right-hand side. The intention recognition problem of finding the correct current intention I_i which explains the current behavior b_i (see definition 2.9) is solved by selecting the intention which is label of the parent node of the i-th leaf node (labeled as b_i) in a parse tree. If there are several possible parse trees that could create $\beta[0,i]$ plan recognition will return an ambiguous result, whereas the same set of trees is not necessarily ambiguous for intention recognition as all possible parse trees might have the same current intention.

Intention recognition with an IS yields in an incremental parsing problem. Simple variations of the well-known Earley parser (Earley, 1970) will incrementally parse CFG sequences in $O(n^3)$ (with n denoting the number of behaviors). For a description of incremental parsing techniques for CFGs see, e. g., Jurafsky and Martin (2000, p. 377ff) or one of the many other textbooks on formal grammars or NLP. Although intention recognition is less ambiguous than plan recognition, ambiguity for intention recognition with ISs is still a major problem.

3.4.1.2 Probabilistic context-free grammars

Probabilistic Context-Free Grammars (PCFGs) address these ambiguity problems by assigning each production rule a probability (Ellis, 1970). Efficient parsers for PCFGs exist (Stolcke, 1995), grammar structures can be learned (Carroll, 1995), as well as probabilities (Prescher, 2004). A PCFG parser will not just return a set of possible parse trees but also the likeliness of each. By assuming that the most likely parse tree is the correct one we can reduce ambiguity, and in most cases even avoid it completely. However, as we saw in the hijacking example in section 3.3 this assumption may lead to total failure. Requirement 4, which was fulfilled by normal CFGs and ISs, is not fulfilled by PCFGs any more. In general, the same considerations about using probabilities as stated about probabilistic networks in section 3.3.1 apply to PCFGs.

PCFGs have, not very surprisingly, been applied in NLP (Suppes, 1970), but also in activity recognition (Ivanov and Bobick, 2000; Minnen et al, 2003; Lymberopoulos et al, 2006). These approaches are related to mobile intention recognition as they can be used in the preprocessing (see Fig. 2.2). A non context-free probabilistic grammar formalism that has been proposed for plan recognition is discussed in section 3.5.1.

3.4.1.3 A note on Vilain (1990) and Sidner (1985)

Schlieder (2005) was not the first to phrase the intention/plan recognition problem as parsing (and, as we will see in section 3.4.2, the parsing itself was not his main argument). Fifteen and twenty years before Schlieder there were two other noteworthy papers on this topic with conclusions supporting the motivation of this thesis:

Vilain (1990)'s starting point are Kautz's event hierarchies (section 3.2.2) and their algorithmic complexity:

> "Finally, since general plan recognition in Kautz' framework is intractable, there is intrinsic interest in identifying those aspects of his approach that cause this intractability, and those that avoid it." (p. 190)

His conclusion comes pretty close to what should be clear after the discussion of partitioning vs. composition in section 2.3.3: "There is a $O(n^3)$-time plan recognition algorithm for hierarchies with ordered, unshared steps, and for disjunctive or abstract observations" (p. 196), i. e., for behavior sequences without interleaving intentions, and he concludes that Kautz's algorithm "is computationally much more onerous, but may turn out to be unavoidable if one wants to allow for sharing and interleaving of steps" (p. 197). This thesis' argument, however, is to choose a way in between: allowing for *some* interleaving while still avoiding Kautz's complexity.

Sidner (1985) is an article that does not provide an algorithm or formalism, and thus reads much less technically. Still, Sidner makes an interesting point.

He discusses on a general level how a human-machine discourse interpreter can make sense of a user's utterances by means of parsing. He approaches the problem of determining the relationship between intentions in several utterances, like creating a sub-plan, delaying an old plan and creating a new one, or finishing a plan. He identifies the interleaving problem and the insufficiencies of CFGs:

> "The parsing scheme described so far may be modeled by a context-free parser, but a context-free parser will not be usable in general because the plan parser must also be able to deal with plans that are interleaved" (p. 4)

It is not clear which concrete grammar formalism the article proposes to solve this problem. However, it suggests a discourse marker mechanism which should perform a preprocessing before the actual plan parsing:

> "Parsing the speaker's intention as part of a plan requires information that can be provided by discourse markers. They are needed to reduce the processing load in parsing the intentions conveyed in utterances." (p. 10)

Discourse markers are selected phrases humans typically use to indicate a relationship between intentions in voice commands, e. g., the words "First" (delaying a plan) and "OK" (end of a plan) in the following discourse between user and system (S):

> "User: 1. I want to add a new definition to the knowledge base.
>   2. First, give me a list of all the users and systems.
>   S: 3. Do you want to know which systems each user uses?
> User: 4. Yes, but just list one if there are several.
>   S: 5. (System prints information out.)
> User: 6. OK, now I want to define a system user as a person who uses
>   any of these systems.
>   7. Then assert that all the people above are system users." (p. 5)

Due to the "OK" at the beginning of sentence 6, for instance, the system can assume that the previous plan has successfully ended. These dedicated segmentation points at which the parser knows that the intention changes are "a way to restrict our attention" (Charniak and Goldman, 1993, p. 67). This idea is similar to the spatial composition restrictions which were shown to reduce the worst-case number of possible groupings in section 2.3.3. In other words: the segmentation points that Sidner (1985) needs to identify algorithmically for discourse understanding come for free in mobile intention recognition if the spatial specificity assumption holds.

3.4.2 Spatially Grounded Intentional Systems

3.4.2.1 The idea of spatial disambiguation

As mentioned in the previous section the main contribution of Schlieder (2005) was not the IS formalism but a "spatialized" version of it:

Definition 3.2. A *spatially grounded intentional system* SGIS $= (B, I, P, S, SM, G)$ is an intentional system (B, I, P, S) enhanced by a spatial model SM $= (R, SRT, SR)$ (see definition 2.6), and a relation $G \subseteq P \times R$ describing the regions in which a production rule is applicable. SM is a partonomy.

An SGIS restricts the applicability of production rules to certain regions which enables spatial disambiguation for mobile intention recognition. Regions in the SGIS formalism are structured partonomically. This representational formalism for the BIM in a mobile recognition algorithm (section 2.3.2) connects intentions and space, as illustrated in principle in Fig. 2.17. The input of an SGIS parser is a spatial behavior sequence, for instance a spatio-temporal behavior sequence β_{st} from definition 2.7 (in which the temporal information is ignored). A production rule p is only applicable if all behaviors in the parse tree that occur as leaf nodes of the partial tree headed by the left-hand intention of p happen in a region consistent with the grounding:

Let $p_x = (I \rightarrow \sigma \mid R_x)$ be a production rule from intention $I \in I$ to a right-hand side, a sequence σ of behaviors from B and intentions from I, grounded in regions $R_x \subseteq R$. An SGIS parse tree using p_x is valid if there exists a region $R_x \in R_x$ which is element of all region sets $R_{x0} \dots R_{xi}$ of the spatio-temporal behavior sequence $\beta_{st}[x0,xi]$ headed by the node with label I.

An example for the idea of spatial disambiguation is presented in Kiefer and Schlieder (2007). It is reproduced in the following because of its simplicity and clarity. Imagine, we observe a car driver on her way from start (R_S) to destination (R_D), with R_S located in R_{area1} and R_D located in R_{area2}. Our sensors allow us to discriminate only two behaviors, parking and driving. We know that the driver is going to give another person a ride who is traveling between the same two areas. She will pick up that person in R_1, and drop her in R_2. However, the start and the pick location, as well as destination and drop location, may coincide, i. e., the passenger may start from the same place and/or have the same destination. An IS for this example, and the four options for identical regions are given in Fig. 3.1 (top, center). The bottom part of Fig. 3.1 shows that, without spatial knowledge, there are two parse trees for the behavior sequence of length five.

An SGIS that resolves this ambiguity is listed in Fig. 3.2 (top): as we know that the passengers are traveling between the same areas we can "ground" the *Pick* rules in R_{area1}, and the *Drop* rules in R_{area2}. Figure 3.2 (bottom) shows the disambiguation effect: rule (5) is not applicable, given the behavior sequence with spatial information. The pick/drop-example is, of course, a

Production Rules P		
$Trip$ →	$Pick$ driving $Drop$	(1)
$Pick$ →	parking	(2)
$Pick$ →	parking driving parking	(3)
$Drop$ →	parking	(4)
$Drop$ →	parking driving parking	(5)

Start	Destination	Observed Behavior Sequence
$R_S \neq R_1$	$R_D \neq R_2$	parking driving parking driving parking driving parking
$R_S = R_1$	$R_D \neq R_2$	parking driving parking driving parking
$R_S \neq R_1$	$R_D = R_2$	parking driving parking driving parking
$R_S = R_1$	$R_D = R_2$	parking driving parking

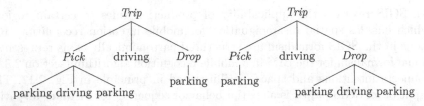

Fig. 3.1 A very simple intentional system (top), the language it defines (center), and ambiguity for a behavior sequence (bottom). Taken from Kiefer and Schlieder (2007), Figs. 1 and 2.

very simple one with low-level intentions, and in no way realistic for mobile assistance systems. However, it clearly illustrates the basic principle of spatial disambiguation. A more complex and realistic example is presented in Kiefer et al (2010). A further example, including an analysis of the disambiguation effects of SGISs, is discussed in chapter 5.

3.4.2.2 SGIS for mobile intention recognition

Schlieder does not formally specify a parsing algorithm but proposes to use a variant of the Earley algorithm, and argues about the runtime that "By exploiting the spatial specificity of intentional behavior there is a simple way to reduce rule conflicts and thereby speed up the parsing process" (Schlieder, 2005). Thus, requirement 1 is met. A parsing algorithm for SGIS is specified in chapter 4.

As any CFG, SGISs are cognitively easy to understand (requirement 3) and allow for exclusive/definite assertions (requirement 4). The SGIS formalism is also the first one in this chapter which definitely fulfills requirement 2 (spatial portability): the rules in an SGIS are connected with qualitative regions, and thus independent of the absolute coordinates in a certain spatial environment. A domain expert can model the spatial behavior and intention constraints in an BIM independently from the spatial model (see Fig. 2.17).

Production Rules P with Spatial Grounding G			
Trip $\rightarrow$	*Pick* driving *Drop*	(1)	$\{R_\Omega\}$
Pick $\rightarrow$	parking	(2)	$\{R_{area1}\}$
Pick $\rightarrow$	parking driving parking	(3)	$\{R_{area1}\}$
Drop $\rightarrow$	parking	(4)	$\{R_{area2}\}$
Drop $\rightarrow$	parking driving parking	(5)	$\{R_{area2}\}$

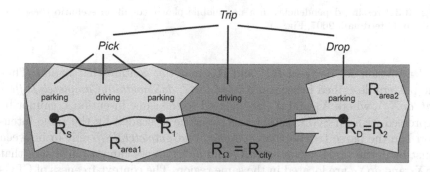

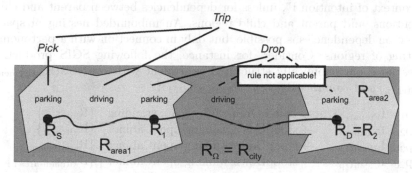

Fig. 3.2 SGIS (top) and spatial disambiguation (bottom) for the example from Fig. 3.1. Taken from Kiefer and Schlieder (2007), Fig. 3.

This is very intuitive as we can often state general rules, like "you can play baseball only in the baseball field", independent of the absolute geographic position of the baseball field. This is also the reason why we formulated the rules in the pick/drop-example (Fig. 3.2) independent from whether R_S and R_1 coincide or not. We could simply use the same SGIS rule set for another spatial environment in which, for instance, the four regions R_S, R_1, R_2, and R_D do not coincide. However, some of the spatial relations must hold in the spatial model as they are intrinsic to the pick/drop use case (e.g., it would not make much sense to place R_S outside of R_{area1}).

The expressiveness requirement is not fulfilled (requirement 5). As described above, the grounding of a rule p leads to a whole partial spatio-temporal behavior sequence $\beta_{st}[x0,xi]$ being restrained to a certain region,

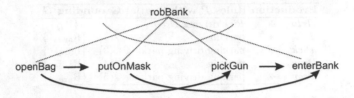

Fig. 3.3 Crossing dependencies in a non-mobile plan recognition scenario (based on Geib and Steedman, 2007, Fig. 2).

and no region set between $\mathbf{R}_{x0}$ and $\mathbf{R}_{xi}$ may *not* contain that region. Thus the pattern described in section 2.3.4, $\langle doX_1, doSomethingCompletelyDifferent, doX_2 \rangle$, where X_1 and X_2 are related to the same intention I, cannot be expressed with an SGIS. Either this sequence is headed by the same intention I in the parse tree so that *doSomethingCompletelyDifferent* in between must be in the same region as doX_1 and doX_2, or we cannot make sure that doX_1 and doX_2 are located in the same region. The context-freeness of CFGs inhibits dependencies between "inside of context of intention I" and "outside of context of intention I", unless for dependencies between parent and child intentions, and parent and child regions. An unbounded nesting of space-intention dependencies is possible, but only in connection with a partonomic nesting of regions. Consider, for instance, the following SGIS production rules for a partonomically structured apartment with $contains(\mathrm{R}_{\mathrm{apartment}}, \mathrm{R}_{\mathrm{kitchen}})$ and $contains(\mathrm{R}_{\mathrm{kitchen}}, \mathrm{R}_{\mathrm{kitchen\text{-}area1}})$:

$$p_1:\ \mathrm{I}_{\mathrm{PrepareMeal}} \rightarrow \mathrm{switchOnStove}\ \mathrm{I}_{\mathrm{CleanUp}}\ \mathrm{standing}\ |\ \{\mathrm{R}_{\mathrm{kitchen}}\}$$
$$p_{2a}:\ \mathrm{I}_{\mathrm{CleanUp}} \rightarrow \mathrm{stoopDown}\ \mathrm{walking}\ \mathrm{openCabinet}\ |\ \{\mathrm{R}_{\mathrm{kitchen}}\}$$
$$p_{2b}:\ \mathrm{I}_{\mathrm{CleanUp}} \rightarrow \mathrm{stoopDown}\ \mathrm{walking}\ \mathrm{openCabinet}\ |\ \{\mathrm{R}_{\mathrm{apartment}}\}$$
$$p_{2c}:\ \mathrm{I}_{\mathrm{CleanUp}} \rightarrow \mathrm{stoopDown}\ \mathrm{walking}\ \mathrm{openCabinet}\ |\ \{\mathrm{R}_{\mathrm{kitchen\text{-}area1}}\}$$

In this example, only p_{2a} and p_{2c} can be inserted in the $\mathrm{I}_{\mathrm{CleanUp}}$ non-terminal of p_1 because the spatial grounding of p_{2b} ($\mathrm{R}_{\mathrm{apartment}}$) is not a sub region of $\mathrm{R}_{\mathrm{kitchen}}$. Thus, our rules bind the agent to clean up in the kitchen, not outside. (Although it may be sensible to constantly keep an eye on the cooking we should not force her to stay in the kitchen.)

This nesting-property makes SGISs so efficient and intuitive on the one hand, but restricts their expressiveness on the other hand. Crossing dependencies and dependencies of different type than *contains* are not possible with an SGIS.

3.4.3 Towards More Context-Sensitivity

The need for modeling crossing dependencies in general plan recognition has recently been identified in Geib and Steedman (2007). The example in Fig. 3.3

is taken from this paper: entering the bank depends on two preconditions (putting on a ski mask, and picking up the gun), whereas each of the two depends on opening the bag. The paper draws a parallel to NLP where similar dependencies occur in syntactic structures, and proposes to have a closer look at the family of Mildly Context-Sensitive Grammars (MCSGs) which are typically used in NLP for these kinds of structures. The paper is a position paper that emphasizes parallels between NLP and plan recognition, but does not propose one specific formalism.

As the parallel between plan/intention recognition and NLP is also the basis of one of the grammar formalisms proposed in chapter 4, the class of MCSGs is discussed in section 4.3.1.

3.5 Combining Formal Grammars and Bayes

This section reports on two approaches which combine formal grammar models with Bayesian inference. Plans are formalized as grammar rules, thus adopting the cognitive understandability advantage of grammars. These plans are then converted into a Bayesian representation for inference to get the disambiguation advantages of reasoning under uncertainty.

3.5.1 Probabilistic State-Dependent Grammars

The discussion of SGISs in section 3.4.2 has revealed that an agent's behavior in a realistic mobile scenario is not context-free. This is also the motivation of Pynadath and Wellman (2000) who propose *Probabilistic State Dependent Grammars* (PSDGs). A PSDG is a PCFG with a state variable $q \in \mathbf{Q}$, and more elaborate probability definitions:

q describes the state of the environment, e. g., the lane of a car on the highway {left, center, right} (Pynadath and Wellman, 2000), or the number of books currently carried by the user of a public library {0, ..., 5} (Kiefer et al, 2009). q is time-indexed, i. e., q_0 describes the initial state of the environment, q_1 the state after the first terminal is parsed, and q_t the state after the tth terminal. For all non-terminals in the parse tree its time is defined as the time of its leftmost child terminal. Production probabilities for each rule are not constant but a function $p(q)$ of the state (where the state q_{t-1} is used for a given non-terminal with time t). For instance, if the library user is already carrying five books, the probability of another *pickBook* behavior is smaller than if she was carrying only one book. The state variable is hidden like in an HMM, i. e., the agent has a belief about the state of the environment. The initial value of q follows the probability distribution π_0, and the probability distribution π_1 describes the state transition probability from q_{t-1} to q_t caused by a certain terminal.

The expressiveness of an PSDG heavily depends on the domain $\mathbf{Q}$. In general, no specific constraints apply so that $\mathbf{Q}$ may be a complex multidimensional set of states. In a realistic scenario we would have to model more than one feature of the environment. For instance, the probability that the user picks another book may be influenced by the time of the day, the weight of the books carried, her spatial closeness to a book shelf, the number of books in that book shelf, the thematic closeness between the books on the shelf and those carried, her currently being in a conversation or not, and so on. The more features we include in $\mathbf{Q}$, the more probabilities will have to be determined for $p(q)$, π_0, and π_1. In the worst case, the features of $\mathbf{Q}$ are not independent of each other so that a full probability distribution must be specified. The understandability of such a model will probably be low (requirement 3). As discussed in section 3.3.1 it is also often difficult to acquire probabilities at all.

Pynadath (1999) describes a method for efficiently answering intention recognition queries by converting a given PSDG description into a DBN and exploiting the particular independence properties of the PSDG language. Bui (2003) claims that "the existing exact inference method for the PSDG in [Pynadath, 1999] has been found to be flawed and inadequate [Bui, 2002]"[5]. In addition, Pynadath and Wellman (2000) restrain themselves to examples with finite domains, and say that for more general languages "although inference [...] is possible, it is impractical in general". However, we would need an infinite domain to express long-ranging space-intention dependencies: by choosing $\mathbf{R}$ as domain for $\mathbf{Q}$ it is possible to create a dependency of the current region. A dependency of the region history would be expressed by an infinite cartesian product over $\mathbf{R}$ which would lead to an explosion of the state space. And even this is not enough to express long-ranging space-intention dependencies because the productions that were chosen along the region history are also relevant (see also Kiefer, 2009)

Thus, a PSDG will either have a finite domain and not be able to express long-ranging space-intention dependencies (violating requirement 5), or have an infinite domain and be cognitively and algorithmically complex (violating requirements 3 and 1).

3.5.2 Plan Tree Grammars and Pending Sets

Geib and Goldman (2009) have recently presented an algorithm for plan recognition called PHATT. It adds the algorithmic approach to an idea which was published in prior work ten years before: "We do not pretend to provide a

---

[5] Bui's technical report in which he provides detailed information on this issue (Bui, 2002) was not available at the time of writing this thesis from the URL specified by Bui.

solution to either the algorithmic or implementation problems, only an understanding at the 'knowledge level'." (Goldman et al, 1999). A short summary of the PHATT algorithm can be found in Goldman et al (2010). PHATT is especially relevant as it addresses the interleaving of plans.

Plans in PHATT are represented as partially ordered trees. These trees can be written like CFG rules, with the difference that the right hand symbols are not ordered by definition. Ordering constraints must be specified explicitly between right-hand symbols of the rules. This plan representation follows the idea of hierarchical task networks (Ghallab et al, 2004). Start symbols are denoted "top-level goals". All other nodes in the trees are called "actions", terminals are specialized as "basic actions".

PHATT is based on a model of plan execution: first, the agent commits to a number of top-level goals, and to a set of methods for achieving these goals. In terms of formal grammars, committing to a method means building a (partially-ordered) parse tree by choosing a rule application for each non-terminal on the right-hand side of a production rule. The algorithm is centered around so-called pending sets. A pending set contains all basic actions which can be chosen next. Initially, all basic actions without preconditions are in the pending set. For the fully ordered case of CFGs, the initial pending set would contain the left-most terminals of all possible parse trees for all top-level root goals. In each time step the agent chooses one action from the pending set, which changes the pending set by removing that action and adding new ones (those which are successors of the executed action according to the ordering constraints). This process continues until the agent stops performing actions.

A Bayesian model is used for inference: in an HMM-fashion, the performed actions are treated as observations, and the pending sets, method choices, and root-level goals as hidden states. "We assume that our input plan library is augmented with probabilities, specifically prior probabilities of root goals, method choice probabilities, and probabilities for picking elements from the pending sets" (Geib and Goldman, 2009, p. 1106). A uniformity assumption is made for these probabilities. "However this is in no way an inherent feature of the model; had one good reasons to choose different probabilities, they could easily be incorporated" (Goldman et al, 2010). It is not discussed where these probabilities come from in realistic use cases, and how they would influence the cognitive understandability of the model.

As the pending set may contain basic actions for several top-level goals, PHATT supports an arbitrary crossing and nesting of top-level goals. This makes the approach very general but, not surprisingly, also algorithmically complex. In a theoretical complexity evaluation Geib and Goldman (2009) state:

"Previous results in the complexity of plan-recognition demonstrate that the PHATT algorithm must be at least NP-Hard [...]. PHATT must be at least as hard as approaches like Kautz' which use heuristic methods to find a single approximately optimal explanation for a set of observations. However, if we also ask PHATT to

1. a1, b1, a2, b2, b3, a3, c1, c2, c3, **b4**, a4, c4
2. a1, b1, a2, b2, b3, a3, c1, c2, **b4**, c3, a4, c4
3. a1, b1, a2, b2, b3, a3, c1, **b4**, c2, c3, a4, c4
4. a1, b1, a2, b2, b3, a3, **b4**, c1, c2, c3, a4, c4
5. a1, b1, a2, b2, b3, **b4**, a3, c1, c2, c3, a4, c4

Fig. 3.4 Five abstract test cases for the early plan closing test (see Geib and Goldman, 2009, p. 1126).

compute the posterior probability of explanations, given the set of observations, then there is an additional NP-complete computation to compute the posterior probabilities. This is essentially a Bayes net probabilistic inference problem, which has also been shown to be NP-complete." (Geib and Goldman, 2009, p. 1120)

This causes them to "turn away from universal claims about PHATT's performance and focus on the actual performance encountered in particular cases." (p. 1122). An empirical evaluation of the key parameters on PHATT's performance reveals that the depth of the plan tree influences run times exponentially. The authors argue that "application experience suggests that the depth of hierarchical plans in most real world applications is limited to a relatively small value" (p. 1124). This application experience may be true for the examples in their paper (a computer network security domain) but not in general. The SGIS-rules for the location-based game CityPoker listed in Kiefer et al (2010, Fig.2), for instance, have a depth of eight which is already out of the scale of the authors' statistics in (Geib and Goldman, 2009, Fig. 7) which show only values for depths three to six.

Another finding of their empirical evaluation especially interesting here is that an early closing of plans significantly reduces runtimes. They test the abstract action sequences listed in Fig. 3.4 which differ only in b4 moving to the front. Each token in this listing denotes a basic action, where actions with the same letter belong to a common top-level goal, and each top-level goal consists of four basic actions. The earlier closing of plan b leads to a decreased amount of overlap (if we define overlap as the sum of the number of concurrent active plans over all time slices). The runtimes decrease significantly, from approx. 21 seconds for sequence 1, to approx. four seconds for sequence 5.

A key feature of PHATT is that it gets evidence from actions it does NOT observe (Peot and Shachter, 1998). Consider, for instance, a temporal version of the hijacking example from section 2.3.3: if we observe a *buyGun* behavior one day, a *buySkis* behavior just the other day, but no *buyTicket* behavior for a very long time interval, we may assume that the interpretations *PracticeBiathlon* or *KillCoyotes* ∧ *GoSkiing* are more probable than *PlanWinterOlympics*. In other words: the probability of an explanation for which observations are missing decreases over time. Although this is an interesting feature for many domains we have seen in the examples in section 2.3.4 that, in many mobile intention recognition scenarios, interleaving intentions may frame the whole behavior sequence, e. g., when a tourist returns to the bus stop where she has entered the city (Fig. 2.19, bottom left). Giving the intention *FindRestaurant* a higher probability than *FindBus*, just because the *GetOffBus* intention was very long ago, would return a wrong result. The spatial closeness of $R_{carpark2}$ to $R_{busterminal}$ should be a more convincing indicator.

Interesting is also the article's discussion on the assumption that all root goals are equally likely:

> "For some goals, this is absurd: for example the pairs 'brewing tea' and 'making toast'; and 'bungee jumping' and 'brewing tea' are unlikely to be independent. The former are probably positively correlated, and the latter negatively. Positive correlations can be handled relatively easily by introducing new top-level goals that activate combinations of the original goals. For example, one might have an 'afternoon tea' goal with a method that involved both brewing tea and making toast." (p. 1112)

IAMSs are always focused on one specific use case. A mobile mapping system for preservation scientists (Matyas and Schlieder, 2005), for instance, will not support a tourist looking for a restaurant, and vice versa for the mobile tourist guide. This is why ISs and SGISs assume that there is only one highest-level intention. This is comparable to introducing the "afternoon tea" goal on top of two initially independent goals "making toast" and "brewing tea". In contrast to the general PHATT approach, the context of an IAMS is known. Even interleaving intentions can be seen as part of a top-level intention. For instance, the *BusTransfer* intention, which combines *GetOffBus* and *FindBus*, is part of a top-level intention *VisitCity*, just as all behaviors between bus arrival and departure (Fig. 2.19, bottom left). Still, the spatial context identifies the two framing behavior sequences as belonging together. Regarding context, Geib and Goldman (2009) continue:

> "PHATT's model is much less friendly to negatively correlated goals. In order to accommodate them, one could make a more elaborate version of the approach for positively correlated goals. In this more elaborate version, one would specify probabilities for combinations of subgoals, that we call contexts. For example, one might have an 'extreme sports' context and a 'quiet afternoon' context, that would turn on (resp. off) goals like 'bungee jumping' and off (resp. on) goals like 'afternoon tea'." (p. 1112)

This "turning on/off" of intentions by using definite, non-probabilistic, knowledge about spatial context is the key idea of formalisms like SGIS and the grammar introduced in the next chapter.

3.6 Summary

This chapter has discussed related approaches in plan and intention recognition under the perspective of the requirements for mobile intention recognition given in section 2.4.

We have seen that very general approaches that allow for arbitrary inter-leaving of plans, incomplete behavior sequences, temporally unordered observations, or complex context models have often knowledge representations that are cognitively difficult to understand, and always suffer from high algorithmic complexity. Assumptions are necessary to reduce the search space, such as the temporal ordering, temporal completeness, and spatial consistency intrinsic to the mobile intention recognition problem. Probabilistic approaches are, in general, a good choice for disambiguation but probabilities are often hard to determine, especially for IAMSs which need to be ready to use for new users immediately. In addition, algorithms for probabilistic approaches, like DBNs, are either not efficient or only approximate. In particular, any current approach that approximates the past, e. g., as a compact belief state, will not be able to capture the long-ranging space-intention dependencies we need to model for realistic mobile intention recognition use cases.

Spatial grammars, such as the SGIS formalism (section 3.4.2), are a cognitively appealing representational formalism to model knowledge about the connection of space and intentions. This allows for spatial disambiguation which is an elegant way "to restrict our attention" (Charniak and Goldman, 1993, p. 67) while parsing these grammars. Geib and Goldman (2009) argue against parsing in their related work section:

> "The major problem with parsing as a model of plan recognition is that it does not treat partially-ordered plans or interleaved plans well." (p. 1104)

Although this applies to SGIS we will see in the following chapter this is not generally true.

Chapter 4
Mobile Intention Recognition with Spatially Constrained Grammars

Extending the idea of spatially grounded grammars of section 3.4.2, this chapter introduces two new spatial grammars which extend SGISs: Spatially Constrained Context-Free Grammars (SCCFGs), and Spatially Constrained Tree-Adjoining Grammars (SCTAGs). These grammars have higher expressiveness than SGISs which allows for modeling long-ranging space-intention dependencies frequently occurring in mobile intention recognition, like those illustrated in the examples in section 2.3.4.

Parsing algorithms for all three spatial grammars, SGISs, SCCFGs, and SCTAGs, are provided. The algorithms in this chapter use a partonomy as spatial model. Section 4.4 then discusses the implications of relaxing this assumption by allowing regions to overlap.

4.1 Parsing Spatial Behavior Sequences

4.1.1 A State Chart Parser for SGISs

SGISs were introduced in section 3.4.2 of the previous chapter as a context-free grammar enhanced by spatial grounding constraints (Schlieder, 2005). Mobile intention recognition with an SGIS yields in an incremental parsing problem which can efficiently be solved with variants of standard CFG parsing algorithms. However, no parsing algorithm for SGISs has been published yet. This section introduces a simple extension of the Earley algorithm (Earley, 1970) for SGIS parsing. The new algorithm exemplifies the main ideas of spatial parsing which also apply to the algorithms in later sections of this chapter: the clear separation of hypotheses generation and behavior parsing, efficient spatial constraint propagation, and the exploitation of certain invariants that hold for partonomically structured spatial models.

4.1.1.1 Earley chart entries with spatial grounding

The Earley parser is a dynamic programming algorithm which works on a state chart. States in this chart consist of a dotted production rule, and two indices $[i, j]$. A dotted production rule $p_\bullet$ is a production rule $p \in \mathbf{P}$ with a $\bullet$ between two symbols on the right-hand side of the rule. The algorithm applies rules to these states which moves the $\bullet$ step-by-step through the right-hand side. Dotted rules in the SGIS parser extend the standard dotted rules by spatial information:

$$p_\bullet = (I \to \sigma_0 \bullet \sigma_1 \mid \mathbf{GC})$$

σ_0 and σ_1 are sequences of symbols from $\mathbf{B} \cup \mathbf{I}$, where at most one of the two may be empty. σ_0 has already been recognized, σ_1 is yet to be reconized. $\mathbf{GC}$ is the set of regions $R_{gc} \in \mathbf{R}$ for which a (p, R_{gc}) in the spatial grounding constraints $\mathbf{G}$ of the SGIS exists. We say, "p is grounded in $\mathbf{GC}$". As short notation the spatial grounding is written behind the rule, separated with a vertical line. Examples for spatially grounded SGIS rules have been given in section 3.4.2 (Fig. 3.2, top).

The indices $[i, j]$ in a chart entry indicate the part of the input behavior sequence subsumed by σ_0. The SGIS parser extends the standard Earley chart entries by a set $\mathbf{GCI} \subseteq \mathbf{GC}$, the *grounding constraints instantiation*. It indicates in which regions the remaining behavior sequence, i.e., the behaviors subsumed by σ_1, may happen. Thus, the SGIS parser works on chart entries

$(p_\bullet, [i, j], \mathbf{GCI})$ or, as full notation: $(I \to \sigma_0 \bullet \sigma_1 \mid \mathbf{GC}, [i, j], \mathbf{GCI})$

4.1.1.2 Turning the recognizer into an incremental parser

Most descriptions of Earley introduce the algorithm as a recognizer that checks whether a given input sequence is part of the language. For mobile intention recognition the algorithm needs to be adapted to the general mobile intention recognition algorithm introduced in Fig. 2.14 so that it returns intention hypotheses (see Fig. 4.1):

- In method initialize() the normal Earley initialization is performed, i.e., all rules with S as left symbol are added to the chart. In addition, initialize() runs a first prediction step on all chart entries. This creates new hypotheses for left-most derivations until all unprocessed entries have the $\bullet$ in front of a terminal.
- Method recognize() takes an incoming spatialized behavior (R_{in}, b_{in}), and scans those entries which have a $\bullet$ in front of terminal b_{in}. Time stamps t_s and t_e are ignored in the SGIS-parser[1]. If the input region complies

---

[1] In fact, the timestamps are used by none of the algorithms presented here. However, they were defined for the general mobile intention recognition algorithm because spatial

// The spatial model SM is a partonomy.
// The behavior intention model BIM is an SGIS = $(\mathbf{B}, \mathbf{I}, \mathbf{P}, S, \mathbf{R}, \mathbf{G})$ (definition 3.2).

int n;
statechart[] chart; *// (time-indexed): an array of sub-charts.*

procedure initialize(domain model *DM*)
begin
    for each $((S \rightarrow \sigma \mid \mathbf{GC}) \in BIM)$ **do**
        Add $((S \rightarrow \bullet \, \sigma \mid \mathbf{GC}), [0,0], \mathbf{GC})$ to chart[0]
    end for
    n $\leftarrow$ 0
    predictAll(0)
end procedure

function recognize(space-time behavior *(t_s, t_e, R_{in}, b_{in})*) **returns** $\mathbf{I}_{\text{hypotheses}}$
begin
    $\mathbf{I}_{\text{hypotheses}} \leftarrow \emptyset$
    for each $(\text{entry} = (I_p \rightarrow \sigma_0 \bullet b_{in} \, \sigma_1 \mid \mathbf{GC}, [i,n], \mathbf{GCI}) \in \text{chart}[n])$ **do**
        boolean recognized $\leftarrow$ scan(entry, R_{in})
        if (recognized) **then** $\mathbf{I}_{\text{hypotheses}}$.add($I_p$)
    end for
    n $\leftarrow$ n + 1
    completeAll(n)
    predictAll(n)
    return $\mathbf{I}_{\text{hypotheses}}$
end function

Fig. 4.1 An incremental SGIS parser based on Earley's state chart parser: methods initialize(), and recognize(), implementing the abstract methods from Fig. 2.14. Methods scan(), completeAll(), and predictAll() are given in Fig. 4.2.

with the spatial constraints, method scan() returns true. The left-hand intention of the rule currently processed is then the parent in the parse tree, i.e., the *current intention*. If more than one entry is successfully scanned there may be ambiguity.

- Finally, the rest of the recognize() method prepares the internal data structures for the incoming of the next behavior. The steps completeAll() and predictAll() can be performed in the background while the user is moving. In the foreground the system could already show an information service that fits to the recognized intention(s).

By structuring the algorithm in a way that predictAll() and completeAll() are running concurrently in the background the runtime requirements for the SGIS parser become apparent: scan() is the time-critical operation while predictAll() and completeAll() have time until the next behavior comes in. Predicting and completing in the background while the user continues to use

---

parsing in its general form easily integrates timestamps (see also section 6.3.1 in the outlook chapter)

the application may slow down computations. This depends on the kind of information service provided: a mobile hotel guide will need less resources than, e. g., a mobile geo information system.

The chart used as data structure in the algorithm is an array of sub-charts. The index of the sub-chart in the array is equal to the index j of all entries in that sub-chart (that is why some descriptions of the Earley algorithm use only one index i). The sub-charts are used as sets in the algorithm. However, an efficient implementation would impose indexing structures that enable an efficient look up of "scannable", "completable", and "predictable" entries (each entry falls in either of these three categories). Thus, the "for each" selection in recognize(), and in the outer loops in completeAll() and predictAll() (see Fig. 4.2) do not iterate over the whole sub-chart.

function scan(chartentry entry, region R_{in}) **returns** boolean
begin
    // entry is of the form ($I \rightarrow \sigma_0 \bullet b_{in} \sigma_2$ | GC, [i,j], GCI)
    $R_g \leftarrow$ The region from **GCI** which is equal to or contains R_{in}
    if (R_g == **null**) **then return** false
    Add ($I \rightarrow \sigma_0 b_{in} \bullet \sigma_2$ | **GC**, [i, j+1], $\{R_g\}$) to chart[j+1]
    return true
end function

procedure completeAll(int k)
begin
    for each (($I_{child} \rightarrow \sigma_3 \bullet$ | **GC**, [j, k], $\{R\}$) $\in$ chart[k]) **do**
        for each (($I_{parent} \rightarrow \sigma_0 \bullet I_{child} \sigma_1$ | GC_p, [i, j], GCI) $\in$ chart[j]) **do**
            $R_p \leftarrow$ The region from **GCI** which is equal to or contains R.
            Add ($I_{parent} \rightarrow \sigma_0 I_{child} \bullet \sigma_1$ | GC_p, [i, k], $\{R_p\}$) to chart[k]
        end for
    end for
end procedure

procedure predictAll(int j)
begin
    for each ((($I_{parent} \rightarrow \sigma_0 \bullet I_{child} \sigma_1$ | GC_{parent}), [i, j], GCI) $\in$ chart[j]) **do**
        for each (($I_{child} \rightarrow \sigma_3$ | GC_{child}) $\in$ SGIS) **do**
            $GCI_{new} \leftarrow$ All R $\in GC_{child}$ which are equal to or contained by a region
            in **GCI**
        if (GCI_{new} is not empty) **then**
            Add ($I_{child} \rightarrow \bullet \sigma_3$ | GC_{child}, [j, j], GCI_{new}) to chart[j]
        end for
    end for
end procedure

Fig. 4.2 Methods scan(), completeAll(), and predictAll() for the SGIS parser.

4.1.1.3 The valid prefix property

All algorithms for mobile intention recognition in this chapter are variants of Earley-like state chart parsers. The original recognizer is turned into an incremental parser, and the parser is enhanced with spatial constraints. Spatial constraint resolution is then added to the parser operations (see section 4.1.2). Though not explored in this thesis this principle is generalizable to many other parsers that use dynamic programming.

However, any parser must have one important property to be useful for mobile intention recognition, the Valid Prefix Property (VPP) (see, e.g., Joshi and Schabes, 1997, p. 50). That means, it must detect errors in an incrementally processed input sequence as early as possible. Consider, for instance, the language $L = \{a^n b^n \mid n \geq 1\} = \{ab, aabb, aaabbb, \dots\}$. A recognizer that only decides that 'aaabbb' is a valid word of the language, whereas 'aab' and 'aba' are not, is not sufficient for mobile intention recognition. It must further be able to decide whether an input sequence is a valid prefix of any word in the language. For instance, no sequence can be added to 'aba' such that the resulting word will be part of L, whereas 'aab' is an incomplete sequence, and adding a 'b' will fix the issue. A parser that maintains the VPP must detect immediately that the current input is wrong, e.g., that appending an 'a' to 'ab' is not allowed. Otherwise, it might accept an arbitrary number of wrong behaviors, such as 'abacdefghijklmn', and recognize wrong intentions for each of them although the sequence was flawed from the very beginning.

The original Earley recognizer maintains the VPP, so there is no problem for SGISs.

4.1.2 Spatial Constraint Resolution

The previous explanation of an incremental Earley algorithm for mobile intention recognition did not treat the spatial aspects. The only spatial adaptation up to now was method initialize() copying the **GC** of the rule to the **GCI** of the according initial chart entry. The three modified Earley operations listed in Fig. 4.2, scan(), predict(), and complete(), resolve spatial constraints[2].

The parser exploits the knowledge that SGISs are defined only for spatial models of type partonomy. Each pair of regions from **R** in a partonomy is either disjunct or in a *contains/isContained* relation. The parser can assume that the regions in each grounding constraint set **GC** are disjunct. If they were not disjunct we could just remove the child regions because that information would be redundant. Accordingly, regions in each **GCI** are disjunct. This leads to the following invariant for all chart entries $(I \rightarrow \sigma_0 \bullet \sigma_1 \mid \mathbf{GC}, [i, j], \mathbf{GCI})$:

---

[2] predict() and complete() denote the inner loops of completeAll() and predictAll().

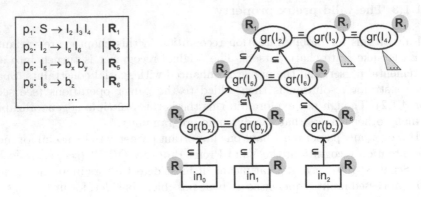

Fig. 4.3 Interpreting SGIS rules as a constraint satisfaction problem (CSP) on a parse tree.

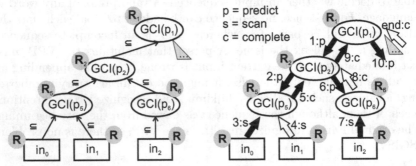

Fig. 4.4 Simplified CSP, and order of constraint propagation in the Earley parser.

$$(\mathbf{GCI} \subseteq \mathbf{GC}) \quad \text{and} \quad ((\sigma_0 \text{ is not empty}) \Rightarrow (|\mathbf{GCI}| == 1))$$

As soon as the first symbol is recognized, exactly one element from **GC** is selected as **GCI**, and this element is the spatial constraint for all following symbols in σ_1.

Resolving spatial constraints in mobile intention recognition relates to the general constraint satisfaction problem (CSP) (see, e.g., Russell and Norvig, 2010, chapter 6). A CSP consists of a number of variables, a domain for each variable, and a set of constraints that specify which combinations of variable values are allowed. A parse tree of SGIS rules can be interpreted as a spatial constraint system (see Fig. 4.3): first, one grounding variable gr(symbol) is added for each right-hand symbol of the starting rule p_1. Their domain is $\mathbf{R}_1$, i.e., the grounding of p_1, and the three variables are connected with "=" which means that they must happen in the same region. In the next step, p_2 is applied to I_2. This adds a new set of variables, again one for each right-hand symbol. These are again connected with "=" among each other, and their domain is taken from the grounding of p_2. They are further connected with "$\subseteq$" constraints with their parent node $gr(I_2)$ which means they must take a value that is equal to, or contained by $gr(I_2)$. In this way, the constraint system takes the form of a parse tree. At the leaf node level, each constraint variable of a behavior $gr(b)$ is connected with an additional variable representing the input region at the respective position in β_{st}. These input variables have domain $\mathbf{R}$ as they may, in principle, happen in any region. By merging those variables that are connected with "=" the constraint system can be simplified (see Fig. 4.4, left). The variables in this simplified figure are the grounding constraint instantiations used by the parser.

Parsers treat inputs sequentially. This is why parsing is well-suited for temporally ordered sequences in mobile intention recognition. Because of the sequentiality, constraint resolution in spatial parsing is rather a constraint propagation problem than a general constraint satisfaction problem, i.e., the order of constraint resolution is given (see Fig. 4.4, right): predict() propagates the spatial constraints from parent to child nodes until the behavior node level is reached. Then, a scan() operation resolves the input region with the behavior node constraint. In the example of Fig. 4.4 (right), the next scan (in_1) is symbolized with a white arrow which means that the constraint is only checked for consistency but will not modify $GCI(p_5)$ because it already contains only one value (see the invariant above, non-empty σ_0). complete() then propagates the result of the children-parse back to the parent, and so on. Constraint propagation problems are known to be solvable in polynomial time. Details for the three operations are provided in the following.

4.1.2.1 Scan

Method scan() checks whether the region R_{in} of the input[3] is equal to, or contained by any of the regions in $\mathbf{GCI}$. As we know that regions in $\mathbf{GCI}$ are disjunct, there may be either exactly one region $R_g \in \mathbf{GCI}$ containing R_{in}, or none. In the latter case, false is returned. In the former case, a new chart entry is created, just as in the original Earley. The $\mathbf{GCI}_{new}$ of this new entry is a set with only R_g as element.

Consider, as an example, a rule for an intention $I_{VisitMovies}$ which is grounded in several cinemas. As soon as the first behavior happens, like the entering or the ticket queuing, we know which cinema the agent is visiting and can exclude the other cinemas. Even if two cinemas touch, the way SGISs were introduced in section 3.4.2 disallows that the part of the behavior sequence subsumed by one $I_{VisitMovies}$ extends spatially to the neighboring cinema. And this also makes sense as crossing the border to the second cinema would either mean two sequential intentions of type $I_{VisitMovies}$, or that the first cinema was not visited but only crossed.

---

[3] Recall that, in partonomies, we choose the smallest region R_{in} as short notation for $\mathbf{R}_{in}$

Determining R_g is easy ($O(1)$) if σ_0 is not empty: **GCI** then contains exactly one potential candidate region R_{gci}, and we just check *equals* and *contains* for (R, R_{gci}) in the spatial model (refer also to the white arrow 4:s in Fig. 4.4, right). For an empty σ_0, we need to iterate over all elements of **GCI** and check their spatial relation to R. This increases the runtime of scan() by |**GC**| which depends on the BIM. In the worst case, the spatial model is a flat POI model, and the rule is grounded in all regions but R_Ω: |**GC**| = |**R**| - 1. However, this is unrealistic as you cannot have every intention everywhere. Assuming a flat POI model and the rule being grounded in a certain percentage of regions (e. g., "20% of our POIs are cinemas"), we would still have a complexity increase of $O(|R|)$. However, in "real" partonomies, i. e., those with more than one parent and one child level, not all rules will be grounded on the bottom level. For instance, $I_{VisitMovies}$ is not grounded in the entrance or the queuing area. Other examples are intentions to cross a certain area. Thus, in an average scenario, the runtime increase is dependent on the branching factor and depth of the partonomy. In any case, the runtime increase is a constant depending on the spatial structure (more specifically: on the connection of space and intentions in the BIM) but not dependent on the length of the input sequence.

4.1.2.2 Complete

Method complete() is called when the dot is at the end of a rule, i. e., all non-terminals and terminals of the right-hand side have been recognized. We know that, as no ϵ (empty string) is allowed as terminal, at least one input (R_{in}, b_{in}) must have been recognized by the rule. Thus, there is exactly one element R in the grounding constraint instantiation of the completable chart entry. Just as in the original Earley, the algorithm looks for each parent chart entry with the • in front of the correct non-terminal, and correct indices [i, j]. The **GCI** of that parent chart entry is now matched against R by selecting the region from **GCI** which is equal to, or contains R. We know that there is exactly one region because the consistency of the region input has been checked by all scans of behaviors subsumed by σ_3. If σ_0 of the parent rule is not empty, we trivially know that this only element of **GCI** is R so that no spatial constraint resolution is necessary (refer also to the white arrow 8:c in Fig. 4.4, right). Otherwise, we look for R_p just as for R_g in scan().

In the movies example, consider the following rules:

$$I_{VisitMovies} \rightarrow I_{Queuing} \; \sigma_0 \mid \{R_{Cinema1} \cdots R_{Cinema50}\}$$
$$I_{Queuing} \quad \rightarrow \sigma_3 \qquad\qquad \mid \{R_{QArea1\text{-}1} \cdots R_{QArea50\text{-}4}\}$$

Consider now, the • being after σ_3, i. e., the parsing of $I_{Queuing}$ being finished, and **GCI** = $\{R_{QArea41\text{-}2}\}$. The complete() method now decides that, if queuing was in $R_{QArea41\text{-}2}$, the visit movies intention must be happening in the parent region $R_{Cinema41}$. This, in turn, restricts the happening of all symbols in σ_0.

4.1.2.3 Predict

The predict() method generates hypotheses about possible rule applications for each chart entry with a • in front of a non-terminal I_{child} by looking up fitting child rules with I_{child} as left-hand symbol. The spatial version restricts the possible regions for each of these fitting child rules such that they adhere to the parent **GCI**.

In the example, there might be a higher-level intention $I_{GoOutInTown}$, grounded in $\{R_{Town1}, ..., R_{Town5}\}$. From some previous behavior, like visiting a bar, we know that $I_{GoOutInTown}$ happens in R_{Town3}. After the bar visit, we hypothesize an intention $I_{VisitMovies}$, and predict() selects those cinemas as grounding constraint instantiation which are located in R_{Town3}, e.g., $\{R_{Cinema5}, ..., R_{Cinema17}\}$. This is, like in scan() and complete(), an operation on one region and a set of regions. However, in the next step we run predict() on $I_{VisitMovies} \rightarrow \bullet I_{Queuing} \sigma_1$, and must select all queuing areas located in one of the pre-selected cinemas.

Thus, in general, the algorithm operates on two sets, e.g., $\{R_{Cinema5}, ..., R_{Cinema17}\}$, and $\{R_{QArea1-1} ... R_{QArea50-4}\}$. A nested loop that compares each two elements of the two sets is one possible solution if the sets are small. As **R** is finite, another option would be to represent region sets as bit strings, and to compare the two sets with an AND operation. A third option would be a look up table for $\mathbf{P} \times 2^{\mathbf{GC}_{parent}} \times \mathbf{P} \rightarrow 2^{\mathbf{GC}_{child}}$ (from parent production rule, parent **GCI**, and child production rule to $\mathbf{GCI}_{new}$). This is, because of the size of the power set $2^{\mathbf{GC}_{parent}}$, not space-optimal. Luckily, not all sets are possible for **GCI**, but only those that correspond to one parent region in the partonomy, just as set $\{R_{Cinema5}, ..., R_{Cinema17}\}$ is not an arbitrary collection, but determined by the parent region R_{Town3}. Thus, the worst case space complexity of the look up table is $O(|R| \cdot |P|^2)$.

4.1.2.4 Conclusions on the runtime of the SGIS parser

The runtime increase for spatial constraint resolution for all three parser operations does not depend on the length of the input sequence n, but is a constant depending on the structure of the BIM. Thus, the worst case complexity is not worse than the $O(n^3)$ of the original Earley algorithm. In addition, if σ_0 is empty, spatial constraint resolution is only constraint checking for scan() and complete(), and very efficient for predict(). The number of chart entries with empty σ_0 depends on the branching factor of the production rules. As plans usually structure an intention into more than one sub-intention, the branching factor will typically be at least 2. In that case, already half of the operations work on non-empty σ_0.

The unchanged worst case complexity is complemented with an expected hypotheses reduction for the average case because scan() and predict() exclude hypotheses from the search that are not consistent with the spatial grounding. In the worst case, all rules are grounded in R_Ω in which case spatial parsing is identical to non-spatial parsing. However, this worst case is only a theoretical one (see also the behavioral specificity assumption in section 2.1.2).

4.2 Non-Local Constraints: A Generalization of Spatial Grounding

One important restriction of SGIS is that the regions are propagated hierarchically through the parse tree. This allows only a restricted subset of spatial configurations to be expressed. For instance, the pattern $\langle doX_1, doSomethingCompletelyDifferent, doX_2 \rangle$, where sub sequences $\langle doX_1 \rangle$ and $\langle doX_2 \rangle$ belong to the same intention, cannot be expressed with SGIS rules (see section 3.4.2). This section introduces a new grammar which allows for expressing long-ranging dependencies like these.

4.2.1 Spatially-Constrained Context-Free Grammars

Definition 4.1. A *Spatially Constrained Context-Free Grammar* is defined as SCCFG = (SGIS, **NLC**), where

- SGIS = (**B**, **I**, **P**, S, SM, **G**) is a Spatially Grounded Intentional System (see definition 3.2)
- **NLC** is a set of *spatial non-local constraints*. Each spatial non-local constraint (p, $index_1$, $index_2$, type) $\in$ **NLC** has a spatial relation type $\in$ **SRT**, and is defined for two intentions of the right-hand side of the same elementary production rule p $\in$ **P** ($index_1 \neq index_2$).

We identify the left and right member of a non-local constraint with their indices as an intention may occur more than once in a production rule. Non-local constraints are notated behind the rule as ($index_1$, $index_2$, type) triples. A rule system for the "return to bus" example in Fig. 2.19 (bottom left), for instance, could look as follows:

$$I_{VisitTown} \rightarrow I_{GetOffBus}\, I_{GoShopping}\, I_{FindBus} \mid \{R_\Omega\}, \{(0,\, 2,\, touches)\}$$
$$I_{GetOffBus} \rightarrow \sigma_0 \mid \{R_{busterminal1},\, \ldots,\, R_{busterminal5}\}, \{\ \}$$
$$I_{GoShopping} \rightarrow \sigma_1 \mid \{R_\Omega\}, \{\ \}$$
$$I_{FindBus} \rightarrow \sigma_2 \mid \{R_{carpark1},\, R_{carpark2},\, R_{20},\, \ldots,\, R_{30}\}, \{\ \}$$

The first rule has a non-local constraint which frames the whole behavior sequence: the $I_{FindBus}$ intention must happen in a region that touches the region of $I_{GetOffBus}$. The second rule states that there are five bus terminals at which the user may get off. The third rule is the shopping intention and will probably have a sophisticated hierarchy of sub-intentions. The fourth rule, the returning to the bus terminal, is grounded in all regions that touch any of the five bus terminals (the two car parks from Fig. 2.19, and plenty others). However, it depends on the bus terminal selected at runtime for $I_{GetOffBus}$, which subset of $\{R_{carpark1}, R_{carpark2}, R_{20}, \ldots, R_{30}\}$ is possible. The selecting of one bus terminal will disable those regions that do not touch that region.

SGISs can be seen as a special case of SCCFGs, i. e., the language expressed by an SGIS can also be expressed with an according SCCFG. An SGIS is converted into a corresponding SCCFG by simply choosing $\mathbf{NLC} = \emptyset$.

The example above has illustrated that the SCCFG formalism allows for modeling of long-ranging space-intention dependencies, like those occurring when the user returns to a certain region. By inserting multiple rules with non-local constraints into each other arbitrary nesting relations can be achieved. In the clothes shop example from Fig. 2.19 (bottom right), for instance, a basic rule set that expresses the user picking a number of pullovers, and returning some of them later, might look as follows:

$$
\begin{array}{llll}
I_{BuyPullover} & \rightarrow I_{Pick}\ I_{ContinueShopping}\ I_{Drop} & | \ \{R_\Omega\}, & \{(0,\ 2,\ equals)\} \\
I_{BuyPullover} & \rightarrow I_{Pick}\ I_{ContinueShopping} & | \ \{R_\Omega\} & \\
I_{ContinueShopping} & \rightarrow I_{TryOn} & | \ \{R_\Omega\} & \\
I_{ContinueShopping} & \rightarrow I_{Pick}\ I_{ContinueShopping}\ I_{Drop} & | \ \{R_\Omega\}, & \{(0,\ 2,\ equals)\} \\
I_{ContinueShopping} & \rightarrow I_{Pick}\ I_{ContinueShopping} & | \ \{R_\Omega\} &
\end{array}
$$

All right-hand intentions, of course, need to be specified in additional rules which would be grounded in the regions around shelves, in the fitting area queue, and in the fitting rooms. The expressiveness of this rule set is equivalent to $a^n x b^m$ (in the example: $pick^n$ try $drop^m$), with $n \geq m$. It is known that patterns like these can be expressed with CFGs. SCCFGs, however, additionally identify which picks and drops belong together. The sequence $\langle$ pick, pick, pick, drop, drop $\rangle$, for instance, could yield in three possible SCCFG interpretations,

$$
\langle pick_1,\ pick_2,\ pick_3,\ drop_3,\ drop_1 \rangle,
$$
$$
\langle pick_1,\ pick_2,\ pick_3,\ drop_3,\ drop_2 \rangle,
$$
$$
\langle pick_1,\ pick_2,\ pick_3,\ drop_2,\ drop_1 \rangle,
$$

where the indices indicate that tokens belong together[4]. This nesting with SCCFGs is unrestricted, i. e., the n and m in ($pick^n$ try $drop^m$) have no theoretical upper bound.

---

[4] Note that this is the inverse notation of that chosen by Geib and Goldman (2009) in the early-closing example of Fig. 3.4 where identical *letters* indicate that tokens belong together.

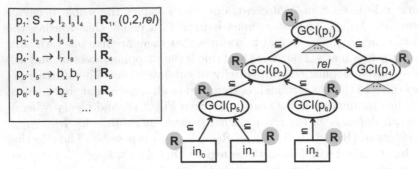

Fig. 4.5 CSP for an SCCFG parse tree.

Unfortunately, a crossing of long-ranging space-intention dependencies cannot be expressed with an SCCFG. In the example, this would be the sequences

$$\langle \text{pick}_1, \text{pick}_2, \text{pick}_3, \text{drop}_1, \text{drop}_2 \rangle,$$
$$\langle \text{pick}_1, \text{pick}_2, \text{pick}_3, \text{drop}_1, \text{drop}_3 \rangle,$$
$$\langle \text{pick}_1, \text{pick}_2, \text{pick}_3, \text{drop}_2, \text{drop}_3 \rangle.$$

The only way to express crossing dependencies is to define them statically in the rule set but this is not possible in an unrestricted way because the rule set would blow up dramatically.

As the crossing of long-ranging space-intention dependencies is essential for many mobile intention recognition scenarios (e. g., we cannot force the customer to return the pullovers in a certain order) a formalism with higher expressiveness becomes necessary. This is the aim of section 4.3.

4.2.2 A State Chart Parser for SCCFGs

The spatial constraint resolution in SGISs described in section 4.1.2 is exclusively local: from parent intention to child intention (predict), from behavior to its sibling (scan), and back to the parent intention as soon as the child intention is finished (complete). The non-local constraints in SCCFGs allow for another kind of spatial constraint resolution in a parse tree: from node with index_1 (left node) to the node with index_2 (right node)[5]. As these nodes are parsed sequentially, resolving non-local constraints is again a constraint propagation problem (see Fig. 4.5).

---

[5] In the following, it is assumed that the spatial relation is directed from non-terminal with index_1 to that with index_2. If the relation in the grammar is modeled in the other direction, it can be replaced by the inverse relation if available in **SRT**. If not, the order of arguments in the algorithm while checking **SR** could be made dependent on the direction of the relation. These details are left out for reasons of clarity.

// *The spatial model SM is a partonomy.*
// *The behavior intention model BIM is an SCCFG = (sgis, **NLC**), with sgis = (**B, I, P, S, R, G**) (definitions 3.2 and 4.1).*

int n;
statechart[] chart; // *(time-indexed): an array of sub-charts.*

procedure initialize(domain model *DM*)
begin
    for each $((S \rightarrow \sigma \mid \textbf{GC, NLC}) \in$ BIM) **do**
        Add $((S \rightarrow \bullet \sigma \mid \textbf{GC, NLC}), [0,0], \textbf{GC, NLI}_{n/spec})$ to chart[0]
    end for
    $n \leftarrow 0$
    predictAll(0)
end procedure

function recognize(space-time behavior *(t_s, t_e, R_{in}, b_{in})*) **returns** $\textbf{I}_{hypotheses}$
begin
    $\textbf{I}_{hypotheses} \leftarrow \emptyset$
    for each (entry =
        $(I_p \rightarrow \sigma_0 \bullet b_{in} \sigma_1 \mid \textbf{GC, NLC}, [i,n], \textbf{GCI, NLI}) \in$ chart[n]) **do**
        boolean recognized $\leftarrow$ scan(entry, R_{in})
        if (recognized) **then** $\textbf{I}_{hypotheses}$.add(I_p)
    end for
    $n \leftarrow n + 1$
    completeAll(n)
    predictAll(n)
    return $\textbf{I}_{hypotheses}$
end function

Fig. 4.6 An incremental SCCFG parser based on Earley's state chart parser: methods initialize(), and recognize(), implementing the abstract methods from Fig. 2.14. Methods scan(), completeAll(), and predictAll() are given in Fig. 4.7.

There are two decisive moments for parsing a non-local constraint:

1. The • "jumps" over the intention with $index_1$ during the execution of complete(). In this moment, we put the region in which the child intention happened into memory.
2. The • starts to parse the intention with $index_2$ with predict(). In this moment, the spatial constraint is resolved.

This "memory" for storing the non-local constraint is modeled as an additional element in the chart entry, the non-local constraint instantiations **NLI**. The **NLI** contains one region for each non-local constraint. **NLI**(nlc) denotes the non-local constraint instantiation for the non-local constraint nlc. A special value *n/spec* indicates that the non-local constraint has not yet been instantiated. This yields in the following chart entries for the SCCFG parser:

$$(p_\bullet, [i, j], \textbf{GCI, NLI})$$
or, as full notation: $(I \rightarrow \sigma_0 \bullet \sigma_1 \mid \textbf{GC, NLC}, [i, j], \textbf{GCI, NLI})$

Figure 4.6 lists the basic structure of the SCCFG parser which is almost the same as that for SGISs in Fig. 4.1. $\mathbf{NLI}_{n/spec}$ denotes an **NLI** initialized with $n/spec$ for all non-local constraints. Method scan() is exactly the same as for SGIS because it does not use the non-local constraints. The Earley methods complete() and predict() are modified as follows (see Fig. 4.7).

function scan(chartentry entry, region R_{in}) **returns** boolean
// same method as scan() in Fig. 4.2

procedure completeAll(int k)
begin
    for each $((I_{child} \to \sigma_3 \bullet \mid \mathbf{GC}, \mathbf{NLC}, [j, k], \{R\}, \mathbf{NLI}_c) \in \text{chart}[k])$ **do**
        for each $(I_{parent} \to \sigma_0 \bullet I_{child} \sigma_1 \mid \mathbf{GC}_p, \mathbf{NLC}_p, [i, j], \mathbf{GCI}, \mathbf{NLI}_p)$
            $\in$ chart[j] **do**
            $R_p \leftarrow$ The region from **GCI** which is equal to or contains R.
            $\mathbf{NLI}_{new} \leftarrow \mathbf{NLI}_p.\text{clone}()$
            for each (nlc $\in \mathbf{NLC}_p$ with $index_1 ==$ index of I_{child}) **do**
                $\mathbf{NLI}_{new}(nlc) \leftarrow R$
            Add $(I_{parent} \to \sigma_0 I_{child} \bullet \sigma_1 \mid \mathbf{GC}_p, \mathbf{NLC}_p, [i, k], \{R_p\}, \mathbf{NLI}_{new})$
              to chart[k]
        end for
    end for
end procedure

procedure predictAll(int j)
begin
    for each $(((I_{parent} \to \sigma_0 \bullet I_{child} \sigma_1 \mid \mathbf{GC}_p, \mathbf{NLC}_p), [i, j], \mathbf{GCI}_p, \mathbf{NLI}_p)$
        $\in$ chart[j]) **do**
        for each $((I_{child} \to \sigma_3 \mid \mathbf{GC}_c, \mathbf{NLC}_c) \in \text{SGIS})$ **do**
            $\mathbf{GCI}_{new} \leftarrow$ All $R \in \mathbf{GC}_c$ which are eq. to or contained by a region in $\mathbf{GCI}_p$
            if ($\mathbf{GCI}_{new}$ is not empty) **then**
                for each (nlc $\in \mathbf{NLC}_p$ with I_{child} as right node) **do**
                    Remove those regions from $\mathbf{GCI}_{new}$ not consistent with nlc.
                end for
                Add $(I_{child} \to \bullet \sigma_3 \mid \mathbf{GC}_c, \mathbf{NLC}_c, [j, j], \mathbf{GCI}_{new}, \mathbf{NLI}_{n/spec})$ to chart[j]
            end if
         end for
    end for
end procedure

Fig. 4.7 Methods scan(), completeAll(), and predictAll() for the SCCFG parser.

4.2.2.1 Complete

A call of complete() means that the child intention I_{child} has been fully parsed. Thus, we know the region in which I_{child} happened. As in the SGIS parser, that must be exactly one region (R in Fig. 4.7). All non-local constraints nlc in the rule for the parent intention I_{parent} which have the I_{child} node as left node are now instantiated by assigning R to $\mathbf{NLI}_{new}(nlc)$. This simple assignment does not increase the runtime noteworthily as the number of non-local constraints starting at one node is very limited.

4.2.2.2 Predict

The predict() method in the SCCFG parser first resolves the constraint from parent to child, just as in the SGIS parser. Then, the set $\mathbf{GCI}_{new}$ is further reduced by removing those elements which contradict any of the non-local spatial constraints ending at the predicted node. The algorithm in Fig. 4.7 implements this as loop over $\mathbf{NLC}_p$, containing another loop over the remaining $\mathbf{GCI}_{new}$ ("Remove those..."). Note that, if σ_0 is empty (• at the beginning), the non-local constraints have not been initialized and are not relevant. On the other hand, if non-local constraints may be relevant (i.e., σ_0 is not empty) there is only one region in $\mathbf{GCI}_p$ so that resolution from parent to child is a loop on only one set.

4.2.2.3 Conclusions on the runtime of the SCCFG parser

The worst case runtime complexity is, as in the SGIS parser, $O(n^3)$ with n denoting the length of the input sequence. Following the same line argumentation as for the SGIS parser, in an average case there will be even more hypotheses that are thrown away which further reduces the search space.

4.3 Intersecting Spatial Dependencies

4.3.1 Towards More Context-Sensitivity: A Parallel to NLP

Intersecting dependencies are a well-known problem in NLP. They occur in the syntax of natural languages, such as Dutch, when the words of different constituents appear interleaved in a sentence. Consider, for instance, the Dutch sentence in Fig. 4.8 (top left): "ik" and "zag" make up one constituent ("I saw"), "Cecilia" and "voeren" another one ("Cecilia feeding"). The grammatical form of one word, e.g., first person singular, must be reflected by the other part of the constituent. Thus, a formal grammar for modeling such languages must be able to represent interleaved syntactic structures, and a parser that validates or interprets a sentence must maintain the knowledge between the different words. An investigation on how much interleaving may appear in the syntax of a given natural language both, in theory and in

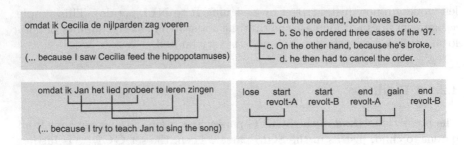

Fig. 4.8 Crossing dependencies in NLP and beyond: syntax in Dutch (left top: de la Clergerie, 2008; left bottom: Geib and Steedman, 2007), discourse semantics (right top: Webber et al, 1999), and argument construction (right bottom: Sprado and Gottfried, 2008).

practice, is beyond the scope of this thesis. However, it is clear that NLP faces problems in which interleaving is not restricted to two overlapping constituents, as becomes apparent in the example given by Geib and Steedman (2007) (see Fig. 4.8, bottom left).

On a higher semantic level, overlapping dependencies occur in discourse semantics when sentences (or clauses) that make up a story refer to other sentences further away in the same text. As an example, consider the construct "On the one hand ... on the other hand" (see Fig. 4.8, top right). This comes close to the discussion of Sidner's (1985) human-machine discourse interpreter in section 3.4.1 although discourse semantics in general is not restricted to recognizing plans. A third area with structural interleaving has been identified by Sprado and Gottfried (2008): they consider argument construction in historical theories which can be seen as the problem of assigning meaning to a temporally ordered sequence of events, just as in mobile intention recognition. A historicist might, for instance, have access to documents about the changing wealth of a given person (events "gain" and "lose"), and about revolts that started at that time. The explanations for the wealth gain and lose are typically unknown. The example in Fig. 4.8 (bottom right) shows an argument construction for a sequence of events which explains that a person's loss of wealth caused him to participate in revolt-A, and the end of revolt-A made him richer, whereas revolt-B had nothing to do with that person.

As mentioned in section 3.4.3, NLP has addressed the problem of interleaving by extending the Chomsky hierarchy (Chomsky, 1959) with grammars that are more expressive than CFGs and less expressive than CSGs (Context Sensitive Grammars), see Fig. 4.9: the first grammar in between, but closer to type 1 grammars, are Indexed Grammars developed by Aho (1968). In Indexed Grammars a stack is attached to each node in the parse tree and handed on to all children when a production rule is applied. Production rule application may trigger push and pop operations that modify the stack. In-

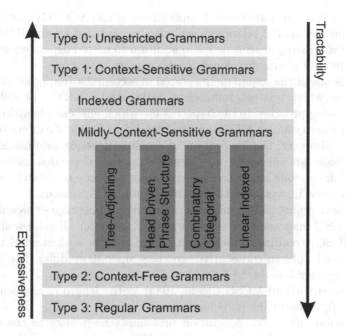

Fig. 4.9 Extended Chomsky hierarchy.

dexed Grammars can express crossing dependencies but the parsing problem for Indexed Grammars is NP-complete.

A restricted type of Indexed Grammars are Linear Indexed Grammars (LIG). They were first used, but not yet designated as LIG, in Gazdar (1988). In contrast to Indexed Grammars, the stack in LIGs is handed on only to one child node. This allows them to be parsed in polynomial time. Other grammatical formalisms falling in between Indexed Grammars and CFGs are Tree Adjoining Grammars (TAG, Joshi and Schabes, 1997), Head Driven Phrase Structure Grammars (HDPSG, Sag and Pollard, 1987), and Combinatory Categorial Grammars (CCG, Steedman, 1985). Vijay-Shanker and Weir (1994) have shown that these formalisms are weakly equivalent to LIGs, i. e., their expressiveness allows them to produce the same languages. Thus, LIG, TAG, HDPSG, and CCG can be subsumed under a common class of language formalisms which was called Mildly Context Sensitive Grammars (MCSG) by Joshi (1985). He defined four common properties for MCSGs: containment of context-free languages, limited crossing dependencies, constant growth, and polynomial parsing:

- *Containment of context-free languages*: all MCSGs have higher expressiveness than CFGs. Thus, the nesting dependencies which appear in mobile intention recognition, and which are already captured by SGISs (with respect to partonomial containment), and SCCFGs (with respect to arbitrary spatial relations), will also be captured by an MCSG.

- *Limited crossing dependencies*: in addition to nested dependencies, a limited number of crossing dependencies can be expressed.
  This is one of the requirements stated in section 2.4 (requirement 5), and the one which was not fulfilled by SGISs and SCCFGs, as well as not by those approaches from chapter 3 for which efficient algorithms exist. This property makes MCSGs a good candidate for mobile intention recognition. However, the limitedness of crossing dependencies needs further discussion: are the kinds of expressible crossing dependencies really sufficient for mobile intention recognition, or are they too restrictive? This is discussed in section 4.3.3 for Tree-Adjoining Grammars.
- *Constant growth*: The sentences of the string language expressible with an MCSG may not grow unboundedly. If we order all valid sentences of an MCSG according to their length there must be a constant K by which the lengths of two consecutive sentences maximally differ. For instance, the language $L = \{a^{2n} \mid n \geq 1\} = \{a, aa, aaaa, aaaaaa, \dots\}$ cannot be expressed with an MCSG (Joshi, 1985) as the length of one sentence in L is a function of the previous sentence.
  For mobile intention recognition problems, this relates to the question whether, given a fully expanded plan P (i.e., a parse tree), it is possible to create an acceptable plan from P by appending only a limited number of behaviors to the behavior sequence. Consider, for instance, one possible behavior sequence for the intention $I_{CleanUpFlat}$ consisting of k behaviors $\langle b_0, \dots, b_{k-1} \rangle$ for cleaning only the kitchen. If afterwards cleaning the corridor is also a valid expansion for $I_{CleanUpFlat}$, we could append another sequence $\langle b_k, \dots, b_{l-1} \rangle$, and maybe another one for cleaning the bathroom $\langle b_l, \dots, b_{m-1} \rangle$, and so on. It is clear that cleaning the second room (or third room respectively) does not take more behaviors just because there was another room before. In other words, the order of cleaning the rooms does not influence the number of behaviors needed. Thus, this mobile intention recognition domain fulfills the constant growth property. Although this is only an example, it seems intuitive that most mobile intention recognition domains are structured this way.
- *Polynomial parsing*: MCSGs can be parsed in polynomial time. This makes them attractive for mobile intention recognition (requirement 1).

To conclude, the class of MCSGs seems to be a good candidate for modeling mobile intention recognition problems. In the following, a formalism based on TAGs is proposed as TAGs allow for an intuitive modeling of plans (requirement 3).

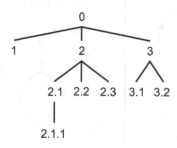

Fig. 4.10 Identification of nodes in an elementary tree of a TAG.

4.3.2 Spatially Constrained Tree-Adjoining Grammars

4.3.2.1 Tree-Adjoining Grammars

With slight notational modification of the definition given in Joshi and Schabes (1997), TAGs can be defined as follows:

Definition 4.2. A *Tree-Adjoining Grammar* is defined as TAG $= (\Sigma, \boldsymbol{NT},$
$\boldsymbol{IT}, \boldsymbol{AT}, \mathrm{S})$, where

- Σ are *terminals*, $\boldsymbol{NT}$ are *non-terminals*, $\mathrm{S} \in \boldsymbol{NT}$ is the *starting symbol*.
- $\boldsymbol{IT}$ is a finite set of *initial trees*. In an initial tree the root and inte-
  rior nodes are labeled with non-terminals. Leaf nodes are either labeled
  with terminals, with ϵ, or with non-terminals marked for substitution.
  Substitution nodes are marked with a downarrow ($\downarrow$).
- $\boldsymbol{AT}$ is a finite set of *auxiliary trees*. An auxiliary tree has exactly one
  special leaf node, the *foot node*, which must have the same label as the
  root node. The foot node is marked with an asterisk (*).

All trees are finite. Initial and auxiliary trees together are the *elementary
trees* of a TAG. As in CFGs non-terminals are typically written in upper case,
terminals in lower-case. Trees are identified with small greek letters[6]. Each
node in the grammar is identified by *node* $= (\alpha, nodeid)$, where α is the tree,
and *nodeid* is determined as follows: the root node is referred to as *nodeid*
$= 0$, child nodes of the root are numbered from left to right starting with 1,
and all other child nodes are identified by appending a number to the *nodeid*
of their parent node (see Fig. 4.10).

---

[6] The notation introduced in the previous chapters and sections is not changed: τ:
trajectory, μ: motion track, β: behavior sequence, ι: intention sequence, ρ: intention
hypotheses sequence, σ: sequence of non-terminals and terminals. All other small greek
letters are used to denote elementary trees.

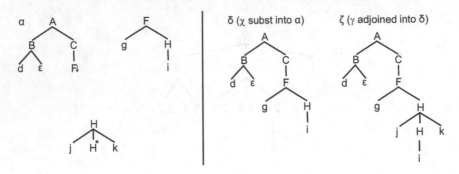

Fig. 4.11 Example for substitution and adjunction in a TAG with two initial trees (α, χ) and one auxiliary tree (γ).

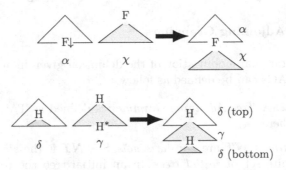

Fig. 4.12 Schematic visualization of substitution (left) and adjunction (right) (similar to Joshi and Schabes, 1997, Fig. 2.2)

The label of a certain node of tree α, which may be a behavior, intention, or ϵ, is referred to as *symbol(node)* or *symbol(α, nodeid)*. The terms "label" and "symbol" are used as equivalent. Figure 4.11 (left) displays a simple example TAG with three elementary trees. The operations defined on a TAG are *substitution* and *adjunction*: a substitution node F↓ may be replaced by a tree whose root node has the same non-terminal F as symbol (see δ in Fig. 4.11, right). This operation is equivalent to rule application in CFGs.

The second operation, adjunction, causes the additional expressiveness of TAGs: an auxiliary tree γ headed with non-terminal H (and footed with H*) may be adjoined into a tree (δ in the example) at an inner node with the same non-terminal H. Adjunction first cuts off the partial tree δ (bottom) below H and attaches it to the foot node H* of γ. The resulting tree is then attached to the inner node H of δ (top). An example is illustrated in Fig. 4.11, right. Root and foot node cut an auxiliary tree into two parts. The way from root to foot node of an auxiliary tree is called *spine*, and the two parts of the tree are refered to as "left of the spine" and "right of the spine". Figure 4.12

(right) illustrates how the two parts left and right of the spine "embrace" the cut-off part of the original tree.

Joshi and Schabes (1997) further introduce three types of adjunction constraints that can hold for any inner node: a *selective adjunction constraint* SA($\mathbf{T}$) states that only auxiliary trees from $\mathbf{T} \subseteq \mathbf{AT}$ may be adjoined into the node. An *obligatory adjunction constraint* OA($\mathbf{T}$), on the contrary, forces to adjoin a tree from $\mathbf{T} \subseteq \mathbf{AT}$ into the node. Of course, all trees in $\mathbf{T}$ must have a fitting non-terminal as symbol of their root node. A *null adjunction constraint* NA disallows any adjunction on the node. Joshi and Schabes use their TAGs sometimes with an implicit *one adjunction constraint*, i.e., one may perform *at most one* adjunction operation on a node.

The set of trees that can be created from a TAG by starting from all initial trees rooted with the start symbol and performing substitution and adjunction defines the *tree language* of a TAG. The according string language is defined as all strings that yield from a tree in the tree language by performing a left-to-right tree-traversal. For instance, the string language defined by the TAG in Fig. 4.11 (assumed a one-adjunction constraint) is {dgi, dgjik}. The string language of a TAG is relevant when using a TAG for intention recognition as it defines the set of behavior sequences we can recognize. The tree language, however, defines the representable plans.

4.3.2.2 Adding Spatial Constraints to TAGs

The definition of TAGs (definition 4.2) is extended by including spatial constraints (similar to the definitions given in Kiefer, 2008b,a):

Definition 4.3. A *Spatially Constrained Tree-Adjoining Grammar* is defined as SCTAG = (TAG, SM, $\mathbf{GC}$, $\mathbf{NLC}$), where

- TAG = ($\mathbf{B}$, $\mathbf{I}$, $\mathbf{IT}$, $\mathbf{AT}$, S) is a Tree-Adjoining Grammar with behaviors $\mathbf{B}$ as terminals, and intentions $\mathbf{I}$ as non-terminals.
- SM = ($\mathbf{R}$, $\mathbf{SRT}$, $\mathbf{SR}$) is a spatial model (see definition 2.6)
- $\mathbf{GC} \subseteq (\mathbf{IT} \cup \mathbf{AT}) \times$ node $\times \mathbf{R}$ is a set of *grounding constraints*. Each grounding constraint is defined for one node in one initial or auxiliary tree.
- $\mathbf{NLC}$ is a set of *spatial non-local constraints*. Each spatial non-local constraint (α, nodeid$_1$, nodeid$_2$, type) $\in \mathbf{NLC}$ has a spatial relation type $\in \mathbf{SRT}$, and is defined for two nodes in the same elementary tree from $\mathbf{IT} \cup \mathbf{AT}$ (nodeid$_1 \neq$ nodeid$_2$, no ϵ-nodes).

SCTAGs combine the idea of SCCFGs (non-local spatial constraints) with the mild context-sensitivity of TAGs. Any SCCFG can be converted into an according SCTAG by simply writing one initial tree for each context-free rule, and turning each right-hand intention into a substitution node. These initial trees created from a SCCFG would have a depth of 1. In an

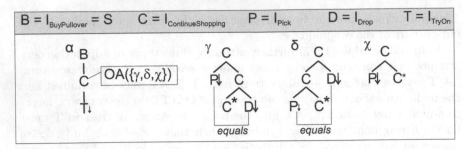

Fig. 4.13 An SCTAG for the clothes shop example.

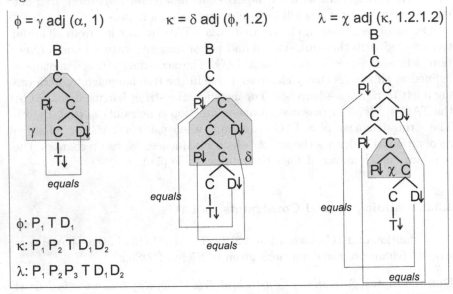

Fig. 4.14 Derivation of P_1 P_2 P_3 T D_1 D_2 with the SCTAG of Fig. 4.13.

SCTAG written from scratch the modeler will typically build larger initial trees. If there is only one tree that can be substituted for a given intention these trees will typically be merged already while modeling. In an SCCFG, it is not possible to merge rules as this would remove the semantics of the intermediate intention. Thus, a fewer number of primitive structures is needed in an SCTAG than in context-free formalisms, making them cognitively easier to understand.

Re-building the expressiveness of an SGIS or SCCFG with a cognitively understandable formalism is, of course, not the main idea of SCTAGs. Interesting are especially those SCTAGs which allow for adjunction as this operation allows to express crossing dependencies. Consider, for instance, the SCTAG in Fig. 4.13 which models the picking and dropping in the clothes store (see also sections 2.3.4 and 4.2.1): derivation always starts with the initial tree α as it is the only tree headed by start symbol S. Because trying on clothes (T) without picking is not a sensible plan, an obligatory adjunction constraint on node $(\alpha, 1)$ ensures that at least one tree will be adjoined in the node with label C. The auxiliary trees γ, δ, and χ are adjunction candidates. Each of these auxiliary trees itself contains nodes with label C in which further adjunctions can take place, with further (instances of) γ, δ, and χ, just as a recursive application of rules in a CFG. In principle, an infinite number of adjunctions is possible. A one-adjunction constraint is not assumed.

The derivation in Fig. 4.14 illustrates how three adjunctions can generate a tree for the string P_1 P_2 P_3 T D_1 D_2 (three pickings, then a try on, and finally two droppings with crossing dependencies) which is a sequence that could not be expressed with the SCCFG in section 4.2.1. The notation $\phi = \gamma$ adj $(\alpha, 1)$ means that tree γ is adjoined into tree α at node with id 1, and the resulting tree is called ϕ. Node ids in derived trees are assigned using the same scheme as in elementary trees. Figures 4.13 and 4.14 illustrate the basic idea of creating crossing dependencies. A full SCTAG would contain trees that can be substituted in P↓, T↓, and D↓, and grounding constraints **GC** for all nodes.

In contrast to SGISs and SCCFGs, SCTAGs allow for ϵ terminals. These ϵ-terminals are skipped during parsing. This does not make much sense for trees like α in the simple TAG example in Fig. 4.11 in which the ϵ node (id 1.2) could just be left out. However, ϵ helps to model that an adjoinable intention has no children of its own: consider the pick/drop example without an I_{TryOn}. This can easily be modeled by replacing the T↓ by ϵ in tree α of the SCTAG in Fig. 4.13.

4.3.3 SCTAGs and the Mobile Intention Recognition Problem

We have seen in the clothes shop example (Figs. 2.19, 4.13 and 4.14) that it is possible to express crossing dependencies of the form P_1 P_2 P_3 T D_1 D_2 between picks and drops in the language $pick^n$ try $drop^m$ $(n \geq m)$. However, it is yet unclear which general types of crossing dependencies SCTAGs allow for, which not, and whether the expressiveness is sufficient for typical scenarios in mobile intention recognition.

In a first step, let us consider a generalization of the pick/drop example in which a pick/drop pair may occur behind one of the drops before. This is similar to the "Visit-Revisit" pattern occurring very frequently in mobile assistance. The examples given at the end of chapter 2 in Fig. 2.19 are of that kind, where Revisit does not necessarily mean the identical region but a region with a certain spatial relation, like the region with a good view on the cathedral. Figure 2.20 (top) has also illustrated how these plans could appear nested in, and crossing with each other. This pattern can be modeled with the SCTAG shown in Fig. 4.15. It is very similar to that in Fig. 4.13, with

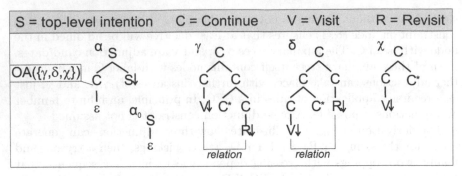

Fig. 4.15 An SCTAG for the "Visit-Revisit" pattern.

additional parent nodes for $V\downarrow$ and $R\downarrow$ which give more freedom for adjoining. This, for instance, allows to express $V_1 V_2 R_1 V_3 R_3 R_2$. For a certain scenario, such as the mobile tourist guide, there will be one triple of (γ, δ, χ), for each possible plan, e.g., one triple of auxiliary trees for visiting the cathedral, and one for joining the whale watching tour. The bus transfer plan, however, must be treated extra because it may not interleave arbitrarily with the other plans, but embrace the whole sequence. This can simply be integrated into tree α, or there may be several initial trees headed with S, one for arriving by bus, one for arriving by car, and so on. To conclude, TAGs are not restricted to patterns in which all Visits must occur before all revisits, $V^n R^m$ ($n \geq m$), but allows some Visit-Revisit plans to close before others start.

Following the expressiveness discussions given by Joshi (1985), the set of all V-intentions, and the set of a R-intentions are called "dependent sets" because a V must always appear with an R. Without loss of generality, let us now ignore the case that a single V may appear; it can always simply be added with an auxiliary tree like χ in Fig. 4.15. For one pair of dependent sets (such as the set of all Visits, and the set of all Revisits), mixed dependencies can be expressed with a TAG, some nested, some crossing (see also Joshi, 1985, p. 222). But what will happen for a triple of dependent sets? Consider, for instance, a whale watching customer who first checks the ticket price, but does not buy the ticket yet as she is unsure whether the price is appropriate. Later, she might return, buy the ticket, and again leave the ticket counter, before she finally enters the boat: $\langle I_{CheckTicketPrice}, Continue, I_{BuyTicket}, Continue, I_{EnterBoat} \rangle$. This could easily be modeled with an auxiliary tree containing two spatial relations, and it would be possible to adjoin other plans into the "Continue" place holders. However, it is not possible to arbitrarily interleave other three-elementary plans around this one, unless by blowing up the number of auxiliary trees (see also Joshi, 1985, p. 223). The same applies, of course, to plans with more than three dependent sets. This is the first restriction of SCTAGs for mobile intention recognition: no arbitrary interleaving with more than two dependent sets can be expressed.

The second restriction concerns cases with more than one pair of dependent sets:

"however, any two pairs of such dependent sets are either disjoint or one is properly nested inside the other. Thus, we have either

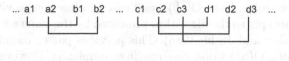

or

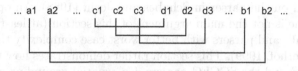

" (Joshi, 1985, p. 223)

Following Joshi's argumentation, this excludes crossing dependencies between two pairs of dependent sets:

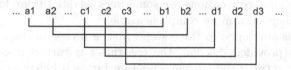

In contrast to four dependent sets, the relations in this example are binary. And, in contrast to the binary "Visit-Revisit" pattern in Fig. 4.15, the four sets may not interleave arbitrarily, but all "a" elements must happen before the "c" elements, "c" before "b", and "b" before "d". In mobile intention recognition this kind of structure is very rare. A tourist, for instance, may decide freely about the order in which she visits (and revisits) POIs. As a counter-example we could require the customer in the clothes shop to first pick all pullovers ("a"), then pick all jeans ("c"), and later first drop all pullovers ("b"), then all jeans ("d"). However, most customers will not stick to this fixed order which would, from a formal point of view, merge the "a"-set and the "c"-set, and "b"/"d"-sets accordingly.

To conclude, there are restrictions on the expressiveness of SCTAGs. This is not very surprising as an arbitrary interleaving, i.e., no restrictions on the number of sets participating in one dependency, and no restrictions on crossing, would lead to an explosion of the state space (see also the partitioning/composition discussion in section 2.3.3) and obviate efficient parsing. Although these restrictions of SCTAGs are not very severe in most mobile intention recognition domains, the type of grammar for a certain domain should be chosen with the restrictions of the respective formalism in mind.

4.3.4 A State Chart Parser for SCTAGs

The SCTAG-parser is again based on an Earley-like parsing algorithm. As only parsers that maintain the VPP are useful for mobile intention recognition (see section 4.1.1) the algorithm proposed by Joshi and Schabes (1997, pp. 36–53) is no option. The recognizer has a $O(n^6)$ worst case runtime complexity. It is based on the same concepts as the algorithm presented by the same authors in previous work (Schabes and Joshi, 1988). This previous parser maintains the VPP, for the sake of a $O(n^9)$ worst case runtime complexity. However, as the VPP is fundamental for mobile intention recognition, the parser proposed in this section is based on the parser in Schabes and Joshi (1988). An optimization of the runtime is not the main argument of this section (at least as long as it is polynomial), and parsers with better worst case complexity than $O(n^9)$ exist (e. g., Nederhof, 1999). This section rather demonstrates how the main ideas of the SGIS and the SCCFG parsers, i. e., spatial grounding and non-local constraints, are combined by a parser for SCTAGs. TAG parasers, in general, are much harder to comprehend than CFG parsers. The parser of Schabes and Joshi (1988) is used as it most closely resembles the original Earley algorithm. Notational conventions are sometimes adapted from Joshi and Schabes (1997) if they seem more comprehensible.

The SCTAG-parser is developed in three steps: first, a review of the original TAG recognizer is provided. Second, the recognizer is turned into an incremental parser that returns the current intention for each behavior. Finally, spatial constraints are integrated for the parsing of SCTAGs.

4.3.4.1 The original TAG recognizer (Schabes and Joshi, 1988)

The algorithm in (Schabes and Joshi, 1988) follows the idea of Earley's (1970) chart parser: a predictive bottom-up parser that uses top-down information. Like the original parser it consists of rules that work on entries in a chart. As the basic constructs of TAGs are trees, the chart entries for the TAG parser do not consist of "dotted rules" but "dotted elementary trees". The dot position $pos \in \{la, lb, rb, ra\}$ indicates whether the dot is left above, left below, right below, or right above of the node. lb and rb are not allowed for terminals and substitution nodes. There is always exactly one dot in a dotted elementary tree. The dot "separates a tree into two parts: a left context consisting of nodes that have been already traversed and a right context that still needs to be traversed." (Joshi and Schabes, 1997, p. 38).

A tree traversal in depth-first, left-to-right manner defines a linear order on all dot positions in an elementary tree. The algorithm moves the dot along this linear order, as displayed in Fig. 4.16 (left). Succeeding dot positions with different nodes are equivalent (see Fig. 4.16, right), i. e., the dot automatically "jumps" from one dot position to the next along the double-arrows. As an extension to the description in Schabes and Joshi (1988) this section proposes

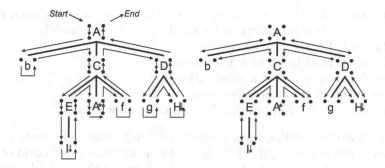

Fig. 4.16 Elementary tree traversal (left), and equivalent dot positions (right) in the TAG recognizer.

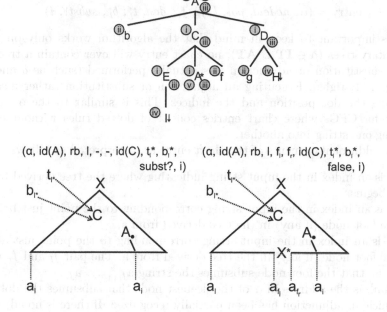

Fig. 4.17 Types of dot positions distinguished by the TAG-recognizer (top). Interpretation of indices on an initial tree (left right), and an auxiliary tree (bottom right).

to combine equivalent dot positions and categorize them into six classes as follows (see Fig. 4.17, left)[7]:

---

[7] The automatic dot jump was modeled as extra rules MOVE DOT UP and MOVE DOT DOWN in Schabes and Joshi (1988). These rules are left out, and the automatic dot jump is ensured by the data structure used for dotted trees.

ⓘ The dot is left above of a non-terminal[8] which is not a substitution node (i.e., either la of an inner non-terminal, or la of a foot node).
ⓘⓘ The dot is left above of a terminal or ϵ.
ⓘⓘⓘ The dot is right below of a non-terminal.
ⓘⓥ The dot is left above of a substitution node.
ⓥ The dot is left below of a foot node.
ⓥⓘ The dot is at the end position (i.e., ra of the root node).

In addition to a dotted tree, a chart entry in Schabes and Joshi (1988) consists of five indices l, f_l, f_r, t_l^*, b_l^*, and a nodeid dan (the nodeid of the "deepest adjunction node"[9]). Versions of the algorithm that use substitution further need a flag $subst?$. Substitution, as equivalent operation to rule application in CFGs, is a very useful operation for mobile intention recognition as it allows to reduce the number of trees needed. For reasons of clarity, this section adds another index i to the chart entry, yielding in an 11-tuple:

$$\text{entry} = (\alpha, \textit{nodeid}, \textit{pos}, l, f_l, f_r, \textit{dan}, t_l^*, b_l^*, \textit{subst?}, i)$$

It is important to keep in mind that the algorithm works only on the elementary trees ($\alpha \in \mathbf{IT} \cup \mathbf{AT}$); no chart entry will ever contain a tree in which substitution or adjunction was actually performed (such as δ and ζ in Fig. 4.11, right). Executing an adjunction or substitution rather means changing the dot position and the indices. This is similar to the original Earley for CFGs where chart entries consist of dotted rules without ever merging one string into another.

The additional elements of the chart entry are interpreted as follows

- "l is an index in the input string indicating where the tree derived from α begins.
- f_l is an index in the input string corresponding to the point just before the foot node (if any) in the tree derived from a.
- f_r is an index in the input string corresponding to the point just after the foot node (if any) in the tree derived from a. The pair f_l and f_r will mean that the foot node subsumes the string $a_{f_l+1} \ldots a_{f_r}$.
- $[dan]$: is the address in α of the deepest node that subsumes the dot on which an adjunction has been partially recognized. If there is no adjunction in the tree α along the path from the root to the dotted node, $[dan]$ is unbound.
- t_l^* is an index in the input string corresponding to the point in the tree where the adjunction on the [deepest adjunction node] was made. If [dan] is unbound, then t_l^* is also unbound.

---

[8] More precise, "left above of a node n with symbol(n) $\in \mathbf{NT}$". In the following, the node and its symbol are sometimes used interchangeably if the meaning is clear.

[9] dan is called "star" in Schabes and Joshi's (1988) chart entries. They called the node with id dan the "starred" node. As the denotation "star" collides with modern notational conventions for TAGs (the star symbolizes the foot node), $star$ is replaced by dan here.

Let G = (Σ, **NT**, **IT**, **AT**, S) be a TAG.
Let $a_0, ..., a_n$ be the input string ($a_0, ..., a_n \in \Sigma$).

begin
    for each $\alpha \in$ **IT** with $symbol(\alpha, 0) = $ S **do**
        add (α, 0, la, 0, -, -, -, -, -, false, 0) to the chart C.
    for (i = 0; i < n; i++) **do**
        Process the states of $C(i)$, performing the operations (1) to (12) from
        Figs. 4.19/ 4.20 until no more items can be added.

        if (C(i+1) is empty and i < n) **then**
            return rejection
    end for
    if there is an item of the form (α, 0, ra, 0, -, -, -, -, -, false, n) in $C(n)$
        with $\alpha \in$ **IT** and root node S
        return acceptance
    else
        return rejection
end

Fig. 4.18 A TAG recognizer (Schabes and Joshi, 1988).

- b_l^* is an index in the input string corresponding to the point in the tree just before the foot node of the tree adjoined at the [deepest adjunction node]. The pair t_l^* and b_l^* will mean that the string as far as the foot node of the auxiliary tree adjoined at the [deepest adjunction node] matches the substring $a_{t_l^*+1} \cdots a_{b_l^*}$ of the input string. If [dan] is unbound, then b_l^* is also unbound." (Schabes and Joshi, 1988, p. 261)
- "*subst?* is a boolean that indicates whether the tree has been predicted for substitution" (Schabes and Joshi, 1988, p. 267)
- The i index denotes the number of terminals recognized up to the dotted node. It is equivalent to the j index in the CFG Earley algorithm. And, also as the CFG Earley algorithm, the TAG recognizer works on a chart C which is an array indexed by i. The sub chart at index i is refered to as $C(i)$.

Figure 4.17 illustrates the interpretation of the indices for an initial and an auxiliary tree. The *subst?* flag is always *false* for auxiliary trees as they cannot be substituted into another tree. It is *false* for chart entries created during initialization, and the rules of the algorithm ensure that it is *true* for all other chart entries with initial trees as these must have been created by a substitution.

The TAG recognizer is listed in Fig. 4.18. The algorithm starts with an initialization loop that creates one chart entry for each initial tree with start symbol S in the root node. The initial chart entries have dot position left above the root node, (0, la), indices l and $i = 0$ (we are expecting input terminal at index 0), and all other indices unbound. After the initialization the algorithm applies the rules (1) to (12) and creates new chart entries until no more rules are applicable. Finally, the algorithm checks if one of the chart

entries contains an initial tree with S as root node and dot position type Ⓥ.
The rules (Figs. 4.19 and 4.20) are the core of the algorithm. They are stated
as inference rules

$$\frac{\text{ChartEntries}}{\text{ChartEntry}_{\text{new}}}, \text{conditions}$$

meaning that if the chart entries above the line are present, and if the *conditions* are true, the algorithm creates the new chart entry specified below the line, and adds it to the chart C. The index i of ChartEntry$_{\text{new}}$ is the index of the sub chart $C(i)$ to which the entry is added.

The following notations are used: $Adj(\alpha, nodeid)$ is the set of auxiliary trees that can be adjoined into node $(\alpha, nodeid)$[10]. $OA(\alpha, nodeid)$ is true if there is an obligatory adjunction constraint on node $(\alpha, nodeid)$. $isFoot(\alpha, nodeid)$ specifies whether $(\alpha, nodeid)$ is a foot node. $Substit(\alpha, nodeid)$ is the set of initial trees that can be substituted into $(\alpha, nodeid)$. Figures 4.19 and 4.20 show each rule with a schematic description. The roman numbers in grey circle refer to the type of dot position according to Fig. 4.17 (left). The new chart entries after the arrow do not have grey circled numbers as most of them have a dot that will automatically jump to an equivalent dot position which is not unique.

---

[10] Where $Adj(\alpha, nodeid) = \emptyset$ if there is a null adjunction constraint on $(\alpha, nodeid)$.

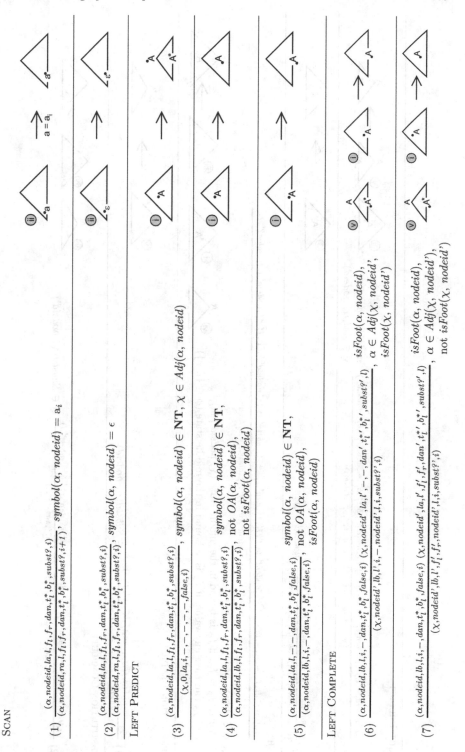

Fig. 4.19 Rules of the TAG recognizer, part 1 (see Schabes and Joshi, 1988).

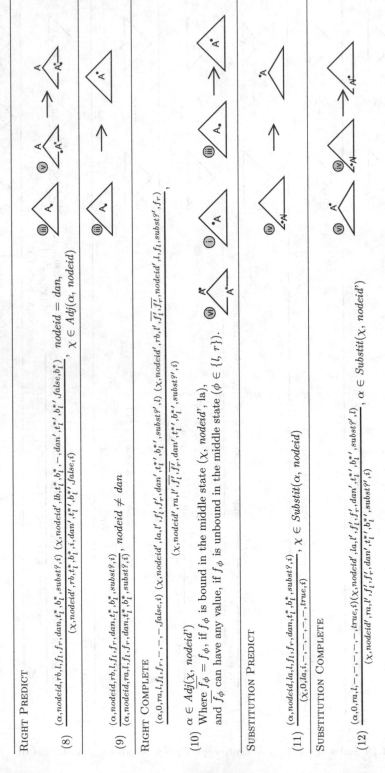

Fig. 4.20 Rules of the TAG recognizer, part 2 (see Schabes and Joshi, 1988).

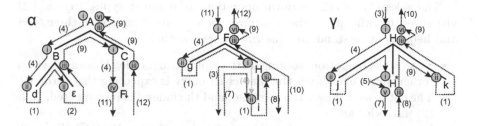

id	input	chart entry	dot pos	created by operation	from
0		$(\alpha,0,la,0,-,-,-,-,false,0)$	ⓘ	init	
1		$(\alpha,1,la,0,-,-,-,-,false,0)$	ⓘ	(4), LEFT PREDICT	0
2		$(\alpha,1.1,la,0,-,-,-,-,false,0)$	ⓘⓘ	(4), LEFT PREDICT	1
3	d	$(\alpha,1.2,la,0,-,-,-,-,false,1)$	ⓘⓘ	(1), SCAN	2
4		$(\alpha,1,rb,0,-,-,-,-,false,1)$	ⓘⓘⓘ	(2), SCAN	3
5		$(\alpha,2,la,0,-,-,-,-,false,1)$	ⓘ	(9), RIGHT PREDICT	4
6		$(\alpha,2.1,la,0,-,-,-,-,false,1)$	ⓘⓥ	(4), LEFT PREDICT	5
7		$(\chi,0,la,1,-,-,-,-,true,1)$	ⓘ	(11), SUBST PREDICT	6
8		$(\chi,1,la,1,-,-,-,-,true,1)$	ⓘⓘ	(4), LEFT PREDICT	7
9	g	$(\chi,2,la,1,-,-,-,-,true,2)$	ⓘ	(1), SCAN	8
10		$(\gamma,0,la,2,-,-,-,-,false,2)$	ⓘ	(3), LEFT PREDICT	9
11		$(\chi,2.1,la,2,-,-,-,-,false,2)$	ⓘⓘ	(4), LEFT PREDICT	9
12		$(\gamma,1,la,2,-,-,-,-,false,2)$	ⓘⓘ	(4), LEFT PREDICT	10
13	j	$(\gamma,2,la,2,-,-,-,-,false,3)$	ⓘ	(1), SCAN	12
14		$(\gamma,2,lb,2,3,-,-,-,false,3)$	ⓥ	(5), LEFT PREDICT	13
15		$(\chi,2.1,la,1,-,-,2,2,3,true,3)$	ⓘⓘ	(7), LEFT COMPLETE	14, 9
16	i	$(\chi,2,rb,1,-,-,2,2,3,true,4)$	ⓘⓘⓘ	(1), SCAN	15
17		$(\gamma,2,rb,2,3,4,-,-,-,false,4)$	ⓘⓘⓘ	(8), RIGHT PREDICT	16, 14
18		$(\gamma,3,la,2,3,4,-,-,-,false,4)$	ⓘⓘ	(9), RIGHT PREDICT	17
19	k	$(\gamma,0,rb,2,3,4,-,-,-,false,5)$	ⓘⓘⓘ	(1), SCAN	18
20		$(\gamma,0,ra,2,3,4,-,-,-,false,5)$	ⓥ	(9), RIGHT PREDICT	19
21		$(\chi,0,rb,1,-,-,-,-,true,5)$	ⓘⓘⓘ	(10), RIGHT COMPLETE	20, 9, 16
22		$(\chi,0,ra,1,-,-,-,-,true,5)$	ⓥ	(9), RIGHT PREDICT	21
23		$(\alpha,2,rb,0,-,-,-,-,false,5)$	ⓘⓘⓘ	(12), SUBST COMPLETE	22, 6
24		$(\alpha,0,rb,0,-,-,-,-,false,5)$	ⓘⓘⓘ	(9), RIGHT PREDICT	23
25		$(\alpha,0,ra,0,-,-,-,-,false,5)$	ⓥ	(9), RIGHT PREDICT	24

Fig. 4.21 An example for the TAG recognizer (see Figs. 4.18, 4.19, and 4.20) running on the example TAG from Fig. 4.11. Bottom: the algorithm creates new chart entries until the final state (id 25) is reached. Top: the trees visualize how rule applications move the dot along the trees. The example only demonstrates non-recursive applications of adjoin (i. e., a null-adjunction constraint is assumed on $(\gamma, 0)$ and $(\gamma, 2)$)

The rules (1) to (12) perform operations of different types. Figure 4.21 visualizes the principle of the recognizer for a small example with three trees and helps to understand how the rules work together:

- SCAN is the operation working on the input string. Rule (1) reads the next terminal and checks whether any chart entry is expecting that terminal. The dot is moved over the terminal, and the index i is incremented. Rule (2) just skips any ϵ.
- LEFT PREDICT creates hypotheses for dot position type ⓘ. Rule (3) hypothesizes that an adjunction might take place on the dotted node. It creates a new chart entry for each auxiliary tree that can be adjoined into that node. In Fig. 4.21 this is visualized with an arrow leaving tree χ and starting with (a new instance of) γ. The indices of the new chart entry indicate that the new chart entry does not subsume any recognized terminals yet, but is expecting the terminal with the same index as the original tree had been expecting last.

  Rule (4) hypothesizes that no adjunction takes place on the dotted node. This is the standard predict operation that moves the dot down inside the tree. If the dot is moved down along the left side of foot node, rule (5) is used instead of rule (4). The indices f_l and f_r must then yet be unbound. Rule (5) sets index f_l to i.

  Rule (3) and one of (4)/(5) can be applicable at the same time. In Fig. 4.21, for instance, the algorithm creates two hypotheses starting from $(\chi, 2, la)$, one with rule (3), and one with rule (4). If there is an obligatory adjunction constraint on the dotted node only (3) is applicable. Also, (3) and (5) would both be applicable in position $(\gamma, 2, la)$. However, the example assumes a null adjunction constraint on node $(\gamma, 2)$.
- After rule (5) we end up in dot position ⓥ. This dot position makes LEFT COMPLETE, rules (6) and (7), applicable. As you can see in Fig. 4.21, the dot at position ⓥ in tree γ has finished the left context of the spine between root and foot node. This is the moment when the algorithm continues with the lower part of the original tree (the terminal i in tree χ in Fig. 4.21). LEFT COMPLETE looks up fitting entries with ⓘ in C(l) and creates an according new chart entry with pushed down dot. Rules (6) and (7) differ in whether the dot in the old chart entry was at the foot node or not, which implies different index values.
- RIGHT PREDICT is applicable for dot position type ⓘⓘⓘ. Rule (8) corresponds to rules (6) and (7): the processing returns to the auxiliary tree, this time on the right side of the foot node, as soon as the middle part of the tree in which we adjoin has been traversed (e. g., as soon as terminal i in Fig. 4.21 has been recognized). Rule (9) is the standard operation pushing the dot upwards without adjunction, thus corresponding to rule (4). This is the point when the value for *dan* is needed: the algorithm uses it to decide whether rule (8) or (9) is applicable.

// The spatial model SM is a partonomy.
*// The behavior intention model BIM is an SCTAG = (tag, SM, **GC**, **NLC**), with tag*
*= (**B**, **I**, **IT**, **AT**, S) (definitions 4.2 and 4.3).*

int n;
statechart[] chart;

procedure initialize(domain model *DM*)
begin
    for each $(\alpha \in \mathbf{IT}$ with $symbol(\alpha,0) = S)$ **do**
        add $(\alpha, 0, la, 0, -, -, -, -, -, \text{false}, 0)$ to the chart C.

    applyRules($C(0)$)

    inputIndex $\leftarrow 0$
end procedure

function recognize(space-time behavior $(t_s, t_e, R_{in}, b_{in})$) **returns** $\mathbf{I}_{\text{hypotheses}}$
begin
    $\mathbf{I}_{\text{hypotheses}} \leftarrow \text{scan}(\text{inputIndex}, b_{in})$
    inputIndex $\leftarrow$ inputIndex $+ 1$
    applyRules(C(inputIndex))
    return $\mathbf{I}_{\text{hypotheses}}$
end function

Fig. 4.22 An incremental SCTAG parser (part 1): methods initialize(), and recognize(), implementing the abstract methods from Fig. 2.14.

- RIGHT COMPLETE, rule (10), is applied as soon as the auxiliary tree has been fully traversed. The adjunction is now finished, and the algorithm continues *ra* of the node in which adjunction has taken place (the H in node $(\chi, 2)$ in the example).
- SUBSTITUTION PREDICT and SUBSTITUTION COMPLETE hypothesize/finish a substitution. Rule (11) creates a chart entry with a new instance of an initial tree, similar to rule (4) for auxiliary trees. The *subst?* flag is set to true. The according complete rule (12) looks up, and "jumps back" to the old entry.

Schabes and Joshi (1988) have proven the correctness of the parser. For further discussions refer to the original paper.

4.3.4.2 Turning the recognizer into an incremental parser.

All rules in the TAG recognizer produce chart entries with an index i greater or equal to the i indices of their input entries. More precisely, the index i of the output is always equal to the index i of the first input, except for the SCAN rule (1). Thus, instead of trying to apply all rules to all entries in each

procedure applyRules(set *chart entries*)
begin
>   *queue* ← *chart entries*
>
>   **while** (*queue* is not empty) **do**
>   *current* ← *queue*.removeFirst()
>   Apply those rules (2) to (13) which are applicable in the dot position type of
>   *current*.
>   If the resulting chart entries are not yet in *C* add them to *queue* and to *C*.
>   **end while**

end procedure

function scan(int *generation*, behavior *b*) **returns** set of intentions
begin
> I_{return} ← ∅
>
>   **for each** (*entry* ∈ *C*(*generation*) with *symbol*(α, *nodeid*) = b) **do**
>   Apply rule (1) to *entry* and add the result to *C*.
>   Add symbol(*entry*.tree, parent(*entry*.nodeid)) to I_{return}.
>   **end for**
>   **return** I_{return}

end function

Fig. 4.23 An incremental SCTAG parser (part 2): methods scan(), and applyRules().
Rules (1) to (13) are given in Fig. 4.24 for SCTAG, and (1) to (12) for normal TAG
parsing in Figs. 4.19 and 4.20.

step, chart entries can be partitioned into generations with increasing i. This
leads to a search strategy equivalent to that of the SGIS parser:

a. Apply rules (2) to (12) on generation 0 until no more entries can be
   added. $i = 0$. The algorithm is now ready for the first terminal.
b. Apply rule (1) on all entries in generation i with dot position ⓘ and
   correct behavior as terminal.
c. Apply rules (2) to (12) on generation $i+1$, goto b.

The incremental SCTAG parser in Figs. 4.22 and 4.23 uses this search
strategy. It is specified similar to the SGIS and the SCCFG parser, separated
into initialize() and recognize(). Again, scan() recognizes the intentions, and
the other operations could be performed in the background while the user
continues to use the application. The algorithm can also be used for a normal
TAG by applying the rules from Figs. 4.19 and 4.20. The rules for SCTAG
are described in the following, and illustrated in Fig. 4.24.

4.3.4.3 An incremental parser for SCTAG

The incremental TAG parser is now modified to a spatial version for SCTAGs
with a partonomy as spatial model. The approach is analog to that of the

SGIS and SCCFG parsers (sections 4.1.1 and 4.2.2). Spatial constraints are again attached to the chart entries:

$entry = (\alpha,\ nodeid,\ pos,\ l,\ f_l,\ f_r,\ dan,\ t_l^*,\ b_l^*,\ subst?,\ i,\ \mathbf{GCI},\ \mathbf{NLI},\ res?)$,

differing from the TAG parser by the following items:

- $res? \in \{true, false\}$ indicates for dot position la whether the spatial constraints of the dotted node have been resolved. Moving a dot to a new node with dot position la automatically sets the flag to $false$. Spatial constraints are then resolved and the flag is set to $true$. The flag $res?$ is always $true$ for dot positions $\{lb, rb, ra\}$. Operations (1) to (12) can only be applied if $res? = true$. Operation (13) changes the flag from $false$ to $true$. In other words, the flag $res?$ splits dot position la into two states: (la, unresolved), (la, resolved). The three dot position types ⓘ, ⓘⓘ, and ⓘⓥ from Fig. 4.17 (left) are now extended with according unresolved dot position types: ⓘ̲, ⓘ̲ⓘ̲, and ⓘ̲ⓥ̲.

- $\mathbf{GCI} \subseteq \mathbf{GC}$ is the instantiation of a grounding constraint, just as in the SGIS- and SCCFG-parser. It relates to the dotted node for $res? = true$ and $dotpos \neq ra$, and to the parent node for $res? = false$ or $dotpos = ra$. It lists the regions in which the behaviors subsumed by the node may happen. Each element in $\mathbf{GCI}$ must be a region from the grounding constraints $\mathbf{GC}$ modeled in the SCTAG for the node[11].

- $\mathbf{NLI}$ is a set of non-local constraint instantiations, just as in the SCCFG-parser. Each non-local constraint $nlc \in \mathbf{NLC}$ of the tree α has one $nli \in \mathbf{NLI}$, denoted as $\mathbf{NLI}(nlc)$. Again, non-local constraint instantiations are initialized with $n/spec$ for "not specified". It gets specified as soon as we know in which region $node_1$ (i.e., the left node) of the according nlc happened. This occurs when the dot is moved to ra. If all leaf nodes subsumed by the dotted node are ϵ, the nli remains $n/spec$.

Figures 4.24, 4.25 and 4.26 define the rules of the SCTAG parser by extending the TAG parser operations, and introducing a new operation, (13). The rules are modified as follows:

- LEFT PREDICT: the "standard" LEFT PREDICT operations, (4) and (5), which move the dot down in one elementary tree do not change the spatial constraints. For operation (4) the successor chart entry will be in dot position la, switching res to $false$, and leading to constraint resolution with rule (13). If the dotted node is a foot node (operation 5) the $res?$ flag remains true as the dot is then in position lb (the two cases are not distinguished in Fig. 4.24 as flag $res?$ is assumed to adapt automatically during the dot jump).
  Operation (3) creates a new auxiliary tree with all elements of $\mathbf{NLI}$ initialized with $n/spec$. The $\mathbf{GCI}$ of the parent tree is inherited, and

---

[11] As notational convenience, the modeler will only specify grounding constraints for some nodes which are inherited by those child nodes without an own spatial grounding. If the root node has no grounding constraint it is grounded in R_Ω.

resolved with the grounding of node $(\chi, 0)$ in the next step (operation 13).

- PREDICT RESOLVE (13): this new operation resolves the spatial constraints for dot position la and $res? = false$ (function $predictResolve()$). It is the only way to move the dot from "- dot position types" to the according dot position type without "-". Resolving the constraints during predict means: select those regions from the grounding constraints modeled in the grammar for the dotted node ($\mathbf{GC}(\alpha, nodeid)$) which are consistent with the grounding constraint instantiation of the parent ($\mathbf{GCI_p}$), and the non-local constraint instantiation ($\mathbf{NLI}$). This is the same spatial constraint resolution as in SCCFG (section 4.2.2).

- SUBSTITUTION PREDICT, (11): from the perspective of spatial constraints, hypothesizing a substitution works exactly as hypothesizing an adjunction (see rule (3)).

- LEFT COMPLETE, (6) and (7): the left spine of the auxiliary tree α is finished, and we "jump" to the cut-off part of the original tree χ. In the resulting tree of an actually performed adjunction this cut-off part is headed by the foot node, so $\mathbf{GCI_\alpha}$ is relevant. The grounding constraints of the node in tree χ in which we adjoin have previously been considered in operation (3) and are automatically obeyed by $\mathbf{GCI_\alpha}$. As we "jump back" to tree χ we now need the non-local constraint instantiations $\mathbf{NLI_\chi}$. The flag $res?$ is set depending on the dot position of the next node in χ.

- RIGHT PREDICT: if the "standard" RIGHT PREDICT operation (9) is applicable all spatialized behaviors subsumed by the node have been recognized, and these are consistent with the grounding constraint instantiation determined when starting with the dotted node in dot position type ⓘ. All behaviors happened in exactly one region R_i. Moving the dot from rb to ra means to resolve this region with the grounding constraint instantiation $\mathbf{GCI'}$ of the parent node, just as complete() in the SGIS parser. This information on the parent is contained in the related chart entry with dot position type ⊙. Thus, operation (9) in the SCTAG parser looks up the according entry which differs to the original TAG parser in which rule (9) takes only one chart entry as input. The according entry has the same dotted node, and the same l index. In a partonomy there must be exactly one region $R_p \in \mathbf{GCI'}$ which contains or is equal to R_i (function $completeResolve()$ selects that region).

In the special case that all terminal nodes subsumed by the dotted node are ϵ we cannot resolve the grounding constraint. In that case, nothing really "happened" below the dotted node so that we cannot select one single region but forward the original $\mathbf{GCI'}$. To identify this special case, the function $completeResolve()$ needs the number of behaviors scanned below the dotted node as input (which is computed using indices i and i').

Besides resolving the grounding constraints, completing a node means that the non-local constraints having the dotted node as left node can be specified. Function *instantiateNLI()* sets the *nli* for each of these non-local constraints to the region in which the dotted node "happened", just as complete() in the SCCFG parser. If the special ϵ case occurs the *nli* remain *n/spec*.

In operation (8), the cut-off part of an adjunction is finished, and we now continue with the right spine of the auxiliary tree (*rb* of the foot node). As in any "tree jump" the new chart entry gets the **NLI** of the old chart entry (**NLI**$_\chi$). As **GCI** must always contain regions from the grounding constraint of the dotted node, a *completeResolve()* becomes necessary.

- SCAN: the spatialized behavior (b, R_i) is scanned. **GCI** of the old entry contains the regions in which b may happen. As in the other parsers, the region R_i of the incoming behavior can either be disjunct with all regions $\in$ **GCI**, or contained by/equal to exactly one region $R_{gci} \in$ **GCI**. The function *scanResolve()* determines R_{gci}, or returns **null** if there is none (in which case operation (1) immediately stops).

  Although this dot position does not exist we can now imagine the dot to be *rb* of the terminal node. Moving the dot to *ra* means that the region R_{gci} of the terminal must be resolved with **GCI**$_{parent}$ of the parent node (which is a complete): we get this **GCI**$_{parent}$ from the chart entry with dot position type ⓘⓘ₋ that belongs to the current chart entry ⓘⓘ (there is a 1:1 relationship between them). That is why (1) in the SCTAG takes two entries as input. We then apply function *completeResolve()* as described above. As a terminal node may also be the left node of a non-local constraint *instantiateNLI()* is also called. The scan() operation is different to scan() in SGIS and SCCFG as a behavior leaf node in an SCTAG may have its own **GC** and be part of a non-local constraint.

  A node with ϵ (rule (2)) is not connected with any spatial information. **GCI** and **NLI** remain unchanged. As an ϵ node never has any grounding constraints in an SCTAG, **GCI** of ⓘⓘ₋ and ⓘⓘ are the same, and no *completeResolve()* is necessary. The *res?* flag is set depending on the dot position of the next node.

- SUBSTITUTION COMPLETE (12): completing a substitution moves the dot at the substitution node to dot position *ra* which means constraints must be resolved with respect to the parent node: **GCI**$_{new}$ is computed from the **GCI** resulting from the substitution tree, and **GCI'** of the parent node which we get from the chart entry with dot position type ⓥ. As the substitution node may be the left side of an *nlc*, we also call *instantiateNLI()*.

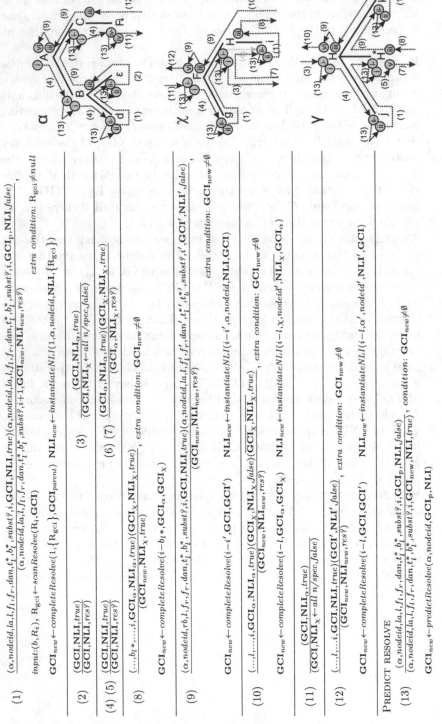

Fig. 4.24 Operations of the SCTAG parser. Unmodified chart entries are listed in short notation (**GCI**, **NLI**, *res?*), enhancing operations from Figs. 4.19/4.20.

function   scanResolve(region R,
                           set of regions GCI)   **returns** a region
begin
    for each (R' $\in$ **GCI**) **do**
        if (*contains*(R', R) $\vee$ *equals*(R, R')) **then**
            return R'
    end for
    return null
end function

function   predictResolve(elementary tree α,
                           node id *node*,
                           set of regions GCI_p,
                           non-local constraint instantiation NLI)   **returns** a set
of regions
begin
    // Resolve grounding constraints from parent (as in the SGIS parser).
    $\mathbf{GCI_c} \leftarrow$ All R $\in$ **GC** of (α, *node*) which are equal to or contained by
        a region in $\mathbf{GCI_p}$

    // Resolve non-local constraints.
    for each (nlc $\in$ **NLC** with nlc = (α, $node_1$, node, *type*)) **do**
        // All nlc ending at node.
        nli $\leftarrow$ **NLI**(nlc)
        if (nli $\neq$ *n/spec*) **then**
            $\mathbf{T} \leftarrow \{R_r \in \mathbf{R} | type(nli, R_r)\}$
            $\mathbf{GCI_c} \leftarrow \mathbf{GCI_c} \cap \mathbf{T}$
            if ($\mathbf{GCI_c} = \emptyset$) **then**
                return $\mathbf{GCI_c}$
        end if
    end for

    return $\mathbf{GCI_c}$
end function

Fig. 4.25 Resolving spatial constraints in the SCTAG parser (scan and predict).

function completeResolve(int *behaviorSpan*,
                          set of regions GCI_{child},
                          set of regions GCI_{parent})   **returns**   a set of regions

begin
     if   (*behaviorSpan* $==0$)   **then**
         // *All terminals subsumed by the dotted node are* ϵ.
         return $\mathbf{GCI}_{parent}$
     end if

     // *At least one terminal subsumed by the dotted node was* $\neq \epsilon$:
     // GCI_{child} *has 1 element.*
     $R_c \leftarrow firstElement(\mathbf{GCI}_{child})$
     for each   ($R_p \in \mathbf{GCI}_{parent}$)   **do**
         if   (*contains*(R_p, R_c) $\vee$ *equals*(R_p, R_c))   **then**
             return $\{R_p\}$
     end for

     return $\emptyset$
end function

function instantiateNLI(int *behaviorSpan*,
                       elementary tree α
                       node id *node*,
                       non-local constraint instantiation $\mathbf{NLI}_{in}$,
                       region set $\mathbf{GCI}$)   **returns**   an NLI

begin
     $\mathbf{NLI}_{out} \leftarrow \mathbf{NLI}_{in}$

     // *Change nli only if at least one behavior was* $\neq \epsilon$.
     // *In that case, GCI.size() must be 1.*
     // *Otherwise, nli remains n/spec.*
     if   (*behaviorSpan* $\neq 0$)   **then**
         for each   (nlc $\in \mathbf{NLC}$ with tree α and left node *node*)   **do**
             $\mathbf{NLI}_{out}(nlc) \leftarrow$ firstElement($\mathbf{GCI}$)
         end for
     end if

     return $\mathbf{NLI}_{out}$
end function

Fig. 4.26 Resolving spatial constraints in the SCTAG parser (complete and instantiateNLI).

- RIGHT COMPLETE (10): finishing an adjunction works, from the perspective of spatial constraint resolution, similar to that of rule (12) for substitution. For the grounding constraint resolution the $\mathbf{GCI}_\chi$ of the second entry is relevant (dot position type Ⓘ-), as this refers to the parent node which is relevant for dot position *ra* in χ to which rule (10) moves the

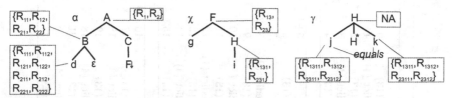

Fig. 4.27 An SCTAG parsing example (grammar).

dot. For the non-local constraint resolution, the $\overline{\text{NLI}}_\chi$ of the third entry (dot position type ⓘⓘⓘ) is relevant as this is the last position in which the algorithm left χ in rule (8). Everything that happened below the dotted node is already incorporated in $\overline{\text{NLI}}_\chi$.

4.3.4.4 Example

An example for an SCTAG parse is shown in Figures 4.27, 4.28 and 4.29: the abstract grammar that guided us throughout the SCTAG section is now annotated with regions from $\{R_1, ..., R_{2312}\}$. A partonomic structure is assumed in a way that R_1 is parent of R_{1k}, and so on. R_1 and R_2 are, of course, children of R_Ω. The "NA" denotes a null-adjunction constraint on $(\gamma, 0)$.

4.3.4.5 Conclusions on the runtime of the SCTAG parser

The worst case runtime complexity of the original TAG parser is $O(n^9)$ (Schabes and Joshi, 1988). Although the chart entries and the parser operations are more complex than for SGISs and SCCFGs the spatial constraint resolution does not differ from that in SCCFGs, i. e., they add to the runtime as constant factors that depend on the structure of the partonomy. Thus, following the same line of argumentation as for the SGIS and SCCFG parser, the worst case complexity is also $O(n^9)$, and, in an average case, the SCTAG parser will be faster than the TAG parser as it considers less hypotheses. As said at the beginning of this section, TAG parsers with lower complexity exist, and the main argument of this section was rather the spatial constraint resolution than an optimal runtime complexity.

#	TAG parser entry		GCI, NLI			res?	action	num
0	α , 0, la	0, -, -, -, --	f	0	{RΩ},	f	init	
1	α , 0, la	0, -, -, -, --	f	0	{R1, R2},	t	Resolve (13)	0
2	α , 1, la	0, -, -, -, --	f	0	{R1, R2},	f	LeftPredict (4)	1
3	α , 1, la	0, -, -, -, --	f	0	{R21, R11, R12, R22},	t	Resolve (13)	2
4	α , 1.1, la	0, -, -, -, --	f	0	{R21, R11, R12, R22},	f	LeftPredict (4)	3
5	α , 1.1, la	0, -, -, -, --	f	0	{R221, R111, R211, R112, R212, R222, R122, R121},	t	Resolve (13)	4
Input: (d, R221)								
6	α , 1.2, la	0, -, -, -, --	f	1	{R22},	f	Scan (1)	5+4
7	α , 1.2, la	0, -, -, -, --	f	1	{R22},	t	Resolve (13)	6
8	α , 1, rb	0, -, -, -, --	f	1	{R22},	f	Scan (2)	7
9	α , 2, la	0, -, -, -, --	f	1	{R2},	f	RightPredict (9)	8+2
10	α , 2, la	0, -, -, -, --	f	1	{R2},	t	Resolve (13)	9
11	α , 2.1, la	0, -, -, -, --	f	1	{R2},	f	LeftPredict (4)	10
12	α , 2.1, la	0, -, -, -, --	f	1	{R2},	t	Resolve (13)	11
13	χ , 0, la	1, -, -, -, --	t	1	{R2},	f	SubstPredict (11)	12
14	χ , 0, la	1, -, -, -, --	t	1	{R23},	t	Resolve (13)	13
15	χ , 1, la	1, -, -, -, --	t	1	{R23},	f	LeftPredict (4)	14
16	χ , 1, la	1, -, -, -, --	t	1	{R23},	t	Resolve (13)	15
Input: (g, R2312)								
17	χ , 2, la	1, -, -, -, --	t	2	{R23},	f	Scan (1)	16+15
18	χ , 2, la	1, -, -, -, --	t	2	{R231},	t	Resolve (13)	17
19	γ , 0, la	2, -, -, -, --	f	2	{R231}, *n/spec*	f	LeftPredict (3)	18
20	γ , 0, la	2, -, -, -, --	f	2	{R231}, *n/spec*	t	Resolve (13)	19
21	χ , 2.1, la	1, -, -, -, --	t	2	{R231},	f	LeftPredict (4)	18
22	χ , 2.1, la	1, -, -, -, --	t	2	{R231},	t	Resolve (13)	21
23	γ , 1, la	2, -, -, -, --	f	2	{R231}, *n/spec*	f	LeftPredict (4)	20
24	γ , 1, la	2, -, -, -, --	f	2	{R2311, R2312}, *n/spec*	t	Resolve (13)	23

Fig. 4.28 An SCTAG parsing example (chart part 1).

	TAG parser entry			GCI, NLI	res?		
Input: (j, R_{2311})							
25	γ, 2, la	2, -, -, -	f 3	{R_{231}}, R_{2311}	f	Scan (1)	24+23
26	γ, 2, la	2, -, -, -	f 3	{R_{231}}, R_{2311}	t	Resolve (13)	25
27	γ, 0, la	3, -, -, -	f 3	{R_{231}}, *n/spec*	f	LeftPredict (3)	26
28	γ, 0, la	3, -, -, -	f 3	{R_{231}}, *n/spec*	t	Resolve (13)	27
29	γ, 2, lb	2, 3, -, -	f 3	{R_{231}}, R_{2311}	t	LeftPredict (5)	26
30	γ, 1, la	3, -, -, -	f 3	{R_{231}}, *n/spec*	f	LeftPredict (4)	28
31	γ, 1, la	3, -, -, -	f 3	{R_{231}}, R_{2312}}, *n/spec*	t	Resolve (13)	30
32	χ, 2.1, la	1, -, 2, 23	t 3	{R_{231}},	f	LeftComplete (7)	29+18
33	χ, 2.1, la	1, -, 2, 23	t 3	{R_{231}},	t	Resolve (13)	32
Input: (i, R_{231})							
34	χ, 2, rb	1, -, 2, 23	t 4	{R_{231}},	t	Scan (1)	33+32
35	γ, 2, rb	2, 3, 4, -	f 4	{R_{231}}, R_{2311}	t	RightPredict (8)	34+29
36	γ, 3, la	2, 3, 4, -	f 4	{R_{231}}, R_{2311}	f	RightPredict (9)	35+25
37	γ, 3, la	2, 3, 4, -	f 4	{R_{231}}, R_{2311}	t	Resolve (13)	36
Input: (k, R_{2311})							
38	γ, 0, rb	2, 3, 4, -, -	f 5	{R_{231}}, R_{2311}	t	Scan (1)	37+36
39	γ, 0, ra	2, 3, 4, -, -	f 5	{R_{231}}, R_{2311}	t	RightPredict (9)	38+19
40	χ, 0, rb	1, -, -, -, -	t 5	{R_{23}},	t	RightComplete (10)	39+17+34
41	χ, 0, ra	1, -, -, -, -	t 5	{R_2},	t	RightPredict (9)	40+13
42	α, 2, rb	0, -, -, -, -	f 5	{R_2},	t	SubstComplete (12)	41+11
43	α, 0, rb	0, -, -, -, -	f 5	{R_2},	t	RightPredict (9)	42+9
44	α, 0, ra	0, -, -, -, -	f 5	{R_Ω},	t	RightPredict (9)	43+0

Fig. 4.29 An SCTAG parsing example (chart part 2).

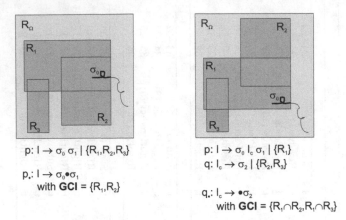

$$p: I \rightarrow \sigma_0\, \sigma_1 \mid \{R_1, R_2, R_3\}$$

$$p_*: I \rightarrow \sigma_0 \bullet \sigma_1$$
$$\text{with } \mathbf{GCI} = \{R_1, R_2\}$$

$$p: I \rightarrow \sigma_0\, I_c\, \sigma_1 \mid \{R_1\}$$
$$q: I_c \rightarrow \sigma_2 \mid \{R_2, R_3\}$$

$$q_*: I_c \rightarrow \bullet \sigma_2$$
$$\text{with } \mathbf{GCI} = \{R_1 \cap R_2, R_1 \cap R_3\}$$

Fig. 4.30 Parsing with overlapping regions: the invariants $((\sigma_0$ is not empty$) \Rightarrow (|\mathbf{GCI}|$ == 1)) (left) and $(\mathbf{GCI} \subseteq \mathbf{GC})$ (right) do not hold any more.

4.4 Beyond Partonomies

SGISs, SCCFGs, and SCTAGs assume a partonomy as spatial model as most mobile intention recognition environments are structured that way. However, there may be rare cases in which this is not true. This section provides an idea of how the parsing algorithms would change if spatial models with overlapping regions would be allowed for. It complements the discussion about the bottom-up worst case complexity of grouping behavior sequences in section 2.3.3 by providing the top-down perspective of a parsing algorithm.

The fundamental difference for spatial models with overlapping regions is that the following invariant introduced in section 4.1.2 does not hold any more (chart entries $(I \rightarrow \sigma_0 \bullet \sigma_1 \mid \mathbf{GC}, [i, j], \mathbf{GCI})$):

$$(\mathbf{GCI} \subseteq \mathbf{GC}) \quad \text{and} \quad ((\sigma_0 \text{ is not empty}) \Rightarrow (|\mathbf{GCI}| == 1))$$

The second part of the invariant, "as soon as the first symbol is parsed, the rest of the string is constrained to only one region", does not necessarily hold because the parsed symbol, or string of symbols (σ_0), may have happened in several regions from $\mathbf{GC}$. Thus, all these regions must stay in the set $\mathbf{GCI}$. For instance, consider the abstract example in Fig. 4.30 (left). The agent has shown behavior σ_0 in the overlapping regions R_1 and R_2. As it is yet open in which of the two regions the rest of the sequence (σ_1) is going to happen both need to stay in $\mathbf{GCI}$, and only R_3 can be excluded.

The first part of the invariant, "a grounding constraint instantiation is always a subset of the grounding constraint", does not necessarily hold because the grounding constraints of the child rule may overlap with the grounding constraints of the parent rule so that an intersection becomes necessary. Again, an abstract example clarifies the principle (Fig. 4.30, right): the agent has entered R_1 and is hypothesized to have intention I_c next which may happen in regions R_2 and R_3, both overlapping with R_1. We cannot just assign R_2 and R_3 to **GCI** of the child rule because the agent is not supposed to leave R_1 (as everything is headed by intention I which is grounded in R_1). Thus, an intersection $R_1 \cap R_2$ ($R_1 \cap R_3$ respectively) becomes necessary. Through further predicts, this intersection may grow so that, in general, an element of **GCI** will be a set of intersected regions $R_1 \cap \ldots \cap R_m$. The number of elements m may, in the worst case when all regions overlap, grow to $|\mathbf{R}|$ - 1.

The missing invariant for spatial models with overlap affects the operations of the SGIS parser (Fig. 4.2). The first effect is that none of the three operations, scan(), predict(), complete(), can ever assume that **GCI** is one-elementary for non-empty σ_0. While in the partonomy algorithm parsing a chart entry with non-empty σ_0 is always more efficient than with empty σ_0, which improves the average complexity, this is not true for spatial models with overlapping regions.

The second effect is caused by the necessity for intersections during predict(). Intersecting the geometries of the polygons (possibly with multi-rings and a huge amount of points) on-the-fly is not very efficient, especially because most of the predicted chart entries will be thrown away as they were only hypothetical. Another option is to not compute the intersection, but to keep each intersection $R_1 \cap \ldots \cap R_m$ as set $\{R_1, \ldots, R_m\}$ in the **GCI**, and to evaluate them in scan() with the input region set $\mathbf{R}_{in}$. However, this would keep many empty intersections, thus unnecessarily blowing up the **GCI** sets. Thus, we should check each newly intersected region R_{m+1} with each region in $\{R_1, \ldots, R_m\}$ for *overlap* in the spatial model to avoid empty intersections. The spatial constraint resolution in all methods would then need three nested loops in the worst case. Another possibility, which requires more complex data structures, is to pre-compute all intersections before runtime and create a tessellation with an according partially ordered set (regions with *contains* relation). Spatial constraint resolution is then mapped to operations for finding the supremum/infimum of regions in this partially ordered set.

4.5 Summary

This chapter has offered four new contributions to mobile intention recognition with formal grammars: first, general issues on using parsing for mobile intention recognition were discussed, in particular the requirement to maintain the VPP, and the separation of hypotheses creation (predict() and complete()) from the input processing (scan()), which relaxes the runtime requirements for mobile intention recognition as the former can be computed in the background while the agent is moving.

Second, the principles of integrating spatial constraints into chart parsers have been provided. As parsing is performed sequentially, spatial constraint resolution for spatial parsers is not a problem of general constraint satisfaction, but one of constraint propagation. As constraint propagation adds to the runtime as constant factors depending on the structure of the BIM the worst-case runtime complexity of the original parsers is not changed, whereas the average runtime is decreased by hypotheses reduction through spatial constraints. Parsers that work on spatial models of type partonomy can exploit the structure of space which makes them more efficient than parsers working on spatial models with overlap.

Third, SCCFG, a new formalism with non-local spatial constraints has been proposed. This formalism allows to express the long-ranging space-intention dependencies of the form $\langle doX_1, doSomethingCompletelyDifferent, doX_2 \rangle$ (with doX_1 and doX_2 belonging to the same intention) that occur in many mobile intention recognition scenarios. The SCCFG formalism exploits that doX_2 can be identified as belonging to doX_1 by the spatial information connected with the behavior sequences. The long-ranging space-intention dependencies in an SCCFG can be nested arbitrarily into each other. The parser for SCCFGs performs long-distance constraint propagation.

Fourth, SCTAG, a spatially-constrained MCSG based on TAGs has been introduced. The mild context-sensitivity adds new expressiveness by allowing long-ranging space-intention dependencies to intersect. These intersections are not possible in an unrestricted way but with respect to the expressiveness of the TAG formalism. An argument, based on the "Visit-Revisit" pattern, has been made that frequently occurring patterns in mobile intention recognition are not severely affected by these limitations.

Chapter 5
Evaluation and Discussion

Long-ranging space-intention dependencies arise as a frequent problem in mobile intention recognition (see section 2.3.4). Approaches to mobile intention recognition which are not capable to formally represent these dependencies will suffer from ambiguity or inexplicability. Chapter 4 has introduced two new representational formalisms, SCCFGs and SCTAGs, and claimed that these are able to represent long-ranging space-intention dependencies typically occurring in mobile intention recognition. This chapter evaluates the formal expressiveness and disambiguation capabilities of SCCFGs and SC-TAGs by parsing exemplary behavior sequences.

As a further contribution, section 5.4 presents the INTENSIVE software tool which can be used to evaluate the different steps of mobile intention recognition as introduced in section 2.1.2.

5.1 The Clothes Shop Example

The clothes shop example was used throughout the thesis to demonstrate how pairs of behaviors (picks and drops) that belong together may embrace a long behavior sequence (see also sections 2.3.4, 4.2.1, and 4.3.2). The clothes shop example is interesting as crossings between picks and drops occur very frequently.

This section evaluates a more sophisticated version of the pick/drop example than used previously (see Fig. 4.13): one that does not hide all details, and that specifies a complete BIM from top-level intention to behaviors. Figure 5.1 lists intentions, behaviors, and gives a decision tree that can be used to classify spatio-temporal behaviors from the speed and curvature of a trajectory. To keep the example simple only a small number of behaviors is used: standing, sauntering, walking, and searching. It is assumed that there exists an indoor positioning technology that is able to deliver data of sufficient quality to distinguish these behaviors. Additionally, the picking and dropping of

Intentions		Behaviors	
B	BuyPullovers	*Spatio-temporal (from trajectory)*	
SS	SearchShelf	se	searching
GP	GetPullover	wa	walking
C	ContinueShopping	sa	sauntering
SE	SearchExit	st	standing
DP	DropPullover		
Try	TryClothes	*Activity (from RFID sensors)*	
SFR	SearchFittingRooms	pick	pick item from shelf
GFR	GetFittingRoom	drop	drop item to shelf
DU	DressUndress		
LFR	LeaveFittingRoom		
Q	Queue		
EFR	EnterFittingRoom		

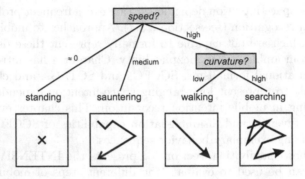

Fig. 5.1 Intentions and behaviors in the clothes shop example.

articles at the shelves is measured as an activity, e. g., with RFID technology. For notational convenience behaviors are not notated as b with suffix, but as tokens starting with lowercase letter (as terminals in formal grammars), and the same applies to intentions accordingly (in uppercase). The example assumes a pullover shop although it does not matter what kind of clothing items is sold.

The spatial model of the clothes shop (see Fig. 5.2) is an extended version of the one presented in chapter 2 (Fig. 2.19): the fitting room area R_{fra} now contains three fitting rooms $R_{fr1}, \ldots, R_{fr3}$. The number of shelves (nine) and fitting rooms (three) could be chosen arbitrarily. In the following, four BIMs for a customer in this shop are presented: IS, SGIS, SCCCFG, and SCTAG.

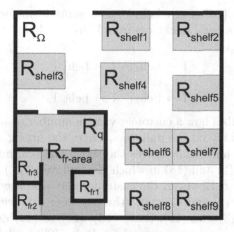

Fig. 5.2 Spatial model of the clothes shop example.

Production Rules with Spatial Grounding		
B → SS GP C SE	$\{R_\Omega\}$	(1)
B → SS GP C SS DP SE	$\{R_\Omega\}$	(2)
B → SS IS C SE	$\{R_\Omega\}$	(3)
SS → {se, wa, sa}$^+$	$\{R_\Omega\}$	(4) ... (9)
GP → IS pick	R_{sh}	(10)
DP → IS drop	R_{sh}	(11)
IS → {sa, st}$^+$	R_{sh}	(12) ... (15)
C → Try	$\{R_\Omega\}$	(16)
C → SS GP C	$\{R_\Omega\}$	(17)
C → SS GP C SS DP	$\{R_\Omega\}$	(18)
C → SS IS C	$\{R_\Omega\}$	(19)
SE → {se, wa}$^+$	$\{R_\Omega\}$	(20) ... (23)
Try → SFR GFR DU LFR	$\{R_\Omega\}$	(24)
SFR → {se, wa}$^+$	$\{R_\Omega\}$	(25) ... (28)
GFR → Q EFR	$\{R_{fr-area}\}$	(29)
GFR → EFR	$\{R_{fr-area}\}$	(30)
Q → {st, sa}$^+$	$\{R_q\}$	(31) ... (34)
EFR → {wa}$^+$	$\{R_{fr-area}\}$	(35), (36)
LFR → {wa}$^+$	$\{R_{fr-area}\}$	(37), (38)
DU → {st}$^+$	R_{fr}	(39), (40)
$R_{sh} = \{R_{shelf1} \ldots R_{shelf9}\}$		
$R_{fr} = \{R_{fr2} \ldots R_{fr3}\}$		

Fig. 5.3 An SGIS for the clothes shop example (top-level intention: B).

5.2 Formalizing the Example with Spatial Grammars

5.2.1 IS and SGIS

Figure 5.3 lists the SGIS rules for the clothes shop example. The according IS is, of course, the same set of rules without the spatial grounding column.

The notation $I \rightarrow \{beh_1, \ldots, beh_k\}^+$ is a short form for "intention I is a sequence of one or several behaviors from $beh_1, \ldots, beh_k$" which yields in $2 \cdot k$ rules:

$$I \rightarrow beh_1, \quad I \rightarrow beh_1\ I$$
$$\ldots$$
$$I \rightarrow beh_k, \quad I \rightarrow beh_k\ I$$

The SGIS describes how a customer visits a number of shelves, then enters the fitting room to try on the pullovers, leaves the fitting room again, drops some of the items, and finally leaves the shop. The pairing of pick and drop is realized in rules (2) and (18) in which GetPullover (GP) and DropPullover (DP) occur together. However, the customer may also keep items (GP without DP), see rules (1) and (17), and the customer may visit a shelf without picking, see rules (3) and (19). Rules (16), (24) to (40) describe the trying on, and all intentions connected with it. Rules (29) and (30), for instance, distinguish whether the customer has to wait in queue or not. The terminalization, i.e., the assignment of behaviors to intentions at the bottom, is chosen closely to the behavior of a typical shopper. For instance, searching a shelf may include *searching*, *walking*, and *sauntering*, whereas *sauntering* will not occur in SearchExit (SE) as searching the exit is more goal directed than checking out clothes. In a realistic scenario, these terminalizations would need to be revised using empirical data. It is also assumed that the customer always buys at least one article, and that the customer will not enter the fitting rooms twice.

5.2.2 SCCFG

The SCCFG is created by modifying rules (2) and (18), see Fig. 5.4: a long-ranging dependency enforces that GP and DP must happen in the same shelf region.

5.2.3 SCTAG

The step from SCCFG to SCTAG (see Fig. 5.5) is not as simple as from SGIS to SCCFG: the grammar has α as only initial tree with start symbol. An obligatory adjunction on C ensures that the customer visits at least one shelf before Try. The auxiliary trees γ_1, γ_2, and γ_2' are variants of the trees γ, δ, and χ in Fig. 4.13. By adjoining these three tress, the overlap of picks and drops is created. An additional auxiliary tree (γ_3) represents Inspect-Shelf without pick. Although not necessary, the rules for GP and DP are directly substituted into the trees. The terminalization rules are converted into according terminalization initial trees ($\phi_{1...6}$, $\varphi_{1...4}$, $\eta_{1...4}$, $\kappa_{1...4}$, $\theta_{1...4}$, $\psi_{1...2}$, $\zeta_{1...2}$, $\varpi_{1...2}$), with an according short notation using ϵ. The grounding of nodes is annotated as sets of regions in boxes.

5.3 Results and Discussion

The expressiveness of the four BIMs (IS, SGIS, SCCFG, SCTAG) is evaluated by processing two spatio-temporal behavior sequences ($\beta_{st,1}$, $\beta_{st,2}$) with the parsers from chapter 4 (the original Earley algorithm is used for ISs, Earley, 1970). The beginning of both sequences is identical: $\beta_{st,1}[0;28]$ = $\beta_{st,2}[0;28]$ (see Fig. 5.6), the ending of the sequences differs; refer to Fig. 5.7 for $\beta_{st,1}[29;49]$, and Fig. 5.8 for $\beta_{st,2}[29;47]$. The figures list the intention hypotheses sets $\mathbf{I}_{i,\text{BIM}}$ for each BIM. These are the intentions the algorithm considers as hypotheses at time i.

5.3.1 Ambiguity Reduction with SGISs

The first part of the sequence (Fig. 5.6) is equivalent to picks in R_{shelf5}, R_{shelf8}, and R_{shelf3}, and a succeeding try on. This part of the sequence is well-suited to demonstrate the disambiguation capabilities of SGIS. Positions in the behavior sequence in which parsing with SGIS ($\mathbf{I}_{i,\text{SGIS}}$) is less ambiguous than with IS ($\mathbf{I}_{i,\text{IS}}$) are highlighted. SGIS, SCCFG, and SCTAG do not differ in this part of the sequence. In detail:

- 0...2: the customer crosses R_{shelf1}. From the type of behavior (searching) the algorithm infers that the customer is not interested in R_{shelf1}, but still has the intention SearchShelf (SS). Thus, in this case, the type of behavior solves the room-crossing problem.
- 3...5: the customer picks an item in R_{shelf5}.
- 6...10: the customer enters R_{shelf7} slowly (sauntering). As it is yet unclear whether the customer is really interested in that shelf, or whether this is just a slow variant of SS, the SGIS parser keeps two hypotheses (IS, SS) until the standing indicates that R_{shelf7} is really the target. The IS parser, however, does not know where the standing occurs. As at least one pick has already occurred the IS parser must consider the hypothesis that the standing could be a sign for a queuing intention (Q). The customer has found no article in R_{shelf7}, so she leaves the region without picking.
- 11...13: a pick in R_{shelf8}. The Q hypothesis stays in the hypotheses sets of the IS parser during all behaviors sauntering and standing, until it is refused when the pick occurs. At this point, the parser could ex-post correct its wrong hypotheses $\mathbf{I}_{8,\text{IS}}...\mathbf{I}_{12,\text{IS}}$ but, due to the incrementality

Production Rules with Spatial Grounding and Non-Local Constraints		
B → SS GP C SS DP SE | $\{R_\Omega\}$, $\{(1, 4, \text{equals})\}$		(2)
C → SS GP C SS DP | $\{R_\Omega\}$, $\{(1, 4, \text{equals})\}$		(18)

Fig. 5.4 An SCCFG for the clothes shop example, modifying the SGIS rules from Fig. 5.3.

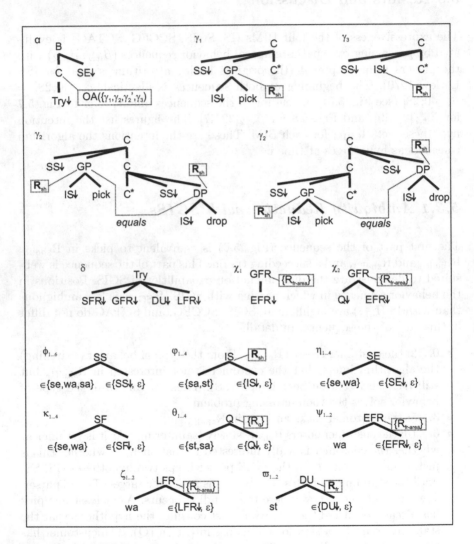

Fig. 5.5 An SCTAG for the clothes shop example.

of mobile intention recognition, it is too late and they remain in the results table.

i	b_i	R_i	$I_{i, IS}$	$I_{i, SGIS}$	$I_{i, SCCFG}$	$I_{i, SCTAG}$
0	wa	R_Ω	{SS}	{SS}	{SS}	{SS}
1	se	R_{shelf1}	{SS}	{SS}	{SS}	{SS}
2	se	R_Ω	{SS}	{SS}	{SS}	{SS}
3	sa	R_{shelf5}	{IS,SS}	{IS,SS}	{IS,SS}	{IS,SS}
4	st	R_{shelf5}	{IS}	{IS}	{IS}	{IS}
5	p	R_{shelf5}	{GP}	{GP}	{GP}	{GP}
6	se	R_{shelf5}	{SFR,SS}	{SFR,SS}	{SFR,SS}	{SFR,SS}
7	se	R_Ω	{SFR,SS}	{SFR,SS}	{SFR,SS}	{SFR,SS}
8	sa	R_{shelf7}	{IS,Q,SS}	**{IS,SS}**	{IS,SS}	{IS,SS}
9	st	R_{shelf7}	{IS,Q}	**{IS}**	{IS}	{IS}
10	sa	R_Ω	{IS,Q,SS}	**{SS}**	{SS}	{SS}
11	sa	R_{shelf8}	{IS,Q,SS}	**{IS,SS}**	{IS,SS}	{IS,SS}
12	st	R_{shelf8}	{IS,Q}	**{IS}**	{IS}	{IS}
13	p	R_{shelf8}	{GP}	{GP}	{GP}	{GP}
14	se	R_{shelf8}	{SFR,SS}	{SFR,SS}	{SFR,SS}	{SFR,SS}
15	se	R_Ω	{SFR,SS}	{SFR,SS}	{SFR,SS}	{SFR,SS}
16	wa	R_{shelf6}	{EFR,SFR,SS}	**{SFR,SS}**	{SFR,SS}	{SFR,SS}
17	wa	R_Ω	{EFR,SFR,SS}	**{SFR,SS}**	{SFR,SS}	{SFR,SS}
18	sa	R_{shelf3}	{IS,Q,SS}	**{IS,SS}**	{IS,SS}	{IS,SS}
19	p	R_{shelf3}	{GP}	{GP}	{GP}	{GP}
20	wa	R_Ω	{SFR,SS}	{SFR,SS}	{SFR,SS}	{SFR,SS}
21	se	R_Ω	{SFR,SS}	{SFR,SS}	{SFR,SS}	{SFR,SS}
22	sa	R_q	{IS,Q,SS}	**{Q,SS}**	{Q,SS}	{Q,SS}
23	st	R_q	{IS,Q}	**{Q}**	{Q}	{Q}
24	sa	R_q	{IS,Q,SS}	**{Q}**	{Q}	{Q}
25	wa	$R_{fr-area}$	{EFR,SFR,SS}	**{EFR}**	{EFR}	{EFR}
26	wa	R_{fr2}	{EFR,SFR,SS}	**{EFR}**	{EFR}	{EFR}
27	st	R_{fr2}	{DU,IS,Q}	**{DU}**	{DU}	{DU}
28	wa	$R_{fr-area}$	{EFR,LFR,SFR,SS}	**{LFR}**	{LFR}	{LFR}

Fig. 5.6 Clothes shop example: disambiguation with SGIS, $\beta_{st,1}[0;28] = \beta_{st,2}[0;28]$ (pick$_5$, pick$_8$, pick$_3$).

- 14...19: a crossing of R_{shelf6}, and a pick in R_{shelf3}. This time, the walking behavior causes the IS parser to hypothesize that the customer has an EnterFittingRoom intention (EFR) which may appear if the customer did not have to wait in queue.
- 20...28: the customer searches the fitting room, stands in the queue, enters fitting room 2, tries on the article, and leaves the fitting room again. Once more, the IS parser cannot decide whether the customer is still searching and inspecting shelves, or whether she is now trying on clothes. At the end of the sequence, the IS parser has a very high ambiguity of $I_{28,IS} = 4$, compared to deterministic parsing with spatial grammars $I_{28,SGIS} = 1$.

The example demonstrates how, in general, the spatial grounding of context-free production rules in SGIS reduces ambiguity. One might argue that a simple LBS also performs spatial disambiguation and could, for instance, decide that intention Queuing is not possible in R_{shelf7}. However,

i	b_i	R_i	$I_{i,\,IS}$	$I_{i,\,SGIS}$	$I_{i,\,SCCFG}$	$I_{i,\,SCTAG}$
29	wa	R_q	{EFR,LFR,SE,SFR,SS}	**{LFR,SE,SS}**	{LFR,SE,SS}	{LFR,SE,SS}
30	wa	R_Ω	{EFR,LFR,SE,SFR,SS}	**{SE,SS}**	{SE,SS}	{SE,SS}
31	sa	R_{shelf3}	{IS,Q,SS}	**{IS,SS}**	{IS,SS}	{IS,SS}
32	st	R_{shelf3}	{IS,Q}	**{IS}**	{IS}	{IS}
33	d	R_{shelf3}	{DP}	{DP}	{DP}	{DP}
34	wa	R_Ω	{SE,SS}	{SE,SS}	{SE,SS}	{SE,SS}
35	sa	R_{shelf1}	{IS,SS}	{IS,SS}	**{SS}**	{SS}
36	se	R_{shelf1}	{SS}	{SS}	{SS}	{SS}
37	se	R_Ω	{SS}	{SS}	{SS}	{SS}
38	sa	R_{shelf4}	{IS,SS}	{IS,SS}	**{SS}**	{SS}
39	wa	R_{shelf4}	{SS}	{SS}	{SS}	{SS}
40	se	R_Ω	{SS}	{SS}	{SS}	{SS}
41	sa	R_{shelf6}	{IS,SS}	{IS,SS}	**{SS}**	{SS}
42	sa	R_Ω	{IS,SS}	**{SS}**	{SS}	{SS}
43	sa	R_{shelf8}	{IS,SS}	{IS,SS}	{IS,SS}	{IS,SS}
44	st	R_{shelf8}	{IS}	{IS}	{IS}	{IS}
45	d	R_{shelf8}	{DP}	{DP}	{DP}	{DP}
46	se	R_Ω	{SE,SS}	{SE,SS}	{SE,SS}	{SE,SS}
47	sa	R_{shelf5}	{IS,SS}	{IS,SS}	{IS,SS}	{IS,SS}
48	d	R_{shelf5}	{DP}	{DP}	{DP}	{DP}
49	wa	R_Ω	{SE}	{SE}	{SE}	{SE}

Fig. 5.7 Clothes shop example: disambiguation with SCCFG, $\beta_{st,1}[29;49]$ (drop$_3$, drop$_8$, drop$_5$). Continuation of the behavior sequence in Fig. 5.6.

SGISs not only disambiguate spatially but have the additional capability to account for the type of behavior in the current region, the behavior shown previously, and the partonomic structure in which the current region is embedded. Although the SGIS formalism is not a contribution of this thesis, as it has previously been published in Schlieder (2005), the disambiguation capabilities have not been evaluated in the original paper.

5.3.2 Ambiguity Reduction with SCCFGs

In the first behavior sequence, $\beta_{st,1}$, the customer leaves $R_{fr-area}$ through the northern door and drops the pullovers in the order drop$_3$, drop$_8$, drop$_5$, which is the shortest way of revisiting the shelves from that door. The listing in Figure 5.7 specifically shows that, in contrast to the SGIS parser, only shelves that have been visited before are considered as candidates for a revisit by the SCCFG parser. The hypotheses sets for SCCFG and SCTAG do not differ.

- 29...33: the customer searches R_{shelf3} and drops a pullover. As soon as the drop occurs, the IS parser knows that the phases of picking and trying on are over.

- 34...42: looking for R_{shelf5} the customer has somehow lost her way, and crosses a number of regions. The SCCFG parser has less ambiguity than the SGIS parser because it has maintained the information that no items were picked in R_{shelf1}, R_{shelf4}, and R_{shelf6}.
- 43...49: the customer drops pullovers in R_{shelf8} and R_{shelf5}, and finally searches for the exit. All formalisms, including IS, are able to count the number of picks and drops, so that the SearchExit (SE) is unambiguous after three drops. Not listed here is a variant of the BIM for regular grammars in which the counting of picks and drops is not possible. A parser for regular grammars (both, spatialized and not) would expect another drop ($I_{49,\text{RegularG}} = \{SS,SE\}$).

The SCCFG example demonstrates the additional disambiguation capabilities of SCCFGs, compared to SGISs. The non-local spatial context information on regions visited previously is used for further disambiguation which, in this case, better solves the room-crossing problem. The spatial relation used by the non-local spatial constraints in this example (*equals*) could easily be replaced by other relations, such as *touches* or *hasCommonParent*. Examples that require such relations have been discussed in section 2.3.4. This is the second advantage of SCCFGs, for SGISs are restricted to *contains or equals* relations between parent and child intentions (refer to the CSPs in Figs. 4.3 and 4.5). Furthermore, SCCFGs allow for more than one non-local constraint to be defined in one rule – nested or crossing – which is also not demonstrated here.

5.3.3 Avoiding Inconsistency with SCTAGs

In this behavior sequence, $\beta_{st,2}$, the customer leaves $R_{fr-area}$ through the southern door and drops the pullovers in the order $drop_8$, $drop_5$, $drop_3$. The parsing results in Fig. 5.8 show that the SCCFG parser is not able to recognize the drops in this order. The reason is that the pattern $pick_5$, $pick_8$, $pick_3$ try $drop_8$, $drop_5$, $drop_3$ of β_2 contains crossings, whereas picks and drops in $pick_5$, $pick_8$, $pick_3$ try $drop_3$, $drop_8$, $drop_5$ of β_1 are nested.

- 29...32: a drop in R_{shelf8}. Although a start with $pick_8$ is not a sign for the reverse order of $pick_5$, $pick_8$, $pick_3$, the SCCFG correctly recognizes the DropPullover (DP) intention. The reason is that the SCCFG parser hypothesizes $pick_3$ to appear alone, yielding either in $pick_5$, $pick_8$, $pick_3$ try $drop_8$, $drop_3$, or in $pick_5$, $pick_8$, $pick_3$ try $drop_8$ which are both nested sequences.
- 33...39: the customer crosses R_{shelf6} and drops in R_{shelf5}. As in $\beta_{st,1}$, the SCCFG and SCTAG parsers know for sure that the customer crosses R_{shelf6}.

i	b_i	R_i	$I_{i,\,IS}$	$I_{i,\,SGIS}$	$I_{i,\,SCCFG}$	$I_{i,\,SCTAG}$
29	wa	R_Ω	{EFR,LFR,SE,SFR,SS}	**{SE,SS}**	{SE,SS}	{SE,SS}
30	sa	R_{shelf8}	{IS,Q,SS}	**{IS,SS}**	{IS,SS}	{IS,SS}
31	st	R_{shelf8}	{IS,Q}	**{IS}**	{IS}	{IS}
32	d	R_{shelf8}	{DP}	{DP}	{DP}	{DP}
33	se	R_Ω	{SE,SS}	{SE,SS}	{SE,SS}	{SE,SS}
34	sa	R_{shelf6}	{IS,SS}	{IS,SS}	**{SS}**	{SS}
35	sa	R_{shelf6}	{IS,SS}	{IS,SS}	**{SS}**	{SS}
36	wa	R_Ω	{SS}	{SS}	{SS}	{SS}
37	sa	R_{shelf5}	{IS,SS}	{IS,SS}	{IS,SS}	{IS,SS}
38	st	R_{shelf5}	{IS}	{IS}	{IS}	{IS}
39	d	R_{shelf5}	{DP}	{DP}	{DP}	{DP}
40	se	R_Ω	{SE,SS}	{SE,SS}	{SE}	**{SE,SS}**
41	wa	R_{shelf4}	{SE,SS}	{SE,SS}	{SE}	**{SE,SS}**
42	sa	R_{shelf4}	{IS,SS}	{IS,SS}	{}	**{SS}**
43	wa	R_Ω	{SS}	{SS}	{}	**{SS}**
44	sa	R_{shelf3}	{IS,SS}	{IS,SS}	{}	**{IS,SS}**
45	st	R_{shelf3}	{IS}	{IS}	{}	**{IS}**
46	d	R_{shelf3}	{DP}	{DP}	{}	**{DP}**
47	wa	R_Ω	{SE}	{SE}	{}	**{SE}**

Fig. 5.8 Clothes shop example: inconsistency avoidance with SCTAG, $\beta_{st,2}[29;47]$ (drop$_8$, drop$_5$, drop$_3$). Continuation of the behavior sequence in Fig. 5.6.

- 40…41: as the SCCFG parser can only recognize nested pick/drop patterns, no drop can be added to pick$_5$, pick$_8$, pick$_3$ try drop$_8$, drop$_5$, and the SCCFG parser has only one hypothesis, SearchExit (SE). Although this is less ambiguous than $I_{40,SGIS}$ and $I_{40,SCTAG}$, the result of the SCCFG parser is wrong because, certainly, the customer may decide to drop in R_{shelf3}.
- 42…47: the SCCFG parser cannot map the sauntering behavior to the SE intention, and no other intention is possible after SE. Thus, the SCCFG parser rejects any further behaviors (indicated with {}). The SCTAG parser, in contrast, correctly disambiguates the crossing in R_{shelf4}, and accepts the drop in R_{shelf3}.

We see in this simple example that SCTAGs are at least as expressive as SCCFGs (which is no surprise as there exists an according SCTAG for each SCCFG, refer to section 4.3.2): they also use non-local information on previously visited regions for better disambiguation. However, the comparison of the results for SCCFG and SCTAG shows that the SCCFG formalism fails to recognize behavior sequences with crossing dependencies. This failing appears as a false classification of a valid behavior sequence as inexplicable.

For practical mobile assistance systems, this false inexplicability is generally worse than high ambiguity as the system may try to handle ambiguity on the level of mapping the intention hypotheses set to an information service: in the clothes shop example, for instance, the system might map the intention SearchShelf to an information service "overview map", the intention SearchFittingRooms to "navigate to fitting rooms", and the set of both ({SFR,SS}) to "overview map with highlighted fitting rooms". Alternatively, the user interface could arrange the possible information services in a queue of screens through which the user could easily switch with a minimal attention interface. Intention recognition would then at least reduce the number of screens in that queue.

Thus, the system designer of an IAMS needs to consider carefully whether non-local constraints definitely appear only in a nested pattern, and should better decide for SCTAGs if there are major doubts.

5.4 INTENSIVE: A Simulation and Testing Environment for the IAMS Framework[1]

The previous sections have evaluated SCCFGs and SCTAGs, the main contribution of this thesis. The second contribution, a framework for IAMSs, has not been evaluated yet. It is difficult to evaluate a framework as it cannot just be compared to another framework by assessing the ambiguity of the output intention hypotheses. The outcome of the whole processing hierarchy (refer to Fig. 2.2) is dependent on a number of factors, and optimizing all of them at the same time yields in searching a multi-dimensional solution space. Even worse, the search space is doubled because the compared framework, such as a DBN, would need to be configured perfectly as well.

Anyway, it is not the aim of a framework to perform better than any other framework for any scenario in terms of hypotheses results, but rather to provide an IAMS engineer or mobile intention recognition researcher a guideline on how to approach and structure the complex problem of interpreting a mobile user's spatio-temporal behavior and activity. Thus, an evaluation of the framework would require empirical user studies with system engineers that are given a certain task, e.g., "use the framework F_1 to structure the mobile intention recognition problem P_1". The quality of the resulting model, if such a quality measure can be defined at all, could be compared with the results of other frameworks and other mobile intention recognition problems. A study like that is very hard to perform as it is difficult to find a sufficient number of test persons with enough background knowledge. Additionally, a number of influence factors may spoil the study, especially the background knowledge (for instance, a dedicated Bayes theorist would probably perform best in the Bayes framework). Because of these difficulties, this section presents a software system that supports the framework (INTENSIVE), and which could be used to evaluate the algorithmic approaches chosen within the framework.

---

[1] The following presentation of the INTENSIVE tool extends the short introduction of the beta-version of INTENSIVE that was presented at the BMI'08 workshop (Kiefer and Stein, 2008).

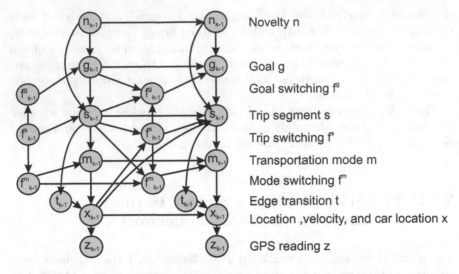

Novelty n

Goal g
Goal switching f^g

Trip segment s
Trip switching f^s

Transportation mode m
Mode switching f^m

Edge transition t
Location ,velocity, and car location x

GPS reading z

Fig. 5.9 Hierarchical DBN (Liao et al, 2007, p. 313).

The section also gives practical advise on how to use INTENSIVE to improve the software engineering process for IAMSs.

The IAMS framework from chapter 2 cuts the semantic gap between low-level input data and high-level intentions into pieces by introducing the intermediate layers motion track, motion track segment, feature list, and behavior. This not only simplifies the task of assigning meaning to the user's trajectory by means of abstraction which, for instance, allows researchers to concentrate on the level of processing they are mostly interested in (such as most of the discussions so far have concentrated only on the step of intention recognition), but also introduces a high degree of flexibility:

- The algorithm chosen for each of the processing steps can be changed without touching the neighboring steps. For instance, the data refinement step could use a probabilistic location estimation method (Bayesian filtering), whereas intention recognition could still choose a non-probabilistic approach, such as the spatial grammars introduced in chapter 4. This distinguishes the framework from other approaches that claim one kind of approach to be the universal solution for all processing steps, such as the multi-layer DBNs discussed in section 3.3.2 of the related work chapter (see Fig. 5.9 for an example from Liao et al, 2007).
- The parameterization of each algorithm can be adapted individually. For instance, there is not necessarily a connection between the criteria chosen for segmentation and the features extracted for behavior classification.
- The framework can easily be adapted to a number of mobile intention recognition scenarios because the data objects handled in the framework, behaviors **B** and intentions **I**, can be defined new for each scenario. This

again is, for instance, different to many approaches discussed in chapter 3 which use hand-made and fixed models for one specific scenario (again, refer to the DBN in Fig. 5.9).

- The framework enables easy spatial portability as all processing steps can share a common spatial model, e. g., the same set of regions can be used for segmentation, behavior classification, and mobile intention recognition[2].

Although the framework structures the search space that needs to be explored when looking for an optimal configuration the flexibility still implicates a number of non-trivial configuration decisions. Some of these decisions can be made analytically, e. g., regarding the complexity of the formal grammar (see the discussions in the previous section), others require an empirical analysis of real motion track data. This concerns, for instance, the types of behaviors a typical customer in the clothes shop shows, and the parameters for classifying these behaviors (refer to the decision tree in Fig. 5.1). A "prototype and revise" software engineering approach that tries a set of parameters on the mobile system with real users, then adjusts these parameters, and continues with user studies until the best set of parameters is found would probably produce the best results. However, this is not feasible because of the high effort connected with the real world testing.

The desktop application INTention SImulation enVironmEnt (INTENSIVE) addresses this problem. It takes the prototyping offline by allowing to configure the steps of the IAMS model in the desktop tool, and test it by playing back motion tracks recorded previously. The system reads a GPS log (currently only outdoor IAMSs are supported), processes the data with the configured IAMS model, and outputs and visualizes the behaviors and intentions the model would recognize. Thus, the system engineer or researcher can perform detailed tests on the desktop before implementing and deploying the algorithms on the real device.

INTENSIVE is a flexible simulation environment whose processing model consists of algorithm blocks encapsulating the computations. Algorithm blocks exchange information with other blocks through typed input and output ports. The type of the port, e. g., "spatio-temporal behavior", defines the type of data accepted (or produced respectively), and defines which blocks can be connected with each other. INTENSIVE comes with a graphical user interface that allows the user to add, connect, and parameterize these blocks (Fig. 5.10). Blocks are defined in plugins, thus allowing a developer to integrate her own algorithms. The meta-data of a block defines the parameters of the algorithm, such as the features used for classification (Fig. 5.13). Geographic models are imported from external files in standard formats (e. g., in the Keyhole Markup language format, KML). The system automatically extracts the spatial relations between the regions in the spatial model which

---

[2] Spatial portability is further discussed in section 6.2.

are, for instance, used by the SCCFG and SCTAG algorithms (see Figs. 5.11 and 5.12).

Having completed the configuration of a model the user of INTENSIVE starts the simulation and switches to the geo visualization screen which contains a zoomable and scrollable map loaded dynamically from Open Street Map[3]. Certain types of blocks, called visualization blocks, define the objects visualized as dynamic overlays on the map. For instance, an AgentVisualizationBlock takes GPS positions as input and uses them to visualize a moving agent on the map. Other visualization blocks show behaviors (see Fig. 5.14) and intentions, where different tokens are distinguished by their color. Thus, the INTENSIVE user can comfortably check the behaviors and intentions recognized at different positions in the motion track.

Since the first beta version of INTENSIVE in 2008 and the time of writing this thesis, the emulators that come with the development tools for mobile platforms, such as Android[4], have developed rapidly. A similar desktop prototyping approach by testing previously recorded motion tracks could as well use an emulator, with the advantage that it runs the real application, including the look-and-feel of the information services. However, emulators are still not completely stable and, for instance, the KML replay feature of Android's DDMS (Dalvik Debug Monitor Server) screen in Eclipse[5] does currently not support timestamps which would be mandatory for analyzing spatio-temporal behavior:

> "Note: DDMS does not support routes created with the ⟨MultiGeometry⟩ ⟨LineString⟩ lat1, long1, lat2, long2, ... ⟨/LineString⟩ ⟨/MultiGeometry⟩ methods. There is also currently no support for the ⟨TimeStamp⟩ node inside the ⟨Placemark⟩. Future releases may support timed placement and routes within a single coordinate element." (Google, 2011)

As additional advantage, INTENSIVE is written in J2SE v.6 which enables to load plugins that contain code from algorithms programmed for some other purpose. Open Source Libraries for J2SE are still much more widespread than for mobile platforms, and the integration of J2SE libraries into Android is often not possible. The third advantage of INTENSIVE is that it also supports the simulation of several agents at the same time, opening up research perspectives for multi-agent intention recognition (see section 6.3.5).

Plugins for the spatial grammar parsers from chapter 4 exist. For the preprocessing steps (data refinement, segmentation, feature extraction, behavior classification) currently only a selected number of processing blocks is available.

---

[3] http://www.openstreetmap.org/

[4] http://developer.android.com/

[5] http://www.eclipse.org/

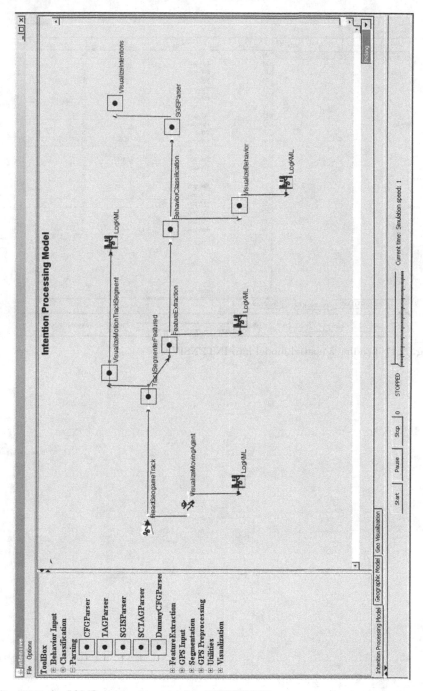

Fig. 5.10 An IAMS processing model in INTENSIVE.

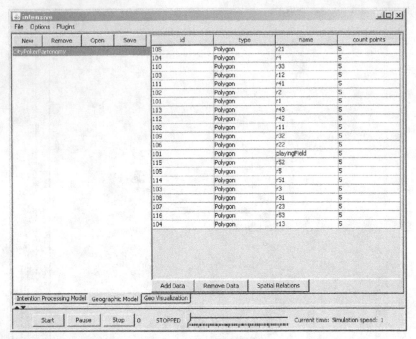

Fig. 5.11 Loading a spatial model into INTENSIVE.

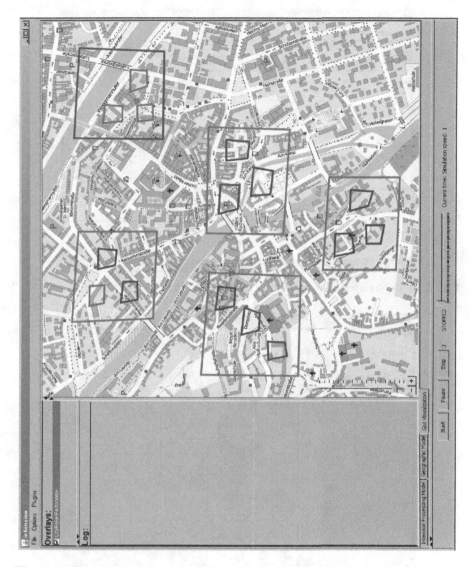

Fig. 5.12 Visualization of a spatial model in the geo visualization screen (map from Open Street Map, http://www.openstreetmap.org/).

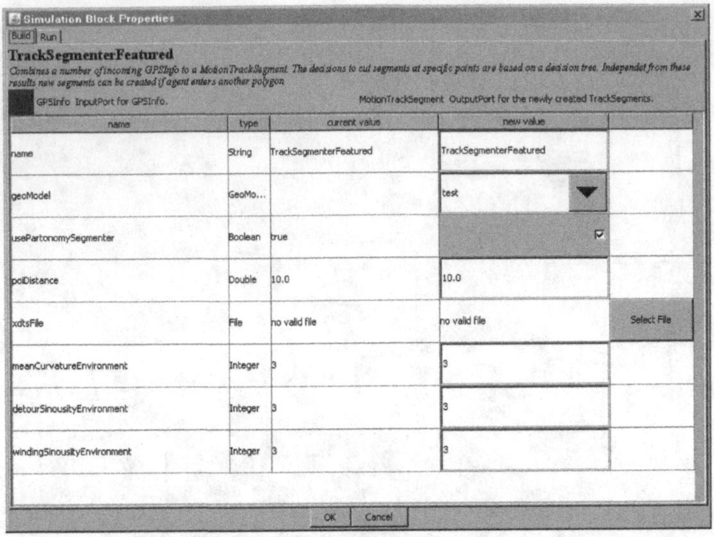

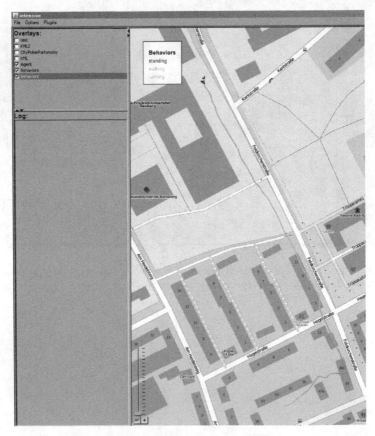

Fig. 5.13 Configuring a processing block in INTENSIVE.

Fig. 5.14 Behavior classification with INTENSIVE (map from Open Street Map, http://www.openstreetmap.org/).

Chapter 6
Conclusion and Outlook

6.1 Mobile Intention Recognition

This thesis has started with the observation that simple proactive LBSs are not able to assist their users adequately as the user's presence at a certain location is not sufficient to unambiguously decide about her information needs. On the other hand, most general context-aware services interpret human behavior on a low semantic level (activity, behavior) which is often not sufficient to fulfill the user's information needs adequately.

Driven by these insufficiencies, chapter 2 has developed the first contribution of this thesis: a framework for mobile services which choose an information service dependent on the user's intention (IAMSs). The framework includes a context-model with primary context location, time, and activity, and secondary context region, behavior, and intentions. The context-model was further developed to a processing architecture that crosses the semantic gap between sensor input and intentions. The architecture specifically focuses on the processing of trajectory data with which the steps data refinement, segmentation, feature extraction, behavior classification, and mobile intention recognition are performed. The challenges and possible approaches for each of these steps have been discussed.

As second contribution of this thesis, chapter 2 has formally defined the mobile intention recognition problem (which is the most important step of any IAMS), and compared it to general intention recognition – a systematic comparison which was missing in the previous literature. As the main feature of mobile intention recognition, the availability of spatial and temporal information on each input has been identified. More specifically, the spatio-temporal behavior sequences used by mobile intention recognition are temporally ordered, temporally complete, and spatially consistent. These properties of mobile intention recognition had implications on all discussions, formalisms, and algorithms presented in the following chapters. To get a first estimate on the different problem complexity of general and mobile intention recognition, chapter 2 has considered the worst case number of possible groupings for a behavior sequence of length n. This number can be estimated by the n-th Bell number for the general case, and 2^{n-1} for the mobile case (where the latter is growing much slower). This difference is due to the temporal ordering in mobile intention recognition. Restricting behavior groupings at the borders of regions further reduces the number of possible groupings. In this context, the concept of BIMs has been introduced which formalize how intentions, behaviors and space are interconnected in a given mobile assistance scenario. Different representational formalisms can be used for an BIM, two of which have been newly introduced in chapter 4, and are revisited in the following section 6.2.

Section 5.4 in the evaluation chapter has briefly introduced the software tool INTENSIVE. This desktop application allows an IAMS designer or mobile intention recognition researcher to test different algorithmic solutions for all steps of the processing architecture using previously recorded trajectory data. The tool features a flexible plugin architecture which makes it easy to integrate new algorithms into the tool, and a graphical user interface with which the developer can create her own combination of algorithms easily, and trace the output of the algorithms in a geo visualization screen. An evaluation of each single processing step in the framework with empirical data using INTENSIVE is one interesting direction of future research, but was out of focus as this thesis concentrated on the last step in the framework, mobile intention recognition, with emphasis on spatial disambiguation.

6.2 Spatially Constrained Grammars

Chapters 3, 4 and 5 were concerned with the main contribution of this thesis: the development of new representational formalisms that capture a larger class of mobile intention recognition problems than previous approaches. In this larger problem class, a user's spatio-temporal behavior sequence cannot be interpreted correctly using a limited sequence of connected spatial contexts, but only under consideration of non-local information, as motivated with the Visit-Revisit pattern in chapter 1. Chapter 2 has described this problem class further and discovered that non-local information, in terms of long-ranging space-intention dependencies, may occur nested and/or crossing, depending on the use case.

A literature review in chapter 3 has shown that the problem of interleaved intentions is a topic of ongoing interest in general plan recognition. However, no approach addresses the spatial aspects of mobile intention recognition. The exception, SGIS, is a context-free formal grammar restricting the applicability of rules to spatial regions. As SGISs are not able to represent long-ranging space-intention dependencies, chapter 4 has introduced two new representational formalisms: SCCFGs and and SCTAGs.

SCCFGs are, just as SGISs, context-free but additionally feature non-local spatial constraints which may be typed by an arbitrary (spatial) relation, such as *touches* or *hasSameParent*. The evaluation of the SCCFG formalism with an exemplary behavior sequence of a customer picking and dropping articles in a clothes shop (chapter 5) has affirmed the claim that SCCFGs suffer from less ambiguity than SGISs due to their ability to maintain information on previously visited regions over a long sequence of behaviors. However, if several long-ranging dependencies occur in the sequence they must be either nested, or statically defined as crossing in the rules. The generation of crossings by rule application is not possible.

SCTAGs are built on the mildly context-sensitive TAG formalism that has proven well for overlapping dependencies in NLP. The adjunction operation of TAGs causes an additional expressiveness which allows to capture a limited number of crossing dependencies. The clothes shop example in chapter 5 has affirmed that SCTAGs are able to represent a richer class of mobile intention recognition problems. Chapter 4 has also discussed the principles of parsing spatial grammars, and how the type of spatial model (partonomic vs. non partonomic) influences the number of operations performed by the parser. Extensions to existing algorithms have exemplified how spatial constraints can be integrated into chart parsers. Returning to the requirements formulated at the end of chapter 2, the contributions of this thesis can mainly seen in SCCFGs and SCTAGs fulfilling the spatial expressiveness requirement:

Requirement 5 *The representational formalism used for the BIM should allow us to express long-ranging space-intention dependencies which may – to a certain degree – nest into and overlap with each other.*

The other requirements are met as follows:

Requirement 1 *Mobile intention recognition algorithms should run efficiently on the limited resources of a mobile device.*

This requirement has not been fully evaluated in this thesis as the algorithms were not tested on a mobile device. However, it has been shown that the runtime complexity of the parsers for spatially constrained grammars is not higher than that of the according parsers for the original grammars. As both, CFGs and TAGs, can be parsed in polynomial time the same applies to spatially constrained grammars. Spatial constraints reduce the number of hypotheses that need to be considered. The exemplary parsers presented were not intended to be the most optimal solution, especially for SCTAGs, but to demonstrate the general principles of integrating spatial constraints into chart parsers.

Requirement 2 *The representational formalism used for the BIM should support easy geographic portability.*

Grounding constraints, as the basis of all spatial grammars, are formulated using sets of regions. The constraints are independent of the geometry of these regions. In many scenarios, the logical connections between intentions, behaviors, and regions formalized in an BIM can easily be ported to a new geographic area just by defining new geometries for the regions. Consider, for instance, the clothes shop company having several subsidiaries with similar arrangements of shelves, fitting rooms, and so on. The portation of an intelligent shopping assistant from one subsidiary to another then basically means to edit the geometries, and possibly to change the number of shelves.

Non-local constraints, as the essential idea of SCCFGs and SCTAGs, are formulated completely independent of the spatial model. For instance, a rule or elementary tree stating that two intentions must happen in regions that *touch* poses only the restriction on the spatial model that it must support the spatial relation type *touches*. The spatial model does not even have to contain regions that *touch*, as in that case the rule would simply not be applicable in this geographic area, but possibly somewhere else. Thus, the spatial model can easily be changed, allowing for easy portability to new regions.

Requirement 3 *The representational formalism used for the BIM should be cognitively understandable, i. e., modifiable by a domain expert.*

Approaches based on formal grammars are, in general, cognitively appealing. CFG and SCCFG rule sets, such as the ones from figures 5.3 and 5.4, are intuitively easy to understand as they follow the human way of describing hierarchical plans. SCTAGs, with their explicit tree representation, describe hierarchies even better. However, modeling sets of auxiliary trees that allow to express a certain type of dependency pattern requires some practice. This can be overcome by providing the knowledge engineer with a set of design patterns, consisting of abstract structures of auxiliary trees. The general pick/drop grammar in Fig. 4.13 is one example for such a design pattern. An in-depth evaluation of cognitive understandability, however, would require extensive HCI studies and is not the main focus of this thesis.

Requirement 4 *The representational formalism used for the BIM should support the formulation of exclusive, definite assertions, i. e., behavior sequences that should definitely be interpreted as one intention, or be classified as irrational.*

This requirement is fulfilled by approaches based on non-probabilistic formal grammars. It has been introduced especially for those assistance scenarios in which certain behavior sequences should trigger an alarm, such as assisting Alzheimer patients with AAL. The outlook in section 6.3.3 discusses the implications of removing this requirement.

To conclude, the two main subjectives of this thesis were achieved, namely the development of a formal framework for mobile intention recognition, and the development of new representational formalisms that allow to represent long-ranging space-intention dependencies with a limited amount of crossings.

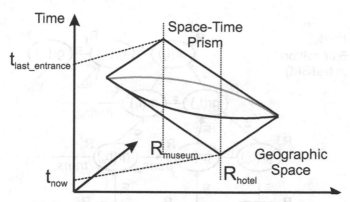

Fig. 6.1 Time Geographic space-time prism, represented as two intersecting cones.

6.3 Future Research

6.3.1 Temporal Constraints

Chapter 2 has identified the availability of temporal information on each behavior as one of the main advantages of mobile intention recognition over general intention recognition, and discussed the implications of temporal ordering on the number of possible behavior groupings. The algorithms of chapter 4 have exploited the ordering to parse behavior sequences, and to efficiently propagate spatial constraints along a parse tree. However, as the focus of this thesis was spatial ambiguity resolution, the absolute time stamps for start and end of each behavior in a spatio-*temporal* behavior sequence β_{st} have been ignored throughout chapter 4.

One possible extension to the proposed parsing approach is to exploit the absolute temporal information for further ambiguity reduction. As mentioned in section 2.2.1 a rational agent's beliefs about space-time mechanics of locational presence, as formalized in the Time Geographic framework (see Hägerstrand, 1970; Miller, 2005), constitute an important part of her beliefs about the world. For instance, an agent will not have the intention to visit the museum if she believes that it is definitely impossible to arrive there before closing time, given her maximum travel speed. The mobile intention recognition algorithm could thus exclude the hypothesis $I_{SearchMuseum}$. Formally, the agent's future space-time path has to lie within the space-time prism resulting from two intersecting cones whose apexes are given by her current space-time position, and the space-time position of the latest acceptable arrival time at the museum. The slope of the cones is determined by her maximum speed. The space-time prism for an agent currently located at a hotel with a possible intention to visit a museum is illustrated in Fig. 6.1.

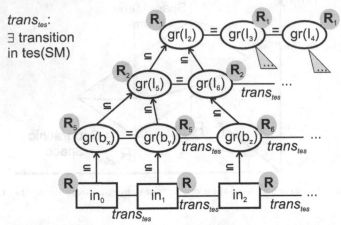

Fig. 6.2 Spatial continuity for spatial constraint satisfaction on the parse tree (refer to the original Fig. 4.3).

If the two cones did not intersect, the agent would not be able to arrive at R_{museum} in time.

A formal grammar that integrates temporal and spatial information for mobile intention recognition has been published in Kiefer et al (2010) (Temporally Restricted and Spatially Grounded Intentional Systems, TR-SGIS). TR-SGISs enhance the SGIS formalism by authority, coupling, and capability constraints that allow to

a. temporally restrict the applicability of a rule (e. g., the agent will not have intention $I_{PrepareBreakfast}$ in the afternoon).
b. temporally restrict certain regions (e. g., the region $R_{fairground}$ is not accessible in the morning, at least with the affordances of a fairground).
c. temporally restrict a combination of rules and regions (e. g., the intention $I_{HaveDinner}$ is not available at the bistro $R_{CityInn}$ in the afternoon, but possibly in other bistros).

TR-SGISs are currently based on SGISs. They allow no overlapping constraints, neither statically defined in the rules, nor as product of a grammar operation. However, there are scenarios in which temporal constraints may overlap with each other, and possibly also with spatial constraints. A mildly context-sensitive approach that combines spatial and temporal constraints could lead to even better ambiguity reduction.

6.3.2 Look-Ahead Parsing

Besides temporal completeness, chapter 2 has identified spatial continuity as one important property of mobile intention recognition. Spatial continuity holds if two succeeding behaviors in β_{st} are located in regions that have an edge in the transition graph of the tessellated spatial model (refer to Fig. 2.13). The following chapters have not exploited this property as it trivially holds for spatio-temporal behavior sequences and needs not be checked for past data.

However, an incremental look-ahead parser could exploit the property by hypothesizing at time i about the next incoming behavior(s). If, for instance, a hypothesis requires the next behavior to happen in R_x, and the last known behavior happened in R_y, this hypothesis is only possible if R_x and R_y touch in the tessellation. As a first step towards a formalization, we could consider extending the CSPs introduced in chapter 4 (see Figs. 4.3 and 4.5) by a constraint $trans_{tes}$ (there exists a transition in the tessellation of SM) which must hold between neighboring nodes that are not already connected via "=" (see Fig. 6.2). Algorithms for look-ahead parsing exist; for instance, the algorithm originally described in Earley (1970) has an integrated look-ahead which is ignored in most implementations, including those of chapter 4.

An algorithm with look-ahead parsing is also necessary for capability disambiguation in TR-SGIS (section 6.3.1) as predicting whether an agent can reach a certain location in time requires a look-ahead into the future.

6.3.3 Probabilistic Spatially Constrained Grammars

The overview on related work in plan recognition (chapter 3) included a number of approaches that considered "the problem of plan recognition [...] largely [as] a problem of inference under conditions of uncertainty" (Charniak and Goldman, 1993, p. 54). Section 3.3.1 has listed some challenges connected with these probabilistic approaches. These include, for instance, the problem of acquiring (conditional) probabilities, the training phase required for personalization, and the problem to assert that an assistance system will not enter an undesired state. These arguments, and the focus of this thesis on space as means of disambiguation, were the reasons not to include probabilities into the representational formalisms. Thus, the aim of the intention hypotheses tables in chapter 5 was not to show how often the algorithms were able to return a non-ambiguous hypotheses set ($|\mathbf{I}_i| = 1$) but to highlight the possibilities of spatial disambiguation by comparing the degree of ambiguity achieved by the different representational formalisms.

Section 5.3.3 has discussed possibilities to resolve ambiguity during the step of mapping intentions to information services. However, these solutions are not perfectly satisfying, especially if the domain is highly ambiguous.

Enhancing the spatial grammar parsing approach with probabilities is definitely an issue worthwhile considering for future work. Probabilistic versions of both, CFGs and TAGs, are known in NLP (Suppes, 1970; Schabes, 1992; Resnik, 1992) and could provide valuable ideas in addition to those approaches discussed in chapter 3 that combine grammars and Bayes (see section 3.5). A specifically mobile aspect in this probabilistic approach could be to integrate transition probabilities between regions (following the Markov idea of Ashbrook and Starner, 2002, section 3.1) into spatial constraint resolution along the $trans_{tes}$ edges in Fig 6.2 that were explained in section 6.3.2.

6.3.4 Grammar Acquisition and Behavioral Corpora

The discussion on probabilistic approaches in section 3.3.1 has also suggested that definite expert knowledge is, in general, superior to learning probabilities. The same applies also to manual modeling vs. learning the structure of a grammar for which approaches exist for both formalisms, CFGs and TAGs, using corpora of natural language (Stolcke and Omohundro, 1994; Chiang, 2000; Xia, 1999). For mobile assistance systems there will hardly be a situation in which the system is supposed to be engineered automatically without a domain expert. It is also not sufficient to identify non-terminals that seem to be somehow structurally relevant for a given dataset, as it is also necessary to assign a meaning to them (in terms of intentions), and to identify those intentions that are relevant for a certain IAMS. This problem of identifying relevancy is especially critical as a behavioral dataset may also feature intentions that are irrelevant for the mobile assistance scenario (refer to section 2.2). However, an expert system might try to help the domain expert to identify typical behavior sequences and plan structures that are relevant for the system, but which the expert is not aware of herself. It is an open question whether grammar learning algorithms tested on corpora of natural language, such as the Penn treebank (Marcus et al, 1993), would perform comparably well for corpora of behavioral data.

Anyway, a sensible evaluation of grammar learning algorithms would require annotated corpora of behavioral data which, up to now, scarcely exist. While other communities have quasi-standard corpora on which a comparable evaluation of approaches is possible, no such standard corpora have yet been established in the plan/intention recognition community. A discussion of the difficulties of acquiring such corpora is given in Blaylock and Allen (2005). Challenges identified by Blaylock and Allen include expensiveness, and confusion between top- and low-level intentions. Indeed, letting a human record her own intentions while she is performing her tasks is time-consuming on the one, and error-prone on the other hand. For the mobile intention recognition problem, recording motion track data with GPS is a rather cheap way of collecting behavioral data. However, publicly available corpora of GPS tracks, such as the GeoLife corpus (Zheng et al, 2008, 2009), are unlabeled. Volunteered Geographic Information (VGI, Goodchild, 2007) may be one solution for the problem of expensiveness: people are acting as voluntary sensors to record geographic data for projects, such as Open Street Map (http://www.openstreetmap.org/), so maybe they are also willing to label their spatio-temporal behavior with intentions.

Besides expensiveness, the discussion in section 2.2 on unconscious and undesired intentions reveals more systematic problems of self-recorded intention data: an agent may not be aware of her intentions at all or, for instance, not regard the unpleasant queuing as an intention, and thus not label her data that way. One way to deal with these problems is to choose a very well-structured domain in which it is clear which intentions the agent can have which at least reduces the likeliness of unforeseen intentions. The rules of a LBG are one way of defining such a well-structured domain (Kiefer et al, 2008). A combination of VGI and LBGs has been proven useful for the semantic labeling of POIs (Matyas, 2007), and could as well for annotating behavioral data with intentions.

6.3.5 Multi-Agent Intention Recognition

Another current research question in plan/intention recognition is the recognition of a common intention of several agents who act cooperatively (see, for instance, Burghardt and Kirste, 2007; Devaney and Ram, 1998; Kaminka et al, 2002; Sadilek and Kautz, 2010). These approaches introduce a new recognition level on top of the individual agent's intentions, mostly referred to as "team intention". An according enhancement could also be added to the architecture for IAMSs proposed in section 2.1.2. For instance, a thesis defense can be seen as a team event in which all actors follow a common intention. Although it is not the primary task of the thesis committee members to act cooperatively with the PhD candidate under all circumstances, the non-spoken activity, such a closing the door, switching on the projector, opening the session, and so on, could be interpreted as indicators for a common intention $I_{DiscussResearch}$. However, the thesis defense example illustrates that a discussion on the implications of assigning a common intention to a group of agents is needed.

The special case of *mobile* team intention recognition in which agents move in geographic space is especially interesting: the Time Geographic constraints discussed in section 6.3.1 then apply to each member of the team and if, for instance, some team intention $I_{meet278}$ requires two agents to meet either in region R_2, R_7, or R_8, the potential path space of both actors (i. e., the interior of the space-time prisms, see Fig. 6.1) must intersect with each other, and with one of the three space-time stations determined by the regions (see Espeter and Raubal, 2009).

An interesting question is also how to cast multi-agent intention recognition as a parsing problem. Grouping the intentions of a group of agents to team intentions yields in yet another combinatory problem: which agents collaborate, which do not? Is there a team intention at all? Another challenge is to keep the balance between expressiveness (e. g., can intentions of different semantic levels be combined to a team intention?) and tractability.

References

Aho AV (1968) Indexed grammars - an extension of context-free grammars. Journal of the ACM 15(4):647–671

Albrecht DW, Zukerman I, Nicholson AE, Bud A (1997) Towards a Bayesian model for keyhole plan recognition in large domains. In: Proceedings of the Sixth International Conference on User Modeling (UM '97), Springer, pp 365–376

Anderson I, Maitland J, Sherwood S, Barkhuus L, Chalmers M, Hall M, Brown B, Muller H (2007) Shakra: Tracking and sharing daily activity levels with unaugmented mobile phones. Mobile Networks and Applications 12(2-3):185–199

Anderson J, Lebiere C (1998) The atomic components of thought. Erlbaum

Asai N, Kubo I, Kuo HH (2000) Bell numbers, log-concavity, and log-convexity. Acta Applicanda Mathematicae 63:79–87

Ashbrook D, Starner T (2002) Learning significant locations and predicting user movement with GPS. In: Proc. of IEEE 6th Int. Symposium on Wearable Computing

Ashbrook D, Starner T (2003) Using GPS to learn significant locations and predict movement across multiple users. Personal and Ubiquitous Computing 7(5):275–286

Audibert P (2010) Mathematics for Informatics and Computer Science, Wiley, chap Parts and Partitions of a Set, pp 275–288

Barkhuus L, Chalmers M, Tennent P, Hall M, Bell M, Sherwood S, Brown B (2005) Picking pockets on the lawn: The development of tactics and strategies in a mobile game. In: Beigl M, Intille S, Rekimoto J, Tokuda H (eds) UbiComp 2005: Ubiquitous Computing, Lecture Notes in Computer Science, vol 3660, Springer Berlin / Heidelberg, pp 358–374

Baus J, Krüger A, Wahlster W (2002) A resource-adaptive mobile navigation system. In: Proc. 7th International Conference on Intelligent User Interfaces, ACM Press, San Francisco, USA, pp 15–22

Bilmes JA (1998) A gentle tutorial on the EM algorithm and its application to parameter estimation for Gaussian mixture and Hidden Markov Models. Tech. Rep. ICSI-TR-97-021, University of Berkeley

Blaylock N, Allen J (2006) Fast hierarchical goal schema recognition. In: Proceedings, The Twenty-First National Conference on Artificial Intelligence and the Eighteenth Innovative Applications of Artificial Intelligence Conference, AAAI Press

Blaylock N, Allen JF (2005) Generating artificial corpora for plan recognition. In: User Modeling 2005, 10th International Conference, UM 2005, LNCS 3538, Springer, pp 179–188

Bobick A, Ivanov Y (1998) Action recognition using probabilistic parsing. In: Proc. of the Conference on Computer Vision and Pattern Recognition, pp 196–202

Bohnenberger T, Jacobs O, Jameson A, Aslan I (2005) Decision-theoretic planning meets user requirements: Enhancements and studies of an intelligent shopping guide. In: Gellersen HW, Want R, Schmidt A (eds) Pervasive Computing, Third International Conference, PERVASIVE 2005, LNCS 3468, Springer, pp 279–296

Bouroubi S (2007) Bell numbers and Engel's conjecture. Rostocker Mathematisches Kolloquium 62:61–70

Brandherm B, Schwartz T (2005) Geo referenced Dynamic Bayesian Networks for user positioning on mobile systems. In: Strang T, Linnhoff-Popien C (eds) Proceedings of the International Workshop on Location- and Context-Awareness (LoCA), LNCS 3479, Springer-Verlag Berlin Heidelberg, Munich, Germany, pp 223–234

Bratman ME (1987) Intention, Plans, and Practical Reasoning. Harvard University Press

Bratman ME (1990) What is intention? In: Cohen P, Morgan J, Pollack M (eds) Intentions in Communication, MIT Press, pp 15–32

Bratman ME (1999) Faces of intention: selected essays on intention and agency. The Press Syndicate of the University of Cambridge

Bratman ME, Israel DJ, Pollack ME (1988) Plans and resource-bounded practical reasoning. Computational Intelligence 4(3):349–355

Buchin M, Driemel A, van Kreveld M, Sacristan V (2010) An algorithmic framework for segmenting trajectories based on spatio-temporal criteria. In: ACMGIS 2010, 18th SIGSPATIAL International Conference on Advances in Geographic Information Systems, ACM Press, pp 202–211

Bui HH (2002) Efficient approximate inference for online probabilistic plan recognition. Technical Report 1/2002, School of Computing Science, Curtin University of Technology, Perth, WA, Australia

Bui HH (2003) A general model for online probabilistic plan recognition. In: Proceedings of the International Joint Conference on Artificial Intelligence (IJCAI)

Bui HH, Venkatesh S, West GAW (2000) On the recognition of abstract Markov policies. In: Proceedings of the Seventeenth National Conference on

Artificial Intelligence and Twelfth Conference on Innovative Applications of Artificial Intelligence, pp 524–530

Bui HH, Venkatesh S, West GAW (2002) Policy recognition in the Abstract Hidden Markov Model. Journal of Artificial Intelligence Research 17:451–499

Burghardt C, Kirste T (2007) Inferring intentions in generic context-aware systems. In: Proceedings of the 6th international conference on Mobile and ubiquitous multimedia, ACM, New York, NY, USA, pp 50–54

Carberry S (1990) Incorporating default inferences into plan recognition. In: Proceedings of the eighth National conference on Artificial intelligence - Volume 1, AAAI Press, pp 471–478

Carberry S (2001) Techniques for plan recognition. User Modeling and User-Adapted Interaction 11(1-2):31–48

Carroll G (1995) Learning probabilistic grammars for language modeling. PhD thesis, Brown University

Carroll G, Charniak E (1991) A probabilistic analysis of marker-passing techniques for plan recognition. In: Uncertainty In Artificial Intelligence, pp 69–76

Chalmers M, Galani A (2004) Seamful interweaving: heterogeneity in the theory and design of interactive systems. In: Proceedings of the 5th conference on designing interactive systems: processes, practices, methods, and techniques, ACM, New York, NY, USA, pp 243–252

Chanda G, Dellaert F (2004) Grammatical methods in computer vision: An overview. Technical Report GIT-GVU-04-29, College of Computing, Georgia Institute of Technology, Atlanta, GA, USA, ftp://ftp.cc.gatech.edu/pub/gvu/tr/2004/04-29.pdf

Charniak E, Goldman RP (1993) A Bayesian model of plan recognition. Artificial Intelligence 64(1):53–79

Chiang D (2000) Statistical parsing with an automatically-extracted tree adjoining grammar. In: Proceedings of the 38th Annual Meeting on Association for Computational Linguistics, Association for Computational Linguistics, Stroudsburg, PA, USA, ACL '00, pp 456–463

Chomsky N (1959) On certain formal properties of grammars. Information and Control 2(2):137–167

de la Clergerie E (2008) Parsing TAGs and +. Tutorial at TAG+9, Tübingen, 6 June, 2008

Cohn G, Gupta S, Froehlich J, Larson E, Patel S (2010) Gassense: Appliance-level, single-point sensing of gas activity in the home. In: Floréen P, Krüger A, Spasojevic M (eds) Pervasive Computing, Lecture Notes in Computer Science, Springer Berlin / Heidelberg, pp 265–282

De Souza E Silva A, Frith J (2012) Mobile Interfaces in Public Spaces - Locational Privacy, Control and Urban Sociability. Routledge, in press

Dee H, Hogg D (2004) Detecting inexplicable behaviour. In: Proc. of the British Machine Vision Conference, The British Machine Vision Association, pp 477–486

Demeester E, Hüntemann A, Vanhooydonck D, Vanacker G, Van Brussel H, Nuttin M (2008) User-adapted plan recognition and user-adapted shared control: A Bayesian approach to semi-autonomous wheelchair driving. Autonomous Robots 24:193–211

Deng M, Cheng T, Chen X, Li Z (2007) Multi-level topological relations between spatial regions based upon topological invariants. GeoInformatica 11:239–267

Devaney M, Ram A (1998) Needles in a haystack: plan recognition in large spatial domains involving multiple agents. In: Proceedings of the fifteenth national/tenth conference on Artificial intelligence/Innovative applications of artificial intelligence, AAAI, Menlo Park, CA, USA, pp 942–947

Dey AK, Abowd GD (1999) Towards a better understanding of context and context-awareness. In: Proceedings of the 1st international symposium on Handheld and Ubiquitous Computing, LNCS 1707, Springer, London, UK, pp 304–307

Dodge S, Weibel R, Lautenschütz AK (2008) Towards a taxonomy of movement patterns. Information Visualization 7:240–252

Earley J (1970) An efficient context-free parsing algorithm. Communications of the ACM 13(2):94–102

Ellis CA (1970) Probabilistic tree automata. In: STOC '70: Proceedings of the second annual ACM symposium on Theory of computing, ACM Press, New York, NY, USA, pp 198–205

Elnekave S, Last M, Maimon O (2008) A compact representation of spatio-temporal data. In: Data Mining Workshops, 2007. ICDM Workshops 2007. Seventh IEEE International Conference on, IEEE, pp 601–606

Espeter M, Raubal M (2009) Location-based decision support for user groups. Journal of Location Based Services 3:165–187

Forbes J, Huang T, Kanazawa K, Russell SJ (1995) BATmobile: Towards a Bayesian automated taxi. In: Proceedings of the 14th International Joint Conference on Artificial Intelligence, Morgan Kaufmann, pp 1878–1885

Fox D, Hightower J, Liao L, Schulz D, Borriello G (2003) Bayesian filtering for location estimation. IEEE Pervasive Computing 2(3):24–33

Frank AU (1992) Qualitative spatial reasoning about distances and directions in geographic space. Journal of Visual Languages and Computing 3(4):343–371

Gazdar G (1988) Natural Language Parsing and Linguistic Theories, D. Reidel, Dordrecht, chap Applicability of indexed grammars to natural languages

Geib CW, Goldman RP (2001) Probabilistic plan recognition for hostile agents. In: Proceedings of the Fourteenth International Florida Artificial Intelligence Research Society Conference (FLAIRS), pp 580–584

Geib CW, Goldman RP (2009) A probabilistic plan recognition algorithm based on plan tree grammars. Artificial Intelligence 173(11):1101–1132

Geib CW, Steedman M (2007) On natural language processing and plan recognition. In: Proc. of the 20th Int. Joint Conference on Artificial Intelligence, pp 1612–1617

Ghallab M, Nau D, Traverso P (2004) Automated Planning: Theory and Practice. Morgan Kaufman

Gibson JJ (1979) The Ecological Approach to Visual Perception. Houghton Mifflin Company

Girardin F, Blat J, Calabrese F, Dal Fiore F, Ratti C (2008) Digital footprinting: Uncovering tourists with user-generated content. Pervasive Computing 7(4):36–43

Giudice NA, Walton LA, Worboys M (2010) The informatics of indoor and outdoor space: a research agenda. In: Proceedings of the 2nd ACM SIGSPATIAL International Workshop on Indoor Spatial Awareness, ACM, New York, NY, USA, pp 47–53

Gogate V, Dechter R, Bidyuk B, Rindt C, Marca J (2005) Modeling transportation routines using hybrid dynamic mixed networks. In: Proceedings of the Twenty-First Conference Annual Conference on Uncertainty in Artificial Intelligence (UAI-05), AUAI Press, Arlington, Virginia, pp 217–224

Goldman RP, Geib CW, Miller CA (1999) A new model of plan recognition. In: Proceedings of the Fifteenth Annual Conference on Uncertainty in Artificial Intelligence, pp 245–254

Goldman RP, Kabanza F, Bellefeuille P (2010) Plan libraries for plan recognition: Do we really know what they model? (position paper). In: Plan, Activity, and Intent Recognition (PAIR) 2010, AAAI Workshop Proceedings, AAAI

Gonzalez RC, Thomason MG (1978) Syntactic Pattern Recognition - An Introduction. Addison-Wesley, Reading, Massachusetts, USA

Goodchild M (2007) Citizens as sensors: the world of volunteered geography. GeoJournal 69:211–221

Google (2011) Using the dalvik debug monitor. http://developer.android.com/guide/developing/tools/ddms.html, [Online; accessed 19-February-2011]

Hägerstrand T (1970) What about people in regional science? In: Papers of the Regional Science Association, pp 7–21

Hightower J, Borriello G (2004) Particle filters for location estimation in ubiquitous computing - a case study. In: Proceedings of the Sixth International Conference on Ubiquituous Computing (Ubicomp), pp 88–106

Holland S, Morse D, Gedenryd H (2002) AudioGPS: Spatial audio navigation with a minimal attention interface. Personal and Ubiquitous Computing 6(4):253–259

Huang CW, Shih TY (1997) On the complexity of point-in-polygon algorithms. Computers and Geosciences 23(1):109 – 118

Ivanov Y, Bobick A (2000) Recognition of visual activities and interactions by stochastic parsing. IEEE transactions on pattern analysis and machine intelligence (PAMI) 22(8):852–872

Jarvis PA, Lunt TF, Myers KL (2005) Identifying terrorist activity with AI plan-recognition technology. AI Magazine 26(3):73–81

Jordan T, Raubal M, Gartrell B, Egenhofer M (1998) An affordance-based model of place in GIS. In: Proc. 8th Int. Symposium on Spatial Data Handling, IUG, Vancouver, pp 98–109

Joshi AK (1985) Tree adjoining grammars: How much context-sensitivity is required to provide reasonable structural descriptions? In: Dowty DR, Karttunen L, Zwicky AM (eds) Natural Language Parsing: Psychological, Computational, and Theoretical Perspectives, Cambridge University Press, Cambridge, pp 206–250

Joshi AK, Schabes Y (1997) Tree-adjoining grammars. In: Rozenberg G, Salomaa A (eds) Handbook of Formal Languages, vol 3, Springer, Berlin, New York, pp 69–124

Jurafsky D, Martin JH (eds) (2000) Speech and Language Processing. Prentice Hall, Upper saddle River, New Jersey, USA

Kaminka GA, Pynadath DV, Tambe M (2002) Monitoring teams by overhearing: A multi-agent plan-recognition approach. Journal of Artificial Intelligence Research 17:83–135

Kautz H (1991) A formal theory of plan recognition and its implementation. In: Allen J, Kautz H, Pelavin R, Tennenberg J (eds) Reasoning About Plans, Morgan Kaufmann Publishers, pp 69–126

Kautz HA (1987) A formal theory of plan recognition. PhD thesis, University of Rochester, Rochester, NY

Kautz HA, Allen JF (1986) Generalized plan recognition. In: Proceedings of the fifth National Conference on Artificial Intelligence (AAAI-86), AAAI press, pp 32–37

Kettani D, Moulin B (1999) A spatial model based on the notions of spatial conceptual map and of object's influence areas. In: Proceedings of the International Conference on Spatial Information Theory: Cognitive and Computational Foundations of Geographic Information Science, LNCS 1661, Springer, London, UK, pp 401–416

Kiefer P (2008a) Modeling mobile intention recognition problems with spatially constrained tree-adjoining grammars. In: Proc. of the 9th Workshop on Tree Adjoining Grammars and Related Formalisms (TAG+9), Tuebingen, Germany, pp 105–112

Kiefer P (2008b) Spatially constrained grammars for mobile intention recognition. In: Freksa C, Newcombe NS, Gärdenfors P, Wölfl S (eds) Spatial Cognition VI, Springer (LNAI 5248), Berlin Heidelberg, pp 361–377

Kiefer P (2009) SCTAG: A mildly context-sensitive formalism for modeling complex intentions in spatially structured environments. In: AAAI Spring Symposium on Human Behavior Modeling, AAAI Technical Report SS-09-04, pp 19–24

Kiefer P, Schlieder C (2007) Exploring context-sensitivity in spatial intention recognition. In: Workshop on Behavior Monitoring and Interpretation, 30th

German Conference on Artificial Intelligence (KI-2007), CEUR Vol-296, pp 102–116, iSSN 1613-0073

Kiefer P, Stein K (2008) A framework for mobile intention recognition in spatially structured environments. In: 2nd Workshop on Behavior Monitoring and Interpretation (BMI08), pp 28–41

Kiefer P, Matyas S, Schlieder C (2008) Geogames - intention recognition and data quality in location-based gaming. KI - Zeitschrift Künstliche Intelligenz (Themenschwerpunkt: Räumliche Mobilität) 3/08:29–33

Kiefer P, Stein K, Schlieder C (2009) Rule-based intention recognition from spatio-temporal motion track data in ambient assisted living. In: Gottfried B, Aghajan H (eds) Behaviour Monitoring and Interpretation in Ambient Environments, IOS Press, pp 235–256

Kiefer P, Raubal M, Schlieder C (2010) Time Geography inverted: Recognizing intentions in space and time. In: ACMGIS 2010, 18th SIGSPATIAL International Conference on Advances in Geographic Information Systems, ACM Press, pp 510–513

Kjaerulff U (1992) A computational scheme for reasoning in dynamic probabilistic networks. In: Proceedings of the Eighth Conference on Uncertainty in Artificial Intelligence, pp 121–129

Kjærgaard M, Blunck H, Godsk T, Toftkjær T, Christensen D, Grønbæk K (2010) Indoor positioning using GPS revisited. In: Floréen P, Krüger A, Spasojevic M (eds) Pervasive Computing, Lecture Notes in Computer Science, vol 6030, Springer Berlin / Heidelberg, pp 38–56

Kortuem G, Bauer M, Segall Z (1999) NETMAN: The design of a collaborative wearable computer system. Mobile Networks and Applications 4(1):49–58

Krüger A, Butz A, Müller C, Stahl C, Wasinger R, Steinberg KE, , Dirschl A (2004) The connected user interface: realizing a personal situated navigation service. In: Proc. of the 9th international Conference on Intelligent User Interfaces, ACM Press, pp 161–168

Küpper A (2005) Location-based Services: fundamentals and operation. John Wiley and Sons

Laube P, Purves RS (2006) An approach to evaluating motion pattern detection techniques in spatio-temporal data. Computers, Environment and Urban Systems 30:347–374

Liao L, Fox D, Kautz HA (2004) Learning and inferring transportation routines. In: Proceedings of the Nineteenth National Conference on Artificial Intelligence, pp 348–353

Liao L, Patterson DJ, Fox D, Kautz H (2007) Learning and inferring transportation routines. Artificial Intelligence 171(5-6):311–331

Longley PA, Goodchild MF, Maguire DJ, Rhind DW (2010) Geographic Information Systems and Science, 3rd edn. Wiley and Sons

Lymberopoulos D, Ogale AS, Savvides A, Aloimonos Y (2006) A sensory grammar for inferring behaviors in sensor networks. In: IPSN '06: Proceedings of the fifth international conference on Information processing in sensor networks, ACM Press, New York, NY, USA, pp 251–259

Marcus MP, Marcinkiewicz MA, Santorini B (1993) Building a large annotated corpus of English: the Penn treebank. Computational Linguistics 19:313–330

Matyas C, Schlieder C (2009) A spatial user similarity measure for geographic recommender systems. In: GeoSpatial Semantics, 3rd Int. Conference, Springer, LNCS, vol 5892, pp 122–139

Matyas S (2007) Playful geospatial data acquisition by location-based gaming communities. The International Journal of Virtual Realities (IJVR) 6:1–10

Matyas S, Schlieder C (2005) Generating content-related metadata for digital maps in built heritage. In: Sanchez-Alonso S (ed) Proceedings of the First on-Line conference on Metadata and Semantics Research (MTSR'05): Advances in Metadata Research, Rinton Press Inc.

Meng L, Zipf A, Reichenbacher T (eds) (2005) Map-based Mobile Services: Theories, Methods and Implementations. Springer, Berlin, Heidelberg

Meng L, Zipf A, Winter S (eds) (2008) Map-based Mobile Services: Design, Interaction and Usability. Springer, Berlin, Heidelberg

Miller GA (1956) The magical number seven, plus or minus two: Some limits on our capacity for processing information. Psychological Review 63(2):343–355

Miller HJ (2005) A measurement theory for Time Geography. Geographical Analysis 37(1):17–45

Minnen D, Essa I, Starner T (2003) Expectation grammars: leveraging high-level expectations for activity recognition. In: Proc. Computer Vision and Pattern Recognition, vol 2, pp 626–632

Mitchell TM (1997) Machine Learning. McGraw-Hill Book Company

Montello D (1993) Scale and multiple psychologies of space. In: Frank A, Campari I (eds) Spatial Information Theory - A Theoretical Basis for GIS (LNCS 716/1993), Springer, Berlin, Heidelberg, pp 312–321

Moya CJ (1990) The Philosophy of Action. Polity Press, Cambridge, UK

Mulder F, Voorbraak F (2003) A formal description of tactical plan recognition. Information Fusion 4(1):47–61

Murphy KP (2002) Dynamic bayesian networks: Representation, inference and learning. PhD thesis, University of California, Berkeley

Murphy KP, Paskin MA (2001) Linear time inference in hierarchical HMMs. In: Proc. of the Conference on Neural Information Processing Systems (NIPS-01), pp 833–840

Musto A, Stein K, Eisenkolb A, Röfer T, Brauer W, Schill K (2000) From motion observation to qualitative motion representation. In: Spatial Cognition II, LNCS 1849, Springer, London, UK, pp 115–126

Nederhof MJ (1999) The computational complexity of the correct-prefix property for tags. Computational Linguistics 25:345–360

Nicholson AE, Brady JM (1994) Dynamic Belief Networks for discrete monitoring. IEEE Transactions on Systems, Man, and Cybernetics 24(11):1593–1610

Nijholt A, Rist T, Tuinenbreijer K (2004) Lost in ambient intelligence? In: Proc. ACM Conference on Compuer Human Interaction (CHI 2004), ACM, New York, USA, pp 1725–1726

Pärkkä J, Ermes M, Korpipää P, Mantyjärvi J, Peltola J, Korhonen I (2006) Activity classification using realistic data from wearable sensors. IEEE Transactions on Information Technology in Biomedicine 10(1):119–128

Patterson DJ, Liao L, Fox D, Kautz H (2003) Inferring high-level behavior from low-level sensors. In: Proceedings of The Fifth International Conference on Ubiquitous Computing (UBICOMP2003), Springer, pp 73–89

Patterson DJ, Liao L, Gajos K, Collier M, Livic N, Olson K, Wang S, Fox D, Kautz H (2004) Opportunity knocks: A system to provide cognitive assistance with transportation services. In: Proceedings of The Sixth International Conference on Ubiquitous Computing (UBICOMP2004), Springer, pp 433–450

Pearl J (1988) Probabilistic Reasoning in Intelligent Systems. Morgan Kaufmann Publishers

Peot MA, Shachter RD (1998) Learning from what you don't observe. In: Proc. of the Fourteenth Conference on Uncertainty in Artificial Intelligence, Morgan Kaufmann Publishers, pp 439–446

Prescher D (2004) A tutorial on the Expectation-Maximization algorithm including maximum-likelihood estimation and EM training of Probabilistic Context-Free Grammars. Presented at the 15th European Summer School in Logic, Language and Information (ESSLLI 2003), http://www.citebase.org/abstract?id=oai:arXiv.org:cs/0412015

Pynadath DV (1999) Probabilistic grammars for plan recognition. PhD thesis, The University of Michigan

Pynadath DV, Wellman MP (2000) Probabilistic State-Dependent Grammars for plan recognition. In: Proceedings of the 16th Annual Conference on Uncertainty in Artificial Intelligence, pp 507–514

Randell DA, Cui Z, Cohn AG (1992) A spatial logic based on regions and connection. In: 3rd Int. Conf. on Knowledge Representation and Reasoning, Morgan Kaufmann, pp 165–176

Raubal M (2011) Cogito ergo mobilis sum: The impact of location-based services on our mobile lives. In: Nyerges T, Couclelis H, McMaster R (eds) Handbook of GIS and Society Research, SAGE Publications, Los Angeles, London, pp 159–173

Raubal M, Winter S, Teßmann S, Gaisbauer C (2007) Time Geography for ad-hoc shared-ride trip planning in mobile geosensor networks. ISPRS Journal of Photogrammetry and Remote Sensing 62(5):366–381

Resnik P (1992) Probabilistic tree-adjoining grammar as a framework for statistical natural language processing. In: Proceedings of the 14th conference on Computational linguistics - Volume 2, Association for Computational Linguistics, Stroudsburg, PA, USA, COLING '92, pp 418–424

Roddick J, Hornsby K, Spiliopoulou M (2001) An updated bibliography of temporal, spatial, and spatio-temporal data mining research. In: Roddick J, Hornsby K (eds) Temporal, Spatial, and Spatio-Temporal Data Mining, Lecture Notes in Computer Science, vol 2007, Springer Berlin / Heidelberg, pp 147–163

Russell S, Norvig P (2010) Artificial Intelligence - A Modern Approach. Prentice Hall

Sadilek A, Kautz H (2010) Recognizing multi-agent activities from GPS data. In: Proc. of the Twenty-Fourth AAAI Conference on Artificial Intelligence

Sag IA, Pollard C (1987) Head-driven phrase structure grammar: An informal synopsis. CSLI Report 87-79, Stanford University, Stanford University

Samaan N, Karmouch A (2005) A mobility prediction architecture based on contextual knowledge and spatial conceptual maps. IEEE Transactions on Mobile Computing 4(6):537–551

Sánchez D, Tentori M, Favela J (2008) Activity recognition for the smart hospital. IEEE Intelligent Systems 23:50–57

Schabes Y (1992) Stochastic lexicalized tree-adjoining grammars. In: Proceedings of the 14th conference on Computational linguistics - Volume 2, Association for Computational Linguistics, Stroudsburg, PA, USA, COLING '92, pp 425–432

Schabes Y, Joshi AK (1988) An earley-type parsing algorithm for tree adjoining grammars. In: Proceedings of the 26th annual meeting on Association for Computational Linguistics, Association for Computational Linguistics, Stroudsburg, PA, USA, ACL '88, pp 258–269

Schaumburg H (2001) Computers as tools or as social actors? - the users' perspective on anthropomorphic agents. International Journal of Cooperative Information Systems 10(1-2):217–234

Schlieder C (2005) Representing the meaning of spatial behavior by Spatially Grounded Intentional Systems. In: GeoSpatial Semantics, First International Conference, Springer, Lecture Notes in Computer Science, vol 3799, pp 30–44

Schlieder C, Werner A (2003) Interpretation of intentional behavior in spatial partonomies. In: Spatial Cognition III, Routes and Navigation, Human Memory and Learning, Spatial Representation and Spatial Learning, Springer, Lecture Notes in Computer Science, vol 2685, pp 401–414

Schlieder C, Kiefer P, Matyas S (2006) Geogames - designing location-based games from classic board games. IEEE Intelligent Systems 21(5):40–46

Schmidt C, Sridharan N, Goodson J (1978) The plan recognition problem: An intersection of psychology and artificial intelligence. Artificial Intelligence 11(1-2):45–83

Shafer G (1990) Perspectives on the theory and practice of belief functions. International Journal of Approximate Reasoning 4(5-6):323–362

Sidner CL (1985) Plan parsing for intended response recognition in discourse. Computational Intelligence 1:1–10

Skiadopoulos S, Sarkas N, Sellis T, Koubarakis M (2007) A family of directional relation models for extended objects. IEEE Transactions on Knowledge and Data Engineering 19:1116–1130

Sloane N (2010) A000110: Bell or exponential numbers: ways of placing n labeled balls into n indistinguishable boxes. The OEIS Foundation Inc. (The On-Line Encyclopedia of Integer Sequences), http://oeis.org/A000110, [Online; accessed 17-December-2010]

Sprado J, Gottfried B (2008) Grammar-based argument construction. In: Lovrek I, Howlett R, Jain L (eds) Knowledge-Based Intelligent Information and Engineering Systems, Lecture Notes in Computer Science, vol 5177, Springer Berlin / Heidelberg, pp 330–340

Steedman M (1985) Dependency and coordination in the grammar of Dutch and English. Language 61(3):523–568

Stein K (2003) Qualitative Repräsentation und Generalisierung von Bewegungsverläufen. PhD thesis, Institut für Informatik der Technischen Universität München

Stein K, Schlieder C (2004) Recognition of intentional behavior in spatial partonomies. In: ECAI 2004 Workshop 15: Spatial and Temporal Reasoning (16th European Conference on Artificial Intelligence)

Stolcke A (1995) An efficient probabilistic context-free parsing algorithm that computes prefix probabilities. In: Computational Linguistics, MIT Press for the Association for Computational Linguistics, vol 21

Stolcke A, Omohundro S (1994) Inducing probabilistic grammars by bayesian model merging. In: Carrasco R, Oncina J (eds) International Conference on Grammatical Inference, Springer, pp 106–118

Storf H, Kleinberger T, Becker M, Schmitt M, Bomarius F, Prueckner S (2009) An event-driven approach to activity recognition in ambient assisted living. In: Tscheligi M, de Ruyter B, Markopoulus P, Wichert R, Mirlacher T, Meschterjakov A, Reitberger W (eds) Ambient Intelligence, Springer, Berlin, Heidelberg, pp 123–132

Suppes P (1970) Probabilistic grammars for natural languages. Synthese 22(1):95–116

Tahboub KA (2006) Intelligent human - machine interaction based on Dynamic Bayesian Networks probabilistic intention recognition. Journal of Intelligent and Robotic Systems 45:31–52

Taylor G, Blewitt G (2006) Intelligent Positioning: GIS-GPS Unification. John Wiley and Sons

Thomas B, Demczuk V, Piekarski W, Hepworth D, Gunther B (1998) A wearable computer system with augmented reality to support terrestrial navigation. In: 2nd International Symposium on Wearable Computers, Digest of Papers, pp 168–171

Veron E, Levasseur M (1991) Ethnographie de l'exposition: L'espace, le corps et le sens. Centre Georges Pompidou Bibliothèque Publique d'Information, Paris, France

Vijay-Shanker K, Weir D (1994) The equivalence of four extensions of context-free grammars. Mathematical Systems Theory 27(6):511–546

Vilain M (1990) Getting serious about parsing plans: a grammatical analysis of plan recognition. In: Proceedings of AAAI-90, The MIT Press, pp 190–197

Webber B, Knott A, Stone M, Joshi A (1999) Discourse relations: A structural and presuppositional account using lexicalised tag. In: Proc. of the 37th. Annual Meeting of the American Association for Computational Linguistics (ACL'99), pp 41 – 48

Wilson D, Atkeson C (2005) Simultaneous tracking and activity recognition (star) using many anonymous, binary sensors. In: Gellersen HW, Want R, Schmidt A (eds) Pervasive Computing, Lecture Notes in Computer Science, vol 3468, Springer Berlin / Heidelberg, pp 62–79

Wing MG, Eklund A, Kellogg LD (2005) Consumer-grade Global Positioning System (GPS) accuracy and reliability. Journal of Forestry 103(4):169–173

Woods W (1990) On plans and plan recognition: Comments on Pollack and on Kautz. In: Cohen P, Morgan J, Pollack M (eds) Intentions in Communication, MIT Press, pp 135–140

Wooldridge M (2000) Reasoning About Rational Agents. MIT Press

Xia F (1999) Extracting tree adjoining grammars from bracketed corpora. In: Proceedings of the 5th Natural Language Processing Pacific Rim Symposium, pp 398–403

Yoon H, Shahabi C (2008) Robust time-referenced segmentation of moving object trajectories. In: Data Mining, 2008. ICDM '08. Eighth IEEE International Conference on, IEEE, pp 1121–1126

Zheng Y, Li Q, Chen Y, Xie X, Ma WY (2008) Understanding mobility based on GPS data. In: Proceedings of the 10th international conference on Ubiquitous computing, ACM, New York, NY, USA, UbiComp '08, pp 312–321

Zheng Y, Zhang L, Xie X, Ma WY (2009) Mining interesting locations and travel sequences from GPS trajectories. In: Proceedings of the 18th international conference on World wide web, ACM, New York, NY, USA, WWW '09, pp 791–800